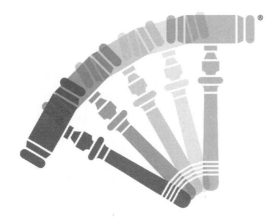

Casenote™ Legal Briefs

COMMERCIAL LAW

Keyed to
Warren and Walt's
Commercial Law, Sixth Edition

ASPEN
PUBLISHERS

1185 Avenue of the Americas, New York, NY 10036
www.aspenpublishers.com

This publication is designed to provide accurate and authoritative information in regard to the subject matter covered. It is sold with the understanding that the publisher is not engaged in rendering legal, accounting, or other professional services. If legal advice or other expert assistance is required, the services of a competent professional person should be sought.

— From a *Declaration of Principles* adopted jointly by a Committee of the American Bar Association and a Committee of Publishers and Associates

© 2004 Aspen Publishers, Inc.
A WoltersKluwer Company
www.aspenpublishers.com

All rights reserved. No part of this publication may be reproduced or transmitted in any form or by any means, electronic or mechanical, including photocopy, recording, or any information storage and retrieval system, without permission in writing from the publisher. Requests for permission to make copies of any part of this publication should be mailed to:

Permissions
Aspen Publishers
1185 Avenue of the Americas
New York, NY 10036

Printed in the United States of America.

ISBN 0-7355-5196-0

1 2 3 4 5 6 7 8 9 0

About Aspen Publishers

Aspen Publishers, headquartered in New York City, is a leading information provider for attorneys, business professionals, and law students. Written by preeminent authorities, our products consist of analytical and practical information covering both U.S. and international topics. We publish in the full range of formats, including updated manuals, books, periodicals, CDs, and online products.

Our proprietary content is complemented by 2,500 legal databases, containing over 11 million documents, available through our Loislaw division. Aspen Publishers also offers a wide range of topical legal and business databases linked to Loislaw's primary material. Our mission is to provide accurate, timely, and authoritative content in easily accessible formats, supported by unmatched customer care.

To order any Aspen Publishers title, go to *www.aspenpublishers.com* or call 1-800-638-8437.

For more information on Loislaw products, go to *www.loislaw.com* or call 1-800-364-2512.

For Customer Care issues, e-mail CustomerCare@aspenpublishers.com; call 1-800-234-1660; or fax 1-800-901-9075.

Aspen Publishers
A Wolters Kluwer Company

FORMAT FOR THE CASENOTE LEGAL BRIEF

PARTY ID: Quick identification of the relationship between the parties.

NATURE OF CASE: This section identifies the form of action (e.g., breach of contract, negligence, battery), the type of proceeding (e.g., demurrer, appeal from trial court's jury instructions) or the relief sought (e.g., damages, injunction, criminal sanctions).

FACT SUMMARY: This is included to refresh the student's memory and can be used as a quick reminder of the facts.

CONCISE RULE OF LAW: Summarizes the general principle of law that the case illustrates. It may be used for instant recall of the court's holding and for classroom discussion or home review.

FACTS: This section contains all relevant facts of the case, including the contentions of the parties and the lower court holdings. It is written in a logical order to give the student a clear understanding of the case. The plaintiff and defendant are identified by their proper names throughout and are always labeled with a (P) or (D).

ISSUE: The issue is a concise question that brings out the essence of the opinion as it relates to the section of the casebook in which the case appears. Both substantive and procedural issues are included if relevant to the decision.

HOLDING AND DECISION: This section offers a clear and in-depth discussion of the rule of the case and the court's rationale. It is written in easy-to-understand language and answers the issue(s) presented by applying the law to the facts of the case. When relevant, it includes a thorough discussion of the exceptions to the case as listed by the court, any major cites to other cases on point, and the names of the judges who wrote the decisions.

CONCURRENCE / DISSENT: All concurrences and dissents are briefed whenever they are included by the casebook editor.

EDITOR'S ANALYSIS: This last paragraph gives the student a broad understanding of where the case "fits in" with other cases in the section of the book and with the entire course. It is a hornbook-style discussion indicating whether the case is a majority or minority opinion and comparing the principal case with other cases in the casebook. It may also provide analysis from restatements, uniform codes, and law review articles. The editor's analysis will prove to be invaluable to classroom discussion.

QUICKNOTES: Conveniently defines legal terms found in the case and summarizes the nature of any statutes, codes, or rules referred to in the text.

PALSGRAF v. LONG ISLAND R.R. CO.
Injured bystander (P) v. Railroad company (D)
N.Y. Ct. App., 248 N.Y. 339, 162 N.E. 99 (1928).

NATURE OF CASE: Appeal from judgment affirming verdict for plaintiff seeking damages for personal injury.

FACT SUMMARY: Helen Palsgraf (P) was injured on R.R.'s (D) train platform when R.R.'s (D) guard helped a passenger aboard a moving train, causing his package to fall on the tracks. The package contained fireworks which exploded, creating a shock that tipped a scale onto Palsgraf (P).

CONCISE RULE OF LAW: The risk reasonably to be perceived defines the duty to be obeyed.

FACTS: Helen Palsgraf (P) purchased a ticket to Rockaway Beach from R.R. (D) and was waiting on the train platform. As she waited, two men ran to catch a train that was pulling out from the platform. The first man jumped aboard, but the second man, who appeared as if he might fall, was helped aboard by the guard on the train who had kept the door open so they could jump aboard. A guard on the platform also helped by pushing him onto the train. The man was carrying a package wrapped in newspaper. In the process, the man dropped his package, which fell on the tracks. The package contained fireworks and exploded. The shock of the explosion was apparently of great enough strength to tip over some scales at the other end of the platform, which fell on Palsgraf (P) and injured her. A jury awarded her damages, and R.R. (D) appealed.

ISSUE: Does the risk reasonably to be perceived define the duty to be obeyed?

HOLDING AND DECISION: (Cardozo, C.J.) Yes. The risk reasonably to be perceived defines the duty to be obeyed. If there is no foreseeable hazard to the injured party as the result of a seemingly innocent act, the act does not become a tort because it happened to be a wrong as to another. If the wrong was not willful, the plaintiff must show that the act as to her had such great and apparent possibilities of danger as to entitle her to protection. Negligence in the abstract is not enough upon which to base liability. Negligence is a relative concept, evolving out of the common law doctrine of trespass on the case. To establish liability, the defendant must owe a legal duty of reasonable care to the injured party. A cause of action in tort will lie where harm, though unintended, could have been averted or avoided by observance of such a duty. The scope of the duty is limited by the range of danger that a reasonable person could foresee. In this case, there was nothing to suggest from the appearance of the parcel or otherwise that the parcel contained fireworks. The guard could not reasonably have had any warning of a threat to Palsgraf (P), and R.R. (D) therefore cannot be held liable. Judgment is reversed in favor of R.R. (D).

DISSENT: (Andrews, J.) The concept that there is no negligence unless R.R. (D) owes a legal duty to take care as to Palsgraf (P) herself is too narrow. Everyone owes to the world at large the duty of refraining from those acts that may unreasonably threaten the safety of others. If the guard's action was negligent as to those nearby, it was also negligent as to those outside what might be termed the "danger zone." For Palsgraf (P) to recover, R.R.'s (D) negligence must have been the proximate cause of her injury, a question of fact for the jury.

EDITOR'S ANALYSIS: The majority defined the limit of the defendant's liability in terms of the danger that a reasonable person in defendant's situation would have perceived. The dissent argued that the limitation should not be placed on liability, but rather on damages. Judge Andrews suggested that only injuries that would not have happened but for R.R.'s (D) negligence should be compensable. Both the majority and dissent recognized the policy-driven need to limit liability for negligent acts, seeking, in the words of Judge Andrews, to define a framework "that will be practical and in keeping with the general understanding of mankind." The Restatement (Second) of Torts has accepted Judge Cardozo's view.

QUICKNOTES
FORESEEABILITY – The reasonable anticipation that damage is a likely result from certain acts or omissions.
NEGLIGENCE - Failure to exercise that degree of care which a person of ordinary prudence would exercise under similar circumstances.
PROXIMATE CAUSE – Something which in natural and continuous sequence, unbroken by any new intervening cause, produces an event, and without which the injury would not have occurred.

NOTE TO STUDENTS

Aspen Publishers is proud to offer *Casenote Legal Briefs*—continuing thirty years of publishing America's best-selling legal briefs.

Casenote Legal Briefs are designed to help you save time when briefing assigned cases. Organized under convenient headings, they show you how to abstract the basic facts and holdings from the text of the actual opinions handed down by the courts. Used as part of a rigorous study regime, they can help you spend more time analyzing and critiquing points of law than on copying out bits and pieces of judicial opinions into your notebook or outline.

Casenote Legal Briefs should never be used as a substitute for assigned casebook readings. They work best when read as a follow-up to reviewing the underlying opinions themselves. Students who try to avoid reading and digesting the judicial opinions in their casebooks or on-line sources will end up shortchanging themselves in the long run. The ability to absorb, critique, and restate the dynamic and complex elements of case law decisions is crucial to your success in law school and beyond. It cannot be developed vicariously.

Casenote Legal Briefs represent but one of the many offerings in Aspen's Study Aid Timeline, which includes:

- Casenotes *Legal Briefs*
- Emanuel *Outlines*
- *Examples & Explanations* Series
- *Introduction to Law* Series
- Emanuel *Law in a Flash* Flashcards
- Emanuel *CrunchTime* Series

Each of these series is designed to provide you with easy-to-understand explanations of complex points of law. Each volume offers guidance on the principles of legal analysis and, consulted regularly, will hone your ability to spot relevant issues. We have titles that will help you prepare for class, prepare for your exams, and enhance your general comprehension of the law along the way.

To find out more about Aspen Study Aid publications, visit us on-line at www.aspenpublishers.com or e-mail us at legaledu@aspenpubl.com. We'll be happy to assist you.

Free access to Briefs on-line!

Download the cases you want in your notes or outlines using the full cut-and-paste feature accompanying our on-line briefs. Please fill out this form for full access to this useful feature. No photocopies of this form will be accepted.

① **Name:** _____ **Phone:** (___) _____

    Address: _____ **Apt.:** _____

    City: _____ **State:** _____ **ZIP Code:** _____

    Law School: _____ **Year (circle one):** 1st 2nd 3rd

② **Cut out the UPC found on the lower left-hand corner of the back cover of this book. Staple the UPC inside this box. Only the original UPC from the book cover will be accepted. (No photocopies or store stickers are allowed.)**

> **Attach UPC inside this box.**

③ **E-mail:** _____ **(Print LEGIBLY or you may not get access!)**

④ **Title (course subject) of this book** _____

⑤ **Used with which casebook (provide author's name):** _____

⑥ **Mail the completed form to:**   Aspen Publishers, Inc.
                                        Legal Education Division
                                        Casenote On-line Access
                                        675 Massachusetts Ave., 11th floor
                                        Cambridge, MA 02139

I understand that on-line access is granted solely to the purchaser of this book for the academic year in which it was purchased. Any other usage is not authorized and will result in immediate termination of access. Sharing of codes is strictly prohibited.

_____

Signature

Upon receipt of this completed form, you will be e-mailed codes so that you may access the Briefs for this Casenote Legal Brief. On-line Briefs may not be available for all titles. For a full list of available titles please check www.aspenpublishers.com/casenotes.

HOW TO BRIEF A CASE

A. DECIDE ON A FORMAT AND STICK TO IT

Structure is essential to a good brief. It enables you to arrange systematically the related parts that are scattered throughout most cases, thus making manageable and understandable what might otherwise seem to be an endless and unfathomable sea of information. There are, of course, an unlimited number of formats that can be utilized. However, it is best to find one that suits your needs and stick to it. Consistency breeds both efficiency and the security that when called upon you will know where to look in your brief for the information you are asked to give.

Any format, as long as it presents the essential elements of a case in an organized fashion, can be used. Experience, however, has led *Casenotes* to develop and utilize the following format because of its logical flow and universal applicability.

NATURE OF CASE: This is a brief statement of the legal character and procedural status of the case (e.g., "Appeal of a burglary conviction").

There are many different alternatives open to a litigant dissatisfied with a court ruling. The key to determining which one has been used is to discover *who is asking this court for what.*

This first entry in the brief should be kept as *short as possible.* The student should use the court's terminology if the student understands it. But since jurisdictions vary as to the titles of pleadings, the best entry is the one that apprises the student of who wants what in this proceeding, not the one that sounds most like the court's language.

CONCISE RULE OF LAW: A statement of the general principle of law that the case illustrates (e.g., "An acceptance that varies any term of the offer is considered a rejection and counteroffer").

Determining the rule of law of a case is a procedure similar to determining the issue of the case. Avoid being fooled by red herrings; there may be a few rules of law mentioned in the case excerpt, but usually only one is *the* rule with which the casebook editor is concerned. The techniques used to locate the issue, described below, may also be utilized to find the rule of law. Generally, your best guide is simply the chapter heading. It is a clue to the point the casebook editor seeks to make and should be kept in mind when reading every case in the respective section.

FACTS: A synopsis of only the essential facts of the case, i.e., those bearing upon or leading up to the issue.

The facts entry should be a short statement of the events and transactions that led one party to initiate legal proceedings against another in the first place. While some cases conveniently state the salient facts at the beginning of the decision, in other instances they will have to be culled from hiding places throughout the text, even from concurring and dissenting opinions. Some of the "facts" will often be in dispute and should be so noted. Conflicting evidence may be briefly pointed up. "Hard" facts must be included. Both must be *relevant* in order to be listed in the facts entry. It is impossible to tell what is relevant until the entire case is read, as the ultimate determination of the rights and liabilities of the parties may turn on something buried deep in the opinion.

The facts entry should never be longer than one to three *short* sentences.

It is often helpful to identify the role played by a party in a given context. For example, in a construction contract case the identification of a party as the "contractor" or "builder" alleviates the need to tell that that party was the one who was supposed to have built the house.

It is always helpful, and a good general practice, to identify the "plaintiff" and the "defendant." This may seem elementary and uncomplicated, but, especially in view of the creative editing practiced by some casebook editors, it is sometimes a difficult or even impossible task. Bear in mind that the *party presently* seeking something from this court may not be the plaintiff, and that sometimes only the cross-claim of a defendant is treated in the excerpt. Confusing or misaligning the parties can ruin your analysis and understanding of the case.

ISSUE: A statement of the general legal question answered by or illustrated in the case. For clarity, the issue is best put in the form of a question capable of a "yes" or "no" answer. In reality, the issue is simply the Concise Rule of Law put in the form of a question (e.g., "May an offer be accepted by performance?").

The major problem presented in discerning what is *the* issue in the case is that an opinion usually purports to raise and answer several questions. However, except for rare cases, only one such question is really the issue in the case. Collateral issues not necessary to the resolution of the matter in controversy are handled by the court by language known as *"obiter dictum"* or merely *"dictum."* While dicta may be included later in the brief, it has no place under the issue heading.

To find the issue, the student again asks *who wants what* and then goes on to ask *why did that party succeed or fail in getting it.* Once this is determined, the "why" should be turned into a question.

The complexity of the issues in the cases will vary, but in all cases a single-sentence question should sum up the issue. *In a few cases,* there will be two, or even more rarely, three issues of equal importance to the resolution of the case. Each should be expressed in a single-sentence question.

Since many issues are resolved by a court in coming to a final disposition of a case, the casebook editor will reproduce the portion of the opinion containing the issue or issues most relevant to the area of law under scrutiny. A noted law professor gave this advice: "Close the book; look at the title on the cover." Chances are, if it is Property, the student need not concern himself with whether, for example, the federal government's treatment of the plaintiff's land really raises a federal question sufficient to support jurisdiction on this ground in federal court.

The same rule applies to chapter headings designating sub-areas within the subjects. They tip the student off as to what the text is designed to teach. The cases are arranged in a casebook to show a progression or development of the law, so that the preceding cases may also help.

It is also most important to remember to *read the notes and questions* at the end of a case to determine what the editors wanted the student to have gleaned from it.

HOLDING AND DECISION: This section should succinctly explain the rationale of the court in arriving at its decision. In capsulizing the "reasoning" of the court, it should always include an application of the general rule or rules of law to the specific facts of the case. Hidden justifications come to light in this entry; the reasons for the state of the law, the public policies, the biases and prejudices, those considerations that influence the justices' thinking and, ultimately, the outcome of the case. At the end, there should be a short indication of the disposition or procedural resolution of the case (e.g., "Decision of the trial court for Mr. Smith (P) reversed").

The foregoing format is designed to help you "digest" the reams of case material with which you will be faced in your law school career. Once mastered by practice, it will place at your fingertips the information the authors of your casebooks have sought to impart to you in case-by-case illustration and analysis.

B. BE AS ECONOMICAL AS POSSIBLE IN BRIEFING CASES

Once armed with a format that encourages succinctness, it is as important to be economical with regard to the time spent on the actual reading of the case as it is to be economical in the writing of the brief itself. This does not mean "skimming" a case. Rather, it means reading the case with an "eye" trained to recognize into which "section" of your brief a particular passage or line fits and having a system for quickly and precisely marking the case so that the passages fitting any one particular part of the brief can be easily identified and brought together in a concise and accurate manner when the brief is actually written.

It is of no use to simply repeat everything in the opinion of the court; the student should only record enough information to trigger his or her recollection of what the court said. Nevertheless, an accurate statement of the "law of the case," i.e., the legal principle applied to the facts, is absolutely essential to class preparation and to learning the law under the case method.

To that end, it is important to develop a "shorthand" that you can use to make margin notations. These notations will tell you at a glance in which section of the brief you will be placing that particular passage or portion of the opinion.

Some students prefer to underline all the salient portions of the opinion (with a pencil or colored underliner marker), making marginal notations as they go along. Others prefer the color-coded method of underlining, utilizing different colors of markers to underline the salient portions of the case, each separate color being used to represent a different section of the brief. For example, blue underlining could be used for passages relating to the concise rule of law, yellow for those relating to the issue, and green for those relating to the holding and decision, etc. While it has its advocates, the color-coded method can be confusing and time-consuming (all that time spent on changing colored markers). Furthermore, it can interfere with the continuity and concentration many students deem essential to the reading of a case for maximum comprehension. In the end, however, it is a matter of personal preference and style. Just remember, whatever method you use, underlining must be used sparingly or its value is lost.

For those who take the marginal notation route, an efficient and easy method is to go along underlining the key portions of the case and placing in the margin alongside them the following "markers" to indicate where a particular passage or line "belongs" in the brief you will write:

N	(NATURE OF CASE)
CR	(CONCISE RULE OF LAW)
I	(ISSUE)
HC	(HOLDING AND DECISION, relates to the CONCISE RULE OF LAW behind the decision)
HR	(HOLDING AND DECISION, gives the RATIONALE or reasoning behind the decision)
HA	(HOLDING AND DECISION, APPLIES the general principle(s) of law to the facts of the case to arrive at the decision)

Remember that a particular passage may well contain information necessary to more than one part of your brief, in which case you simply note that in the margin. If you are using the color-coded underlining method instead of margin notation, simply make asterisks or checks in the margin next to the passage in question in the colors that indicate the additional sections of the brief where it might be utilized.

The economy of utilizing "shorthand" in marking cases for briefing can be maintained in the actual brief writing process itself by utilizing "law student shorthand" within the brief. There are many commonly used words and phrases for which abbreviations can be substituted in your briefs (and in your class notes also). You can develop abbreviations that are personal to you and which will save you a lot of time. A reference list of briefing abbreviations will be found elsewhere in this book.

C. USE BOTH THE BRIEFING PROCESS AND THE BRIEF AS A LEARNING TOOL

Now that you have a format and the tools for briefing cases efficiently, the most important thing is to make the time spent in briefing profitable to you and to make the most advantageous use of the briefs you create. Of course, the briefs are invaluable for classroom reference when you are called upon to explain or analyze a particular case. However, they are also useful in reviewing for exams. A quick glance at the fact summary should bring the case to mind, and a rereading of the concise rule of law should enable you to go over the underlying legal concept in your mind, how it was applied in that particular case, and how it might apply in other factual settings.

As to the value to be derived from engaging in the briefing process itself, there is an immediate benefit that arises from being forced to sift through the essential facts and reasoning from the court's opinion and to succinctly express them in your own words in your brief. The process ensures that you understand the case and the point that it illustrates, and that means you will be ready to absorb further analysis and information brought forth in class. It also ensures you will have something to say when called upon in class. The briefing process helps develop a mental agility for getting to the *gist* of a case and for identifying, expounding on, and applying the legal concepts and issues found there. Of most immediate concern, that is the mental process on which you must rely in taking law school examinations. Of more lasting concern, it is also the mental process upon which a lawyer relies in serving his clients and in making his living.

ABBREVIATIONS FOR BRIEFING

acceptance	acp
affirmed	aff
answer	ans
assumption of risk	a/r
attorney	atty
beyond a reasonable doubt	b/r/d
bona fide purchaser	BFP
breach of contract	br/k
cause of action	c/a
common law	c/l
Constitution	Con
constitutional	con
contract	K
contributory negligence	c/n
cross	x
cross-complaint	x/c
cross-examination	x/ex
cruel and unusual punishment	c/u/p
defendant	D
dismissed	dis
double jeopardy	d/j
due process	d/p
equal protection	e/p
equity	eq
evidence	ev
exclude	exc
exclusionary rule	exc/r
felony	f/n
freedom of speech	f/s
good faith	g/f
habeas corpus	h/c
hearsay	hr
husband	H
in loco parentis	ILP
injunction	inj
inter vivos	I/v
joint tenancy	j/t
judgment	judgt
jurisdiction	jur
last clear chance	LCC
long-arm statute	LAS
majority view	maj
meeting of minds	MOM
minority view	min
Miranda warnings	Mir/w
Miranda rule	Mir/r
negligence	neg
notice	ntc
nuisance	nus
obligation	ob
obscene	obs

offer	O
offeree	OE
offeror	OR
ordinance	ord
pain and suffering	p/s
parol evidence	p/e
plaintiff	P
prima facie	p/f
probable cause	p/c
proximate cause	px/c
real property	r/p
reasonable doubt	r/d
reasonable man	r/m
rebuttable presumption	rb/p
remanded	rem
res ipsa loquitur	RIL
respondeat superior	r/s
Restatement	RS
reversed	rev
Rule Against Perpetuities	RAP
search and seizure	s/s
search warrant	s/w
self-defense	s/d
specific performance	s/p
statute of limitations	S/L
statute of frauds	S/F
statute	S
summary judgment	s/j
tenancy in common	t/c
tenancy at will	t/w
tenant	t
third party	TP
third party beneficiary	TPB
transferred intent	TI
unconscionable	uncon
unconstitutional	unconst
undue influence	u/e
Uniform Commercial Code	UCC
unilateral	uni
vendee	VE
vendor	VR
versus	v
void for vagueness	VFV
weight of the evidence	w/e
weight of authority	w/a
wife	W
with	w/
within	w/i
without prejudice	w/o/p
without	w/o
wrongful death	wr/d

TABLE OF CASES

CHAPTER 1
CREATING A SECURITY INTEREST

QUICK REFERENCE RULES OF LAW

1. **Why Secured Credit?** Under the U.C.C., a secured creditor who obtains a defaulted debtor's property is not subject to restitution for the amount of the value of goods furnished to the debtor by a third party. (Knox v. Phoenix Leasing Incorporated)

2. **The Composite Document Rule.** It is not necessary for a formal grant of a security interest to exist for a security agreement to arise. It is sufficient if, looking at the transaction as a whole, there is a writing, or writings, signed by the debtor describing the collateral which demonstrates an intent to create a security interest in the collateral. (In re Bollinger Corp.)

3. **Description of Collateral.** A bank's financing statement that indicates the bank has a lien on property consisting of "all inventory, chattel paper, accounts, equipment, and general intangibles" is sufficient to perfect its security interest in a Chapter 11 debtor's property. (In re Grabowski)

4. **After-Acquired Collateral.** Washington law presumes security interests in inventory and accounts receivable include after-acquired property, absent evidence of a contrary intent. (In re Filtercorp, Inc.)

5. **Rights in Collateral.** A secured party is a purchaser for value under the U.C.C. and may, therefore, take good title from a transferor who tendered a dishonored check for the original purchase price. (Swets Motor Sales, Inc.v. Pruisner)

KNOX v. PHOENIX LEASING INCORPORATED
Seller (P) v. Financer (D)
Cal. Ct. App., 29 Cal. App. 4th 1357 (1994).

NATURE OF CASE: Appeal from judgment in an unjust enrichment action.

FACT SUMMARY: Phoenix (D), a creditor with a security interest in a winery's property, liquidated all property in the winery, which included property owned by Knox (P), a third party.

CONCISE RULE OF LAW: Under the U.C.C., a secured creditor who obtains a defaulted debtor's property is not subject to restitution for the amount of the value of goods furnished to the debtor by a third party.

FACTS: Domaine Laurier Winery contracted with Mel Knox (P) to purchase 200 seasoned oak wine barrels. Four months later, Domaine sought financing for the purchase from Phoenix Leasing Incorporated (D). Phoenix (D) was protected by a security agreement covering all property owned or later acquired by Domaine. The wine barrels came in two shipments. Upon arrival of the first lot, Knox (P) invoiced Domaine. Domaine forwarded the invoice to Phoenix (D), and Phoenix (D) paid Knox (P). With the second lot, Knox (P) directly invoiced Phoenix (D). Phoenix (D) did not pay the second invoice. Phoenix (D) then declared Domaine in default and liquidated Domain's assets. The second set of barrels was included in the liquidation. Knox (P) sued for restitution on the barrels that were liquidated before payment. The court awarded Knox (P) the resale value of the barrels, totaling $21,350. Phoenix (D) appealed.

ISSUE: Under the U.C.C., is a secured creditor who obtains a defaulted debtor's property subject to restitution for the amount of the value of goods furnished to the debtor by a third party?

HOLDING AND DECISION: (Poche, Assoc. J.) No. Under the U.C.C., a secured creditor who obtains a defaulted debtor's property is not subject to restitution for the amount of the value of goods furnished to the debtor by a third party. To preserve the integrity of the U.C.C. treatment of security priorities, a majority of jurisdictions have declined to require restitution where a secured creditor has liquidated third-party property held by debtors. In this case, Phoenix (D) conducted itself in accord with the U.C.C. Knox (P) could have checked records for a threatening security interest, or could have required cash on delivery. The legislative mandate must prevail over the common-sense notion that Phoenix (D) should pay Knox (P) for the barrels it received and sold. Reversed.

EDITOR'S ANALYSIS: The U.C.C. attempts to protect secured creditors from the costs associated with supervising debtor behavior. A finance company, for example, is not in as good a position to study the daily operations of a debtor as would be a trade creditor that supplies inventory to the debtor at regular intervals. If an unsecured creditor's restitution rights could prevail over a perfected security interest, then much of the value of perfecting the interest would be lost.

NOTES:

IN RE BOLLINGER CORP.
Creditor (P) v. Debtor (D)
614 F.2d 924 (3d Cir. 1980).

NATURE OF CASE: Appeal from review of an order in bankruptcy.

FACT SUMMARY: Z & J (P), which had loaned Bollinger Corporation (D) $150,000, took an assignment of a pre-existing security agreement to cover $65,000 of the debt but insisted it had a secured claim for the full $150,000 because the various documents executed in connection with the loan evidenced an intent to create a security interest even though no formal security agreement covering the remaining $85,000 was ever signed.

CONCISE RULE OF LAW: It is not necessary for a formal grant of a security interest to exist for a security agreement to arise. It is sufficient if, looking at the transaction as a whole, there is a writing, or writings, signed by the debtor describing the collateral which demonstrates an intent to create a security interest in the collateral.

FACTS: Originally, Bollinger Corporation (D) obtained a $150,000 loan from Industrial Credit Company (ICC), for which it executed a promissory note and signed a security agreement giving ICC a security interest in certain machinery and equipment. ICC filed a financing statement to perfect its security interest and Bollinger (D) proceeded to make the loan payments. When there was only $65,000 left to be repaid on the principal, Bollinger (D) sought to obtain additional capital by entering into a loan agreement with Zimmerman & Jansen, Inc. (Z & J) (P). It called for Z & J (P) to pay off the remaining $65,000 owed by Bollinger (D) on the loan from ICC, for which ICC assigned to Z & J (P) the original promissory note and security agreement it had received from Bollinger (D). Bollinger executed a $150,000 promissory note in favor of Z & J (P). The note provided that it was secured by security interests in the original security agreement between Bollinger (D) and ICC and in the financing statement filed by ICC. It then went on to state that it was further secured "by security interests in a certain security agreement to be delivered by Bollinger (D) to Z & J (P) with this Promissory Note covering the identical machinery and equipment as identified in the ICC Agreement and with identical schedule attached in the principal amount of Eighty-Five Thousand Dollars." Although there was correspondence between Z & J (P) which evidenced an intent to create a security interest for the $85,000 not covered by the ICC Agreement, no formal security agreement was ever executed between Bollinger (D) and Z & J (P). Thus, when Bollinger (D) eventually filed for an arrangement under Chapter 11 of the Bankruptcy Act and was adjudicated bankrupt, the bankruptcy judge held that Z & J (P) had a secured claim of $65,000 and that the remaining $85,000 was an unsecured claim due to the absence of a security agreement covering it. When it reviewed the

order in bankruptcy, the district court reversed the bankruptcy court and entered judgment for Z & J (P) in the full amount of the asserted $150,000 secured claim. It reasoned that the promissory note Bollinger (D) had executed in favor of Z & J (P) was in itself sufficient to act as the security agreement between the parties.

ISSUE: In the absence of a formal grant of a security interest, can a security agreement arise if, looking at the transaction as a whole, there is a writing or writings signed by the debtor describing the collateral and demonstrating an intent to create a security interest in the collateral?

HOLDING AND DECISION: (Rosenn, Cir. J.) Yes. A number of courts have declined to follow the rule of the earliest cases and have recognized that it is not necessary for a formal grant of a security interest to exist for a security agreement to arise. It is the Court's conclusion that the Pennsylvania courts would accept the logic of this modern trend and reject the antiquated rule imposing the requirement of a formal grant of a security interest before a security agreement may exist. In those instances where the parties have neglected to sign a separate security agreement, it would appear that the better and more practical view is to look at the transaction as a whole in order to determine if there is a writing, or writings, signed by the debtor describing the collateral which demonstrates an intent to create a security interest in the collateral. When such a writing or writings exist, the requirements set forth in Article 9 of the U.C.C. for perfection of a security interest in a debtor's collateral are met. In this particular case, the promissory note standing alone would not be sufficient to act as a security agreement. It is some evidence that a security agreement was contemplated, but by its own terms, it plainly indicates that it is not the security agreement. However, from the course of dealing between the parties, including their correspondence, there is sufficient evidence that the parties intended a security agreement to be created separate from the assigned ICC agreement with Bollinger (D). Thus, Z & J (P) has a secured claim in the amount of $150,000. Affirmed.

EDITOR'S ANALYSIS: All that Article 9 of the U.C.C. requires for the creation of a perfected security interest in a debtor's collateral is: (1) the existence of a "security agreement" giving the creditor an interest in the collateral, and (2) a "financing statement," *i.e.*, a document signed by the parties and filed for public record. The pro-secured creditor view evidenced in this case is now the rule in most courts. The Ninth Circuit was among the first to adopt it when it held that a financing statement could itself serve as a security agreement if it contained a description of the collateral and was signed by the debtor. Other courts, although reluctant to go that far, did recognize that a financing statement, when read in conjunction with other documents executed by the parties, could meet the requirements Article 9 sets forth for creation of a security agreement.

IN RE GRABOWSKI
Lien creditor (P) v. Secured creditor (D)
U.S. Bankr., 277 B.R. 388 (S.D. Ill. 2002).

NATURE OF CASE: Complaint filed by Chapter 11 debtors to determine the validity, priority, and extent of liens on their farm equipment.

FACT SUMMARY: Bank of America (D) and South Pointe Bank (P) both claimed security interests in three items of farm equipment owned by the bankruptcy debtors. South Pointe (P) contended that Bank of America's (D) financing statement (although prior in time) which indicated that Bank of America (D) had a lien on property consisting of "all inventory, chattel paper, accounts, equipment, and general intangibles," was insufficient under the U.C.C. to perfect Bank of America's (D) security interest in the farm equipment.

CONCISE RULE OF LAW: A bank's financing statement that indicates the bank has a lien on property consisting of "all inventory, chattel paper, accounts, equipment, and general intangibles" is sufficient to perfect its security interest in a Chapter 11 debtor's property.

FACTS: Debtors Ronald and Trenna Grabowski filed a Chapter 11 proceeding to reorganize their farming operation. Their schedules included a list of items of equipment used in their farming operation. There were three items of farm machinery as to which a dispute remained between the creditors Bank of America (D) and South Pointe Bank (P): a John Deere 925 flex platform, a John Deere 4630 tractor, and a John Deere 630 disk. Bank of America (D) claimed a prior security interest in this equipment by virtue of a security agreement signed by the debtors. The Bank's (D) financing statement identified the debtors as "Ronald and Trenna Grabowski" and listed their address as "12047 State Highway # 37, Benton, Illinois 62812." The financing statement described the Bank's (D) collateral as: All Inventory, Chattel Paper, Accounts, Equipment and General Intangibles. South Pointe (P) subsequently obtained a lien on the debtors' equipment. South Pointe's (P) financing statement identified the debtors as "Ronald and Trenna Grabowski" at "P.O. Box 38, Dubois, Illinois 62831" and described South Pointe's (P) collateral as: JD 1995 9600 combine ..., JD 925 FLEX PLATFORM ..., JD 4630 TRACTOR ..., JD 630 DISK 28' 1998. South Pointe (P) asserted that Bank of America's (D) financing statement, although prior in time, was insufficient to perfect the Bank's (D) interest because it failed to place other lenders on notice of Bank of America's (D) interest in the subject equipment. Specifically, South Pointe (P) noted that the Bank's (D) financing statement contained the address of the debtors' farm equipment business rather than that of the debtors' home where their farming operation was located and, further, that it failed to mention any specific items of equipment or even make reference to "farm

equipment" or "farm machinery." South Pointe (P) maintained, therefore, that the Bank's (D) financing statement did not reasonably identify the Bank's (D) collateral as required to fulfill the notice function of a financing statement under the U.C.C. The debtors filed a complaint to determine the validity, priority, and extent of the liens held by the various lenders in this equipment.

ISSUE: Is a bank's financing statement that indicates the bank has a lien on property consisting of "all inventory, chattel paper, accounts, equipment, and general intangibles," sufficient to perfect its security interest in a Chapter 11 debtor's property?

HOLDING AND DECISION: (Meyers, Bankr. J.) Yes. A bank's financing statement that indicates the bank has a lien on property consisting of "all inventory, chattel paper, accounts, equipment, and general intangibles," is sufficient to perfect its security interest in a Chapter 11 debtor's property. The U.C.C. sets forth the requirements for a creditor to obtain and perfect a security interest in personal property of the debtor. Section 9-203 governs the attachment and enforcement of security interests through the parties' execution of a security agreement, while § 9-502 relates to the requisites of a financing statement filed to perfect the creditor's interest against the interests of third parties. Both sections call for a description of the debtor's property. However, the degree of specificity required of such description depends on the nature of the document involved (whether it is a security agreement or a financing statement) and the purpose to be fulfilled by such document. While a security agreement defines and limits the collateral subject to the creditor's security interest, a financing statement puts third parties on notice that the creditor may have a lien on the property described and that further inquiry into the extent of the security interest is prudent. U.C.C. § 9-108 sets forth the test for sufficiency of a description under the U.C.C., stating, that a description of personal property is sufficient, whether or not it is specific, if it reasonably identifies what is described. While § 9-108 provides a flexible standard for determining the sufficiency of a description in a security agreement, U.C.C. § 9-504 provides an even broader standard with regard to a financing statement. This section states that a financing statement sufficiently indicates the collateral that it covers if the financing statement provides a description of the collateral or an indication that the financing statement covers all assets or all personal property. Thus, in the case of a financing statement, a creditor may either describe its collateral by "type" or "category" as set forth in § 9-108 or may simply indicate its lien on

Continued on next page.

"all assets" of the debtor. This exceedingly general standard for describing collateral in a financing statement, is consistent with the "inquiry notice" function of a financing statement. A financing statement need not specify the property encumbered by a secured party's lien, but need merely notify subsequent creditors that a lien may exist and that further inquiry is necessary "to disclose the complete state of affairs." Here, Bank of America's (D) financing statement was sufficient to perfect its security interest in the farm equipment and Bank of America's (D) interest, being prior in time, was superior to that of South Pointe (P). Accordingly, the court finds in favor of Bank of America (D) and against South Pointe (P) on the debtors' complaint to determine the validity, priority, and extent of liens in the debtors' farm equipment.

EDITOR'S ANALYSIS: In the Grabowski bankruptcy, the court noted that while a subsequent creditor should not be required to be a "super-detective" in investigating prior secured transactions, the debtors' address in this case was an accurate and ready means of contacting the debtors. Furthermore, even though the mailing address on the bank's financing statement was that of the debtors' business, the debtors' names were listed as "Ronald and Trenna Grabowski," not "Grabowski Tractor-Benton, Inc.," the name of the debtors' business. Accordingly, the court found that a reasonably prudent lender would not be misled into believing that the collateral listed was property of the debtors' business, rather than that of the debtors individually.

NOTES:

IN RE FILTERCORP, INC.
Creditor (P) v. Debtor (D)
163 F.3d 570 (9th Cir. 1998).

NATURE OF CASE: Appeal from summary judgment in an action to enforce a security interest.

FACT SUMMARY: Paulman (P) sought to enforce a security interest in after-acquired inventory and accounts receivable of Filtercorp (D).

CONCISE RULE OF LAW: Washington law presumes security interests in inventory and accounts receivable include after-acquired property, absent evidence of a contrary intent.

FACTS: Filtercorp (D), a Washington corporation in the business of developing and distributing carbonated pads for filtering cooking oils, took out a series of loans from Paulman (P), a salesman. The final note provided for a security of 75,000 shares of Filter Corp. (D) stock owned by Robin Bernard, Filter Corp.'s (D) accounts receivable and inventory, and John Gardner personally. The parties did not execute a separate security agreement. Paulman (P) perfected his security interest by filing a U.C.C.-1 financing statement identifying the collateral as accounts receivable and inventory. Although the note referred to an inventory listing, none was attached. The parties presented conflicting evidence of their intentions regarding securing after-acquired inventory or accounts receivable. The bankruptcy court and the BAP held that an express after-acquired property clause was required in order to secure after-acquired property. Summary judgment for Filtercorp (D). Paulman (P) appealed.

ISSUE: Does Washington law presume security interests in inventory and accounts receivable include after-acquired property, absent evidence of a contrary intent?

HOLDING AND DECISION: (Schwarzer, Sr. Dist. J.) Yes. Washington law presumes security interests in inventory and accounts receivable include after-acquired property, absent evidence of a contrary intent. The question of whether a security agreement creates a lien on certain assets is determined by state law. Courts are divided as to the requirements of a security agreement to include after-acquired inventory and accounts receivable. The minority view requires an express statement of the intent to include such assets. The majority view, however, holds that a security interest in inventory or accounts receivable presumptively includes an interest in after-acquired inventory or accounts receivable, respectively. The theory is that those assets are continually shifting as the assets are depleted and then subsequently replaced. Both commentators and the U.C.C. support the majority view. Applying the majority view to the present case, Paulman (P) had a security interest in the after-acquired accounts receivable of Filtercorp (D), but not in the after-acquired inventory, because the security agreement evidenced an intent to limit the inventory collateral to the referenced listing. Summary judgment reversed with respect to Paulman's (P) lien on Filtercorp's (D) accounts receivable, and affirmed with respect to the lien on inventory.

EDITOR'S ANALYSIS: The presumption that a security interest in accounts receivable and inventory also extends to after-acquired property is rebuttable. The presumption may be rebutted if the agreement expressly demonstrates the parties' intent to limit the collateral to particular assets; if there is "clear evidence of a contemporaneous intent to limit the collateral"; or if the debtor can show that the nature of his business does not involve the regular turn-over of inventory or receivables.

NOTES:

SWETS MOTOR SALES, INC. v. PRUISNER
Automobile wholesaler (P) v. Retail automobile dealer (D)
Iowa Sup. Ct., 236 N.W.2d 299 (1975).

NATURE OF CASE: Suit seeking declaratory relief and attachment.

FACT SUMMARY: Pruisner (D) purchased vehicles from Swets Motor Sales, Inc. (P) and several of his payments by check were dishonored. Chrysler Credit Corp. (D), which provided financing to Pruisner (D), had a security interest in the vehicles.

CONCISE RULE OF LAW: A secured party is a purchaser for value under the U.C.C. and may, therefore, take good title from a transferor who tendered a dishonored check for the original purchase price.

FACTS: Swets Motor Sales, Inc. (P) sold a number of used cars and trucks to Pruisner (D), who paid for the vehicles at the time of delivery. Pruisner (D) obtained financing for the purchase of the vehicles from Chrysler Credit Corp. (D) and had executed a security agreement giving Chrysler (D) a security interest covering the vehicles. Four of Pruisner's (D) checks to Swets (P) were subsequently dishonored and Swets (P) filed a petition to obtain a writ of attachment. Swets (P) also sought declaratory relief in the form of an order declaring that Swets (P) had an interest in the automobiles superior to that of Chrysler (D). At the time of the issuance of the writ of attachment, Chrysler (D) held the unencumbered titles to the vehicles in question. At trial, Chrysler (D) moved for a summary judgment on the issue of the priority of its security interest. The trial court sustained Chrysler's (D) motion and also found that the value of the cars at the time of attachment was $9,300, and that their value at time of trial was $5,100. The court held that Chrysler (D) was entitled to possession of the attached vehicles and that Swets (P) was obliged to pay the difference between $9,300 and $5,100 out of its attachment bond. Swets (P) appealed.

ISSUE: Where a purchaser has paid for goods by a check which is dishonored, may he nevertheless transfer good title to a good-faith purchaser for value?

HOLDING AND DECISION: (Rees, J.) Yes. A secured party is a purchaser for value under the U.C.C. and may, therefore, take good title from a transferor who tendered a dishonored check for the original purchase price. U.C.C. § 2-403 provides that when goods are delivered under a transaction of purchase, the purchaser has the power to transfer a good title to a good-faith purchaser for value even though the delivery was in exchange for a check subsequently dishonored. In the instant case, Pruisner (D), who purchased the vehicles and whose checks for payment were dishonored, was nevertheless able to transfer a good title to a good-faith purchaser for value. Under §§ 1-201(32) and (33), a purchaser is one who takes "by sale mortgage lien or any other voluntary transaction creating an interest in property." There is no question that the security agreement between Pruisner (D) and Chrysler (D) transferred Pruisner's (D) interest in the vehicles to Chrysler (D). And § 1-201(44)(b) provides that a person gives value for rights if he obtains them as security for a preexisting claim. Chrysler (D) clearly qualifies as a good-faith purchaser for value. Swets (P) argued that if its (P) contract with Pruisner (D) were obtained by fraud or mutual mistake it would be void, and Pruisner (D) would have been unable to transfer any rights in the vehicles and Chrysler (D) could be neither a secured party nor a purchaser. Under the facts of the instant case and under the U.C.C., title to the vehicles passed upon delivery and Swets (P) did not by contract or otherwise reserve any interest in the vehicles. Pruisner (D) has sufficient rights to transfer good title to Chrysler (D). In addition, the U.C.C. provides remedies in the event of a credit sale to an insolvent buyer which were not pursued. The judgment of the trial court was correct in declaring Chrysler's (D) interest superior to Swets' (P). However, there remained a genuine issue of fact regarding the value of the vehicles at the time of attachment and the case must be remanded for further determination of the value of the vehicles. The judgment is therefore affirmed in part, and reversed in part and remanded for further proceedings.

EDITOR'S ANALYSIS: The U.C.C. provided a resolution of the problem of whether voidable title passed to a vendee who gave a bad check by permitting such title to pass. Adoption of this view, which in pre-Code times was a minority position, favors the potential third-party purchaser for value from the vendee. Where goods are delivered to a vendee without reservation of a security interest or any other action by the seller evidencing a desire to retain title until a check has cleared, the vendee would certainly appear to have title and a purchaser from such a vendee is deemed to deserve more protection than the original vendor.

NOTES:

CHAPTER 2
PERFECTION

QUICK REFERENCE RULES OF LAW

1. **Sufficiency of Financing Statement.** Errors in the name and address in a financing statement of record that no longer accurately reflect the secured party after a succession in interest of the secured party has occurred, do not render the financing statement seriously misleading and, therefore, insufficient to perfect the security interest granted. (In re Hergert)

2. **Possession by Agent.** The debtor's attorney may hold collateral as a valid bailee under U.C.C. § 9-305 to perfect the creditor's interest, so long as the attorney is not controlled by the debtor. (In re Rolain)

3. **Location of the Debtor.** Under U.C.C. §9-103, debtors are located in the jurisdiction where persons dealing with the debtor would normally look for credit information. (Mellon Bank v. Metro Communications, Inc.)

4. **What Law Governs Perfection?** The local law of the jurisdiction under whose certificate of title a motor vehicle is covered governs perfection. (Meeks v. Mercedes Benz Credit Corporation)

IN RE HERGERT

[Parties not listed.]

Bankr., 275 B.R. 58 (D. Idaho 2002).

NATURE OF CASE: Determination of perfection of security interests in a bankruptcy proceeding.

FACT SUMMARY: Pacific One Bank (Pacific) filed financing statements to secure Debtor's debt. Pacific was acquired by Bank, rendering the name and address of the secured party in the financing statements incorrect. Debtor claimed that these errors rendered the financing statement seriously misleading, and, therefore, insufficient to perfect the security interests in the financing statements.

CONCISE RULE OF LAW: Errors in the name and address in a financing statement of record that no longer accurately reflect the secured party after a succession in interest of the secured party has occurred, do not render the financing statement seriously misleading and, therefore, insufficient to perfect the security interest granted.

FACTS: Pacific One Bank (Pacific) financed Debtor's farm business through three secured loans: two commercial loans and a consumer loan. The commercial loans were secured by an Agricultural Security Agreement and two Commercial Security Agreements, which cross-collateralized the loan obligations. The consumer loan was secured by Debtor's manufactured home. To perfect the interests under the Agricultural Security Agreement, Pacific filed a U.C.C.-1F (farm products) financing statement. The U.C.C.-1F named Pacific as the secured party, with an Idaho address. To perfect the interests under the Commercial Security Agreements, Pacific filed a U.C.C.-1 financing statement that named Pacific as the secured party, with both the Idaho address and an Oregon address. The same addresses were also shown on the certificate of title (Title) that secured the Debtor's consumer loan, and on which Pacific was shown as lienholder. The addresses were correct when the statements were filed. In 1998, all of Pacific's assets were acquired by Bank, and although the Oregon address remained valid, the Idaho address expired. Neither the name nor the Idaho address was corrected to reflect that Bank was Pacific's successor in interest. In July 2001, Idaho repealed its then-current Article 9 and replaced it with a new Article 9 (New Article 9). In August 2001, a month later, Debtor filed for bankruptcy. New Article 9 provided that a financing statement would be effective despite minor errors or omissions, unless the errors or omissions rendered the statement "seriously misleading." However, it also expressly provided that a statement that failed to sufficiently provide the name of the debtor would be "seriously misleading." Debtor claimed that the errors in the U.C.C.-1F relating to the secured party's name and address rendered it ineffective to perfect the security interests therein.

ISSUE: Do errors in the name and address in a financing statement of record that no longer accurately reflect the secured party after a succession in interest of the secured party has occurred, render the financing statement seriously misleading, and, therefore, insufficient to perfect the security interest granted?

HOLDING AND DECISION: (Myers, J.) No. Errors in the name and address in a financing statement of record that no longer accurately reflect the secured party after a succession in interest of the secured party has occurred, do not render the financing statement seriously misleading, and, therefore, insufficient to perfect the security interest granted. Under New Article 9, a filing officer must refuse to accept a financing statement if it is not in compliance with provisions requiring a name or mailing address for the secured party. However, New Article 9 also protects improper statements provided they are in fact filed and contain certain essential information, even if the filing officer is required to refuse to accept it for filing. Here, the name of the secured party was Pacific, not the Bank. However, New Article 9 makes only a failure to sufficiently provide the name of the debtor a seriously misleading error—not the failure to provide the name of the secured party. Negative inference indicates, therefore, that an error in the name of the secured party is not of the same magnitude as an error in the name of the debtor, so, at a minimum, it is not automatically per se seriously misleading. An Official Comment to New Article 9 also indicates that an error in the secured party's name is not seriously misleading, as searches are not conducted under the secured party's name. Finally, New Article 9 indicates that the secured party identified in the financing statement is the "secured party of record" and will remain so until the situation is altered by amendment. However, nothing in the statute requires such amendment. As regards the address of a secured party, only a limited function is served by the inclusion of that address—it only indicates a place to which others can send any required notifications. Although the absence of an address requires that the statement be rejected for filing initially, such absence does not render the statement ineffective. For these reasons, the errors in the name or address of the secured party on the U.C.C.-1F did not render the filing of that statement ineffective to perfect the security interest covered therein. Therefore, Bank has a valid, perfected, security interest in the property described in the U.C.C.-1 and in the U.C.C.-1F, and in the manufactured home shown on the Title.

Continued on next page.

EDITOR'S ANALYSIS: U.C.C. § 9-502(a) provides that a financing statement is sufficient only if it provides the names of the debtor and secured party (or its representative). However, as this case shows, the structure of the U.C.C. makes the absence of a secured party's name or address grounds for the filing officer to reject the statement, but if the statement is accepted for filing, it will be effective despite such errors—because they are not "seriously misleading." Thus, as the case demonstrates, a financing statement can be effective even if it does not include some information, so long as it meets the basic requirements of § 9-502(a).

NOTES:

IN RE ROLAIN
Trustee in bankruptcy (P) v. Creditor board (D)
823 F.2d 198 (8th Cir. 1987).

NATURE OF CASE: Appeal of partial summary judgment that creditor had perfected a security interest.

FACT SUMMARY: A note securing Norwest's (P) loan to Rolain was held in the possession of Rolain's attorney, Mannikko.

CONCISE RULE OF LAW: The debtor's attorney may hold collateral as a valid bailee under U.C.C. § 9-305 to perfect the creditor's interest, so long as the attorney is not controlled by the debtor.

FACTS: Norwest (P) made a loan to Rolain guaranteed by a note from Owen. The note represented a debt of Owen to Rolain's company. Under U.C.C. § 9-305, a security interest may be perfected by having the secured party or a bailee take possession of the collateral. The interest is not perfected if the collateral is held by the debtor or someone under the debtor's control. Norwest (P) wanted possession of the Owen note to perfect its interest. However, Rolain had a confidentiality agreement with Owen, so Norwest (P) and Rolain agreed in writing that Rolain's attorney, Mannikko, would hold the note as Norwest's (P) agent. Rolain filed for bankruptcy. Norwest (P) moved for partial summary judgment that it had a perfected interest in the Owen note. The bankruptcy trustee, Berquist (D), filed a cross-motion claiming the attorney-client relationship put Mannikko under Rolain's control. Thus, Mannikko could not qualify as a § 9-305 bailee, Norwest's (P) interest was not perfected, and under Bankruptcy Code § 544(a) Berquist (D) could keep the note in the estate . The bankruptcy court granted Norwest's (P) motion, the district court affirmed, and Berquist (D) appealed.

ISSUE: May the debtor's attorney hold collateral as a valid bailee under U.C.C. § 9-305 to perfect the creditor's interest?

HOLDING AND DECISION: (Wright, Cir. J.) Yes. The debtor's attorney may hold collateral as a valid bailee under U.C.C. § 9-305 to perfect the creditor's interest, so long as the attorney is not controlled by the debtor. The purpose of § 9-305 is to give notice that property has been used as collateral and may not be repledged. When collateral is delivered to an agent not controlled by the debtor, the debtor no longer has unfettered use of the property and third parties are warned that the property is encumbered. The debtor's attorney is a valid bailee if he has the debtor's consent to act as a fiduciary to the creditor. In such a case both attorney and client are bound by the terms of the bailment agreement and the attorney is not controlled by the client. Here, Rolain consented to Mannikko's acting as an agent for Norwest (P), so Mannikko was not under Rolain's control. Affirmed.

EDITOR'S ANALYSIS: Berquist (D) claimed Mannikko's personal relationship with Rolain also disqualified him from acting as a § 9-305 bailee. The court disagreed, finding Rolain and Mannikko's joint business ventures and joint vacations, and the fact that they were personal confidants, insufficient to overcome Norwest's (P) determination that Mannikko could act as bailee.

NOTES:

MELLON BANK v. METRO COMMUNICATIONS, INC.

Secured creditor (P) v. Production company (D)

945 F.2d 635 (3rd Cir. 1991).

NATURE OF CASE: Review of bankruptcy court findings to determine the validity and priority of a security interest.

FACT SUMMARY: Mellon Bank (P) held a perfected security interest in Metro (D) assets. Mellon (P) refiled less than four months after Metro (D) announced that it was moving its headquarters to another state and two months before Metro (D) filed for bankruptcy.

CONCISE RULE OF LAW: Under U.C.C. § 9-103, debtors are located in the jurisdiction where persons dealing with the debtor would normally look for credit information.

FACTS: Metro (D) was purchased by TCI in a stock buy out. Mellon Bank (P) financed the buy out and also loaned money to Metro (D) for use as working capital under a line of credit agreement. On April 6, 1984, Metro (D) granted Mellon (P) a security interest in its property including accounts and general intangibles. Mellon (P) perfected by filing in Maryland, where Metro (D) was incorporated. On December 3, 1984, Metro's (D) parent company announced that the chief offices were moving to Pennsylvania. On February 5, 1985, Mellon (P) also filed a security interest in Pennsylvania. On March 15, 1985, Metro (D) filed a bankruptcy petition in Chapter 11. Mellon (P) filed a proceeding against Metro (D) to determine the validity and priority of its security interest. The bankruptcy court found that Mellon (P) had a voidable preference since, according to the court, the filing in Pennsylvania was a reperfection of a lapsed interest that occurred within ninety days of a bankruptcy filing. Since the perfection of an unperfected interest is treated as a transfer of property, and it occurred within ninety days of the filing, it was voidable under § 547(b). Mellon (P) appealed claiming that the Pennsylvania filing was timed under U.C.C. § 9-103(3) and Mellon's (P) perfected interest never lapsed.

ISSUE: Are debtors located in the jurisdiction where persons dealing with the debtor would look for credit information, under § 9-103?

HOLDING AND DECISION: (Rosenn, Cir. J.) Yes. Under U.C.C. § 9-103, debtors are located in the jurisdiction where persons dealing with the debtor would normally look for credit information. In this case, the bankruptcy court determined that Metro (D) moved its home office when it came under control of the parent corporation. Had Metro (D) moved in August, as the court found, Mellon's interest would have lapsed by February of the following year, and the reperfected interest by the Pennsylvania filing could have been set aside as a voidable preference. However, subsidiaries are presumed to be a separate entity. Creditors cannot be expected to analyze and understand the internal structure of related corporations. In fact, it appears from the record that Metro (D) kept its offices in Maryland until December 1984. Additionally, Metro's (D) business operations were conducted out of its Maryland offices until that time. Thus, Maryland is the jurisdiction where creditors normally would have looked for information about Metro (D) until December 1984. Accordingly, Mellon's (P) refiling in Pennsylvania did not constitute the reperfection of its security interest since its interest never lapsed under U.C.C. § 9-103. Reversed.

EDITOR'S ANALYSIS: The bankruptcy court looked at when Metro (D) was acquired by its parent company. The appellate court found that such inquiries were irrelevant to the location issue. This decision supports the notion that this determination under § 9-103 should not be governed by strict rules but by general principles of fairness.

NOTES:

MEEKS v. MERCEDES BENZ CREDIT CORPORATION

Bankruptcy trustee (P) v. Creditor (D)

257 F.3d 843 (8th Cir. 2001).

NATURE OF CASE: Appeal from judgment affirming bankruptcy court judgment upholding a creditor's lien in proceeds from the sale of a debtor's asset.

FACT SUMMARY: Stinnett's (Debtor's) truck was registered and titled in Oklahoma, although his residence was listed as Arkansas on his security agreement for the truck, which was held by Mercedes-Benz Credit Corporation (MBCC) (D). During Debtor's bankruptcy, the bankruptcy trustee, Meeks (Trustee) (P) claimed that Arkansas's laws concerning motor vehicle registration, not Oklahoma's laws, governed, and that under Arkansas's laws, MBCC's (D) security interest in the truck was not perfected.

CONCISE RULE OF LAW: The local law of the jurisdiction under whose certificate of title a motor vehicle is covered governs perfection.

FACTS: Stinnett (Debtor) purchased a truck on credit from Texarkana Truck Center, Inc. (TTC), in Texas. The parties' security agreement indicated that his home address was in Arkansas. The security agreement was assigned immediately to Mercedes-Benz Credit Corporation (MBCC) (D). The truck was registered and titled in Oklahoma, which issued a title reflecting a lien in favor of MBCC (D). However, the truck was operated from Arkansas. Debtor went into bankruptcy, and the bankruptcy court concluded that under Arkansas law, Oklahoma law controlled the perfection of MBCC's (D) security interest. The bankruptcy court then determined that because Oklahoma law requires indication of a security interest on the certificate of title for perfection, MBCC's (D) interest was perfected for purposes of Arkansas law. The district court affirmed. The bankruptcy trustee, Meeks (Trustee) (P) appealed, arguing that Arkansas's statutes concerning motor vehicle registration applied to determine the validity of MBCC's (D) security interest, and that under these provisions, the security interest was not perfected because the truck was never registered in Arkansas. The Court of Appeals granted review.

ISSUE: Does the local law of the jurisdiction under whose certificate of title a motor vehicle is covered govern perfection?

HOLDING AND DECISION: (Per curiam) Yes. The local law of the jurisdiction under whose certificate of title a motor vehicle is covered governs perfection. Under Arkansas law (which parallels U.C.C. § 9-103(2)) where goods are covered by a certificate of title issued under the statute of another jurisdiction, perfection of the security interest is governed by the law of the jurisdiction issuing the certificate of title—where the security interest must be indicated on the certificate as a condition of perfection. Under Oklahoma law (the law of the other jurisdiction) a statement of lien or encumbrance must be included on an Oklahoma certificate of title and is deemed continuously perfected. Trustee's (P) argument that Arkansas motor vehicle law applies instead is incorrect, as the issue is the perfection of a security interest, not compliance with Arkansas's vehicle registration laws, which serve a different purpose. Applying the U.C.C. provisions enables buyers and lenders readily to ascertain the existence of lines on vehicles and promotes the purpose of the U.C.C., which is to promote the uniform recognition of security interests that have been noted on a certificate of title. Affirmed.

EDITOR'S ANALYSIS: Under U.C.C. § 9-311(a)(2), a security interest in goods in which a certificate-of-title law provides for a security interest to be noted on the certificate as a condition or result of perfection, cannot be perfected by filing a financing statement. Thus, compliance with the certificate-of-title law is made in lieu of filing a financing statement, and under § 9-311(b), the security interest so perfected remains perfected notwithstanding a change in the use or transfer of possession of the collateralized goods. Generally, as this case demonstrates, the local law of the jurisdiction under whose certificate of title the goods are covered governs perfection.

NOTES:

CHAPTER 3
PRIORITY

QUICK REFERENCE RULES OF LAW

1. **Purchase Money Security Interests.** A purchase-money creditor need only perfect its interest upon sale, even if the debtor had prior possession of the collateral. (Brodie Hotel Supply, Inc. v. United States)

2. **Requirements for Purchase Money Security Interest in Inventory.** Exercise of after-acquired property and future advances clauses in a security agreement converts a purchase money security interest into an ordinary security interest. (Southtrust Bank v. Borg-Warner Acceptance Corp.)

3. **Double Debtors.** If a debtor transfers collateral without authorization of the creditor, the creditor's perfected security interest in the collateral takes priority over any liens against the purchaser of the collateral. (Bank of the West v. Commercial Credit Financial Services, Inc.)

4. **The New Definitions.** A secured creditor's interest in a debtor's general intangibles gives the creditor an interest in proceeds recovered from a lawsuit sounding in negligence, the gravamen of which is a contract between the debtor and the party who has allegedly committed the negligence. (In re Wiersma)

5. **Effect of Sales of Receivables: The Octagon Heresy.** A sale of accounts leaves a residual interest in the transferor of the accounts after the sale that falls within the transferor's bankruptcy estate. (Octagon Gas v. Rimmer)

6. **Section 9-309(2) Exception.** The filing of an assignment is required to perfect a security interest when the transaction is not casual and isolated. (In re Tri-County Materials, Inc.)

7. **Chattel Paper and Instruments.** According to U.C.C. § 9-308, a purchaser or chattel paper who gives new value and takes possession of it in the ordinary course of his business has priority over a security interest in chattel paper which is claimed merely as proceeds of inventory subject to a security interest, even though he knows that the specific paper is subject to the security interest. (Rex Financial Corp. v. Great Western Bank & Trust)

8. **Pre-Revision Background.** A recipient of a payment made by a debtor in the ordinary course of the debtor's business takes that payment free and clear of any claim a secured creditor may have in the payment as proceeds. (HCC Credit Corporation v. Springs Valley Bank & Trust)

9. **Lowest Intermediate Balance Rule.** Since the U.C.C. offers no guidance as to how to trace funds deposited in a bank account after the sale of secured collateral, the common law "lowest intermediate balance rule" should be used to determine what funds in the account may be claimed by the secured creditor. (Chrysler Credit Corporation v. Superior Court)

10. **§ 6323(c) and (d)s' Exceptions: Post-Lien Transactions.** A security interest has priority over a federal tax lien where it is perfected in property prior to the filing of the notice of the federal tax lien. (McCord v. Petland, Inc.)

11. **PMSIs and Post-Lien Proceeds.** For purposes of the Federal Tax Lien Act's § 6323(c) safe harbor provisions for after-acquired property, a security interest in qualified contract rights covers the proceeds of those rights, even where such proceeds are an account receivable, and the proceeds fall within the scope of the safe harbor's protection. (Plymouth Savings Bank v. Internal Revenue Service)

BRODIE HOTEL SUPPLY, INC. v. UNITED STATES
Supply company (P) v. Federal government (D)
431 F.2d 1316 (9th Cir. 1970).

NATURE OF CASE: Appeal from order setting priority to the proceeds of certain equipment.

FACT SUMMARY: Brodie Hotel Supply (P) took a security interest in certain equipment, which had been possessed by one Lyon on a rental basis, at the time it sold the equipment to Lyon.

CONCISE RULE OF LAW: A purchase-money creditor need only perfect its interest upon sale, even if the debtor had prior possession of the collateral.

FACTS: Brodie Hotel Supply, Inc. (P), acquired title to certain equipment in a hotel restaurant. The equipment remained in the hotel, which was purchased by Lyon. Brodie (P) allowed Lyon to use the equipment, for which Lyon paid rent. This arrangement lasted about five months, whereupon Lyon purchased the equipment, and Brodie (P) took a purchase-money security interest, which it perfected in a timely fashion. However, about two weeks prior to sale, Lyon had borrowed $17,000 from National Bank, which had taken a security interest in the hotel, including the equipment. Lyon defaulted, and the hotel equipment was sold. Brodie (P) sued to obtain the funds generated from the equipment, which had been deposited with the court. The district court held Brodie (P) to have priority, and the federal government (D) appealed.

ISSUE: Must a purchase-money creditor perfect its interest only upon sale, even if the debtor had had prior possession of the collateral?

HOLDING AND DECISION: (Hamley, Cir. J.) Yes. A purchase-money creditor need only perfect its interest upon sale, even if the debtor had prior possession of the collateral. U.C.C. § 9-312(4) gives a purchase-money lender priority over all other security interests if it perfects within ten days after the debtor receives possession of the goods. A debtor becomes a debtor only when a purchase money agreement is executed. If the debtor had previously possessed the collateral under some other arrangement, such as a leasehold interest, he was not a "debtor" and, therefore, the owner of the goods had no security interest to perfect. The government (D) argued that this allows debtors to work frauds upon other creditors. On the contrary, it is incumbent upon lenders to inquire as to the status of goods upon which it lends credit. Here, Lyon did not become a debtor until it purchased the goods, so Brodie's (P) properly perfected interest had priority. Affirmed.

EDITOR'S ANALYSIS: Section 9-312(4) is silent on the issue here, and the official comments provide no further information.

Not unexpectedly, some courts have reached contrary conclusions. The rationale therefor is the same put forth by the government (D), *i.e.*, the rule of this case allows for frauds to be perpetrated upon other creditors. It would appear to be nothing more than a policy judgment as to whether lenders must bear the burden of inquiry.

NOTES:

SOUTHTRUST BANK v. BORG-WARNER ACCEPTANCE CORP.

Priority dispute.
760 F.2d 1240 (11th Cir. 1985).

NATURE OF CASE: Appeal of order establishing creditor priority in bankruptcy action.

FACT SUMMARY: Borg-Warner (D) claimed that its purchase money security interests (PMSIs) in the debtors' inventory took priority over Southtrust's (P) earlier-filed security interests.

CONCISE RULE OF LAW: Exercise of after-acquired property and future advances clauses in a security agreement converts a purchase money security interest into an ordinary security interest.

FACTS: Southtrust (P) filed financing statements perfecting security interests in four commercial debtors' inventories. Later, Borg-Warner (D) made PMSI agreements with the same debtors through which Borg-Warner (D) perfected interests in all the debtors' existing and after-acquired inventories. The agreements provided for future advances for the debtors to purchase more inventory. Borg-Warner (D) regularly purchased inventory for the debtors. The debtors each went bankrupt, and Southtrust (P) sued for a declaration that it had priority over the debtors' remaining inventories because it was first to file. Borg-Warner (D) countered that it was entitled to priority under U.C.C. § 9-312(3), which provides that PMSIs take priority over ordinary security interests. The district court ruled that the after-acquired property and future advances clauses in Borg-Warner's (D) agreements transformed its PMSIs into ordinary security interests. Thus, as first to file, Southtrust (P) was awarded possession of the all of the inventories. Borg-Warner (D) appealed.

ISSUE: Does exercise of after-acquired property and future advances clauses convert a PMSI into an ordinary security interest?

HOLDING AND DECISION: (Tuttle, Sr., Cir. J.) Yes. Exercise of after-acquired property and future advances clauses in a security agreement converts a PMSI into an ordinary security interest. By buying inventory for the debtors, Borg-Warner (D) exercised the clauses. It need not be decided whether mere inclusion of such clauses in an agreement transforms a PMSI. Unlike here, most prior PMSI transformation cases involved consumer bankruptcy, but the U.C.C. provides no statutory basis for distinguishing between consumer and commercial cases. Some courts have allowed creditors in Borg-Warner's (D) position to gain priority on part of the debtor's inventory, to the extent of the PMSI, by determining which part of the debtor's inventory is PMSI inventory and which part is after-acquired inventory. However, unlike here,

the security agreements in those cases provided contractual guidance as to how to draw the distinction. Affirmed.

EDITOR'S ANALYSIS: Under § 9-312(3) a PMSI creditor who was not first to file has priority over the proceeds of collateral inventory only to the extent they are received by the debtor before delivery of inventory to the buyer. This means the creditor does not have priority over proceeds from credit sales, e.g., accounts receivable. The only benefit § 9-312(3) provides to PMSI creditors who were not first to file is priority as to possession of the debtor's unsold inventory at bankruptcy. The *Southtrust* case casts doubt on whether a PMSI creditor will even get that.

NOTES:

17

BANK OF THE WEST v. COMMERCIAL CREDIT FINANCIAL SERVICES, INC.
Priority dispute.
852 F.2d 1162 (9th Cir. 1988).

NATURE OF CASE: Appeal of order subordinating security interest.

FACT SUMMARY: CCFS (D) had a lien on BCI's property, BCI sold some of CCFS's (D) collateral to Allied, and CCFS (D) and the Bank (P), Allied's secured creditor, both claimed first priority over the transferred collateral.

CONCISE RULE OF LAW: If a debtor transfers collateral without authorization of the creditor, the creditor's perfected security interest in the collateral takes priority over any liens against the purchaser of the collateral.

FACTS: In 1982, Bank of the West (P) made a loan to Allied and was granted a security interest in Allied's current and future inventory and accounts. The Bank (P) filed a financing statement, perfecting the interest. In 1984, CCFS (D) made loans to BCI and was granted a security interest in BCI's current and future inventory and accounts. CCFS (D) filed a financing statement, perfecting the interest. Without express or implied approval by CCFS (D), BCI sold its beverage business to Allied, including inventory and accounts in which CCFS (D) had a security interest. Both the Bank (P) and CCFS (D) claimed their security interest took priority as to the transferred collateral. The district court found for the Bank (P) under U.C.C. § 9-312 because its financing statement had been filed first. CCFS (D) appealed.

ISSUE: If a debtor transfers collateral without authorization of the creditor, does the creditor's perfected security interest in the collateral take priority over any liens against the purchaser of the collateral?

HOLDING AND DECISION: (Thompson, Cir. J.) Yes. If a debtor transfers collateral without authorization of the creditor, the creditor's perfected security interest in the collateral takes priority over any liens against the purchaser of the collateral. Under § 9-306(2), CCFS's interest continued because it did not authorize the transfer. The issue is which interest takes priority. Section 1-102(a) directs application of the U.C.C. to promote the purposes of the Code. Section 9-312 has two purposes, neither of which is promoted by applying it to this case. First, § 9-312 protects creditors from prior unfiled security interests of which there is no notice. Here, though, the notice function does not apply since the Bank (P) had a different debtor from CCFS's (D) so there could be no detrimental reliance on a failure to file. Second, § 9-312 protects a creditor who complies with the filing system. Here, however, application of § 9-312 would punish CCFS (D) even though CCFS (D) promptly filed. Since § 9-312 should not be applied, the correct result is reached by applying the common

sense notion that a transferor cannot transfer more than it has. BCI could not, and did not, transfer its beverage business free of CCFS's (D) first priority on its inventory. Reversed.

EDITOR'S ANALYSIS: Under § 9-402(7) the court further held that CCFS (D) not only maintained its first lien on collateral transferred from BCI to Allied, but also had a first lien over any of Allied's assets acquired in the four months after the transfer which could be traced to the beverage business.

NOTES:

IN RE WIERSMA
[Parties not listed.]
Bankr., 283 B.R. 294 (D. Idaho, 2002).

NATURE OF CASE: Motion in bankruptcy proceeding to determine secured status.

FACT SUMMARY: The Wiersmas (Debtors) (P) claimed in their bankruptcy proceeding that the perfected security interest in Debtors' (P) general intangibles held by one of their secured creditors, United California Bank (UCB) (D), did not cover as collateral any interest Debtors (P) had in a negligence lawsuit against Gietzen Electric, Inc. (Gietzen) stemming from Debtors' (P) contract with Gietzen.

CONCISE RULE OF LAW: A secured creditor's interest in a debtor's general intangibles gives the creditor an interest in proceeds recovered from a lawsuit sounding in negligence, the gravamen of which is a contract between the debtor and the party who has allegedly committed the negligence.

FACTS: Debtors (P) owned a dairy. In 1998, they borrowed over $2.2 million from United California Bank (UCB) (D). In connection with that loan, Debtors (P) signed a security agreement in favor of UCB (D), in which they granted UCB (D) a security interest in Debtors' (P) "… General Intangibles …." In addition, the security agreement provided that UCB's (D) "interest in the collateral shall be a continuing lien and shall include all proceeds and products of the collateral including, but not limited to, the proceeds of any insurance thereon." UCB (D) perfected its interest. Debtors (P) filed for bankruptcy in October 2001. A significant factor leading to Debtors' (P) financial problems stemmed from electrical work performed by Gietzen Electric, Inc. (Gietzen) at the Debtors' (P) dairy. Apparently as a result of Gietzen's alleged negligence in completing the job, Debtors' (P) dairy cows were subjected to varying degrees of electric shocks. This ultimately caused the cows to produce a lower quantity and quality of milk, to become sick, and in some cases, to die. Debtors (P) sued Gietzen for, among other things, negligence and breach of contract, in state court for their losses, and Gietzen offered to settle for $2.5 million. (Debtors (P) had also executed a $550,000 promissory note in favor of O.H. Kruse Grain & Milling (O.H. Kruse) (D), secured by an agreement that purported to assign to O.H. Kruse (D) an interest in any proceeds from the Gietzen lawsuit.) UCB (D) claimed that any proceeds from the Gietzen settlement constituted a "general intangible," and, therefore, fell within the scope of the collateral in which UCB (D) had an interest. Debtors (P) argued that their claim against Gietzen was a commercial tort, and was, accordingly, excluded from the definition of a general intangible.

ISSUE: Does a secured creditor's interest in a debtor's general intangibles give the creditor an interest in proceeds recovered from a lawsuit sounding in negligence, the gravamen of which is

a contract between the debtor and the party who has allegedly committed the negligence?

HOLDING AND DECISION: (Pappas, C.J.) Yes. A secured creditor's interest in a debtor's general intangibles gives the creditor an interest in proceeds recovered from a lawsuit sounding in negligence, the gravamen of which is a contract between the debtor and the party who has allegedly committed the negligence. Revised Article 9 controls the court's analysis of the issues presented. Under the U.C.C., a general intangible includes things in action, but excludes commercial tort claims. Under Article 9, for individuals such as Debtors (P), a commercial tort claim must, by definition, arise in tort. The U.C.C. itself does not provide direction for determining whether a claim arises in tort, nor has any state case decided this issue directly under Article 9. Under another line of cases, if a party's claims against another are not premised primarily on tort causes of action, and where a contract between the parties exists, the claims need not be characterized as arising in tort. Applying that reasoning here, Debtors' (P) suit against Gietzen is primarily premised on a contract between Debtors (P) and Gietzen for the provision of electrical services. However, more is required to determine whether Debtors' (P) claim arises in contract than the mere existence of a contract. Here, Debtors' (P) claims for breach of contract and breach of warranty related directly to their contract with Gietzen. Clearly, the contract was integral to these claims. Debtors' (P) other claims, including those for negligence, fraud, and violations of the state's Consumer Protection Act, while not traditional contract claims, are also integrally related to the contract. The presence of these other causes of action in Debtors' (P) complaint did not change the fundamental nature of the action and its genesis in contract law. Because the contract between Debtors (P) and Gietzen was the gravamen of Debtors' (P) claims, the court concludes that those claims arose in contract rather than tort. Therefore, Debtors' (P) right to recover against Gietzen was not a commercial tort claim and, therefore, Debtors' (P) claim against Gietzen was a general intangible, and, therefore, subject to UCB's (D) security agreement. Moreover, a cause of action is a thing in action, which is a type of general intangible. Accordingly, UCB's (D) perfected security interest in Debtors' (P) general intangibles applies to the Gietzen lawsuit.

EDITOR'S ANALYSIS: The court also determined that O.H. Kruse (D) was granted a security interest in Debtors' (D) claim against Gietzen rather than receiving an absolute assignment of

Continued on next page.

Debtors' (P) interest in the claim. An absolute assignment effects a transfer of all an owner's interest in property, whereas a security interest is an interest in personal property or fixtures which secures payment or performance of an obligation. While distinguishing between the two types of transactions is sometimes difficult, courts often look past the express language of the documents evidencing a transaction and treat purported assignments as security agreements to give effect to the true nature of a transaction. Here, although Debtors (P) signed a document entitled "Assignment," which might have suggested the document was intended to effect an absolute conveyance of the Gietzen claim from Debtors (P) to O.H. Kruse (D), the court held that regardless of the form of this instrument, the substance of the relevant documents indicated that both the parties intended to create a security interest rather than an assignment.

NOTES:

OCTAGON GAS v. RIMMER

Successor in interest to debtor (P) v. Purchaser of account (D)

995 F.2d 948 (10th Cir. 1993).

NATURE OF CASE: Appeal from summary judgment granted in a bankruptcy proceeding to the purchaser of an account.

FACT SUMMARY: Rimmer (D) purchased a royalty "account" in the proceeds from the sale of natural gas from Poll Gas, Inc. (Poll), which subsequently declared bankruptcy and was eventually sold to Octagon Gas (Octagon) (P). Octagon (P) refused to make payments to Rimmer (D) on his account.

CONCISE RULE OF LAW: A sale of accounts leaves a residual interest in the transferor of the accounts after the sale that falls within the transferor's bankruptcy estate.

FACTS: Poll Gas, Inc. (Poll) owned an "overriding royalty interest" in proceeds of natural gas sold through its gathering system, and sold Rimmer a 5% share of the royalty. Poll filed for bankruptcy, and under a plan of reorganization, was sold to Octagon Gas (Octagon) (P). Octagon (P) refused to make payments to Rimmer (D) on the ground that Rimmer (D) owned an account, governed by U.C.C. Article 9, that became part of Poll's bankruptcy estate. Rimmer (D), conceding that he had purchased an account, maintained that he, not Poll, owned the interest outright, so that it could never have been part of Poll's bankruptcy estate. The bankruptcy court granted summary judgment to Rimmer (D), holding that Article 9 was inapplicable because Article 9 provides a classification of interests for the purpose of determining competing secured interests, not a classification for the creation of an ownership right in personal property. The district court affirmed, and the court of appeals granted review.

ISSUE: Does a sale of accounts leave any residual interest in the transferor of the accounts after the sale that falls within the transferor's bankruptcy estate?

HOLDING AND DECISION: (Baldock, Cir. J.) Yes. A sale of accounts leaves a residual interest in the transferor of the accounts after the sale that falls within the transferor's bankruptcy estate. Article 9 applies to sales of accounts, because sales of wholly intangible interests in accounts create the same risks of secret liens inherent in secured transactions. Rimmer (D) held an account to which Article 9 is applicable, as Article 9 defines an account as any right to payment for goods sold which is not evidenced by an instrument or chattel paper. Extracted natural gas is a "good" that comes within this definition. Therefore, Rimmer (D) is to be treated, under Article 9, as a secured party, and his interest as a secured interest, whether the transaction was intended to create such an interest or not. The impact of applying Article 9 to Rimmer's (D) account is that Article 9's

treatment of accounts sold as collateral would place Rimmer's (D) account within the property of Poll's bankruptcy estate. The bankruptcy court, siding with Rimmer (D), held that because Rimmer (D) purchased the account, he had title to the account and "owned" it, and, therefore, Poll no longer had any ownership interest in the account, and thus Poll's bankruptcy estate could not include the account. However, the assignment of the account to Rimmer (D) did not transfer all property interests in the account. There is no policy reason or case law that provides that a debtor's sale of an account, prior to filing for bankruptcy, places the account beyond the reach of the bankruptcy trustee. Because Article 9 treats Rimmer (D) as a secured party, Poll, as the seller or assignor of the account, does not part with all transferable rights in the account even following absolute assignment. To hold otherwise, would allow an account buyer to benefit unfairly, at the expense of a bankrupt debtor's other creditors, from the debtor's filing for bankruptcy. Accordingly, the bankruptcy court was wrong in holding that Article 9 was inapplicable to Rimmer's (D) interest, and must determine whether Rimmer's (D) account was perfected. Reversed and remanded.

EDITOR'S ANALYSIS: Most commentators, legislators, and courts believe this decision was wrong. This decision was decided under old Article 9. When Revised Article 9 was drafted, a special section, 9-318(a), was enacted specifically to reject the holding in *Octagon*. Some states went even further, providing special statutory protection for securitization transactions (such as the one involved in this case) by providing that property transferred in a securitization transaction no longer is property of the transferor and does not remain part of the transferor's bankruptcy estate.

NOTES:

IN RE TRI-COUNTY MATERIALS, INC.

Debtor (D) v. Creditor (P)

114 B.R. 160 (C.D. Ill. 1990).

NATURE OF CASE: Appeal of denial of bankruptcy court denial of recognition of a perfected security interest.

FACT SUMMARY: KMB, lessor of equipment to Tri-County, was assigned a part of Tri-County's contract with Ladd but neglected to file a financing statement as required by U.C.C. § 9-302.

CONCISE RULE OF LAW: The filing of an assignment is required to perfect a security interest when the transaction is not casual and isolated.

FACTS: KMB leased equipment to Tri-County in return for Tri-County's assignment of part of its contract with Ladd Construction, although KMB did not usually engage in this type of financing. Ladd was notified of the assignment and received periodic notification of the amount due to KMB under the assignment. KMB failed to file the standard financing statement regarding the assignment. Later, Tri-County filed for bankruptcy, at which time Ladd owed Tri-County $43,413.71, and Tri-County owed KMB $30,484. KMB contended that it had a security interest under the assignment of the funds owed by Ladd. The bankruptcy court ruled that KMB did not have a security interest since it had failed to perfect the interest by filing pursuant to U.C.C. § 9-302. KMB appealed.

ISSUE: Is the filing of an assignment necessary under U.C.C. § 9-302 to perfect a security interest where the transaction is not casual and isolated?

HOLDING AND DECISION: (Mihm, Dist. J.) Yes. Under § 9-302, the filing of an assignment is necessary to perfect a security interest when the transaction is not casual and isolated. The financing statement does not need to be filed if the assignment was casual and isolated and if the assignment represents an insignificant part of outstanding accounts. The party seeking this exception has the burden of proof. KMB's assignment was for approximately $30,000, which represented only 12% of the total outstanding account of the Ladd contract. Twelve percent is considered insignificant for purposes of the § 9-302 exception. Although KMB was not in the business of accepting contract assignments, the assignment at issue was not casual since it was the type of formal agreement regarding which reasonable parties acknowledge the importance of filing. Therefore, KMB did not prove that it was entitled to the exception, and pursuant to § 9-302, the filing of a financing statement was required to perfect its security interest. Affirmed.

EDITOR'S ANALYSIS: Comment 5 to U.C.C. § 9-302 states that the exception to the filing requirement is to save from invalidation assignments which parties would not think to file. It explicitly notes that parties who regularly take assignments of any debtor's accounts without regard to their casual nature should file regardless of the amount. Some courts apply only the casual-and-isolated portion of the test and do not require parties to heed the suggestion made in Comment 5.

NOTES:

REX FINANCIAL CORP. v.
GREAT WESTERN BANK & TRUST
Priority dispute.
Ariz. Ct. App., 23 Ariz.App. 286, 532 P.2d 558 (1975).

NATURE OF CASE: Action involving conflicting interests in chattel paper.

FACT SUMMARY: Rex Financial (P) financed the inventory of a dealer in mobile homes and received a security interest in the vehicles, after which the dealer sold the security agreement contracts signed by the buyers of the homes to Great Western (D) without using the funds to pay off Rex (P).

CONCISE RULE OF LAW: According to U.C.C. § 9-308, a purchaser of chattel paper who gives new value and takes possession of it in the ordinary course of his business has priority over a security interest in chattel paper which is claimed merely as proceeds of inventory subject to a security interest, even though he knows that the specific paper is subject to the security interest.

FACTS: As a result of its agreeing to finance a dealer's inventory of mobile homes, Rex (P) was given certain manufacturer's certificates of origin on the vehicles and a security interest in the vehicles themselves (to secure repayment of the loans). In the regular course of his business, the dealer sold four of the mobile homes on security agreement contracts. He then took those contracts, sold them, and assigned them to Great Western (D), which had knowledge of Rex's (P) security interest. Great Western (D) purchased them in the ordinary course of its business, but the dealer failed to use the funds he thus obtained to pay off his outstanding loans to Rex (P). The litigation that resulted required the courts to establish a priority between the conflicting interests Rex (P) and Great Western (D) had in the security agreements. Treating Great Western's (D) motion to dismiss as a motion for summary judgment, the trial court came down on the side of Great Western (D) after concluding that there was no genuine issue of material fact. On appeal, Rex (P) made several arguments as to why Great Western (D) did not come within the reach of U.C.C. § 9-308, which provides that "a purchaser of chattel paper who gives new value and takes possession of it in the ordinary course of his business has priority over a security interest in chattel paper which is claimed merely as proceeds of inventory subject to a security interest, even though he knows that the specific paper is subject to the security interest."

ISSUE: Under U.C.C. § 9-308, does a purchaser of chattel paper who gives new value and takes possession of it in the ordinary course of his business have priority over a security interest in chattel paper which is claimed merely as proceeds of inventory subject to a security interest, even though he knows that the specific paper is subject to the security interest?

HOLDING AND DECISION: (Donofrio, J.) Yes. As U.C.C. § 9-308 states: "A purchaser of chattel paper who gives new value and takes possession of it in the ordinary course of his business has priority over a security interest in chattel paper which is claimed merely as proceeds of inventory subject to a security interest, even though he knows that the specific paper is subject to the security interest." The argument has been made that the manufacturer's certificates of origin which Rex (P) kept in its possession were a part of the chattel paper and were necessary ingredients along with the security agreements purchased by Great Western (D) to make up the "chattel paper" which must be possessed by the purchaser. It is not a valid point. "Chattel paper" as defined in the U.C.C. clearly must evidence "both a monetary obligation and a security interest in or a lease of specified goods." The manufacturer's certificates of origin do not meet this definition, As to some of the remaining contentions, it is clear that Great Western (D) gave "new value" for the four security agreements it purchased from the dealer and that it purchased the chattel paper "in the ordinary course of his (its) business." It is also clear that Rex's (P) claim was merely to the proceeds of the inventory when sold. It is a reasonable interpretation of the record that Rex (P) did not place a substantial reliance on the chattel paper in making the loan to the mobile home dealer, but rather relied on the collateral (the mobile homes) and the proceeds when the collateral was sold. The proceeds of the sale of the four mobile homes included the chattel paper sold by the mobile home dealer to Great Western (D). Rex (P) could have protected itself by requiring all security agreements executed on the sale of the mobile homes to be turned over immediately to Rex (P), or if sold, that all payments for the security agreements (chattel paper) be made to itself. In any case, the construction and application of U.C.C. § 9-308 to undisputed facts is a question of law for the trial court which was reasonably determined in the instant case. Affirmed.

EDITOR'S ANALYSIS: White and Summers offer a concise explanation of the reasoning behind making the prior secured party's interest subordinate to that of the purchaser of chattel paper. As they put it, "the later party is favored on the assumption that chattel paper is his main course but merely the frosting on the cake for the mere proceeds claimant." White and Summers, Uniform Commercial Code, § 25-17, p. 951 (1972 Edition).

HCC CREDIT CORPORATION v. SPRINGS VALLEY BANK & TRUST

Secured creditor (P) v. Bank (D)

Ind. Sup. Ct., 712 N.E.2d 952 (1999).

NATURE OF CASE: Suit by secured creditor seeking to recover the proceeds of a sale of the creditor's collateral.

FACT SUMMARY: HCC (P) sought to recover $199,122 in proceeds obtained by Lindsey Tractor Sales from the sale of 14 Hesston tractors, in which HCC (P) held a valid and perfected security interest, and which was used by Lindsey to pay off a debt it owed Springs Valley Bank & Trust (D).

CONCISE RULE OF LAW: A recipient of a payment made by a debtor in the ordinary course of the debtor's business takes that payment free and clear of any claim a secured creditor may have in the payment as proceeds.

FACTS: Lindsey purchased wholesale farm equipment from Hesston for resale in Lindsey's farm machinery sales and service business. The financing for these purchases was provided by HCC (P). The relationship between Lindsey and Hesston was governed by written contracts, including a security agreement. The agreement granted HCC (P) a security interest in all the equipment purchased from Hesston and in the proceeds from the sale of that equipment. The agreement also provided for immediate payment from the sale proceeds. In 1991, the Indiana State Department of Transportation agreed to purchase 14 Hesston tractors from Lindsey. The state paid Lindsey $199,122, which was deposited in Lindsey's checking account at Springs Valley (D). The following day, Lindsey wrote a check on the account payable to the bank (D) for $212,104.75 in order to pay debts Lindsey owed Springs Valley (D). The debts were evidenced by four promissory notes that were not yet due. Lindsey filed a bankruptcy liquidation proceeding in December 1991. HCC (P) sought to recover the $199,122 in proceeds from the sale of the tractors that Lindsey had paid Springs Valley (D). The trial court granted summary judgment for Springs Valley (D) and the court of appeals affirmed. HCC (P) appealed.

ISSUE: Does a recipient of a payment made by a debtor in the ordinary course of the debtor's business take that payment free and clear of any claim a secured creditor may have in the payment as proceeds?

HOLDING AND DECISION: (Sullivan, J.) Yes. A recipient of a payment made by a debtor in the ordinary course of the debtor's business takes that payment free and clear of any claim a secured creditor may have in the payment as proceeds. HCC (P) had a valid and perfected security interest in the proceeds from Lindsey's sale of the tractors. Article 9 of the U.C.C. provides that a secured party has priority over any other party, except as otherwise provided by priority rules. The Official Comment 2(c) to

Article 9 states that when cash proceeds are placed in a debtor's checking account and paid out in the ordinary operation of the debtor's business, the recipient of those funds takes free of the secured party's claim in them as proceeds. Payment is in the ordinary course if it is made in the operation of the debtor's business, but not if there was collusion with the debtor to defraud the secured party. The type of relationship between the debtor and the transferee can create a presumption that the transferee was aware that it was acting to the prejudice of the secured creditor, including where the transferee is a lender. A secondary lender is generally presumed to have actual knowledge of prejudice to the secured party. Furthermore, a transfer is free of any claim a secured creditor may have to its proceeds unless the payment would constitute a windfall to the receiver. A windfall occurs when the recipient has no reasonable expectation of receiving payment prior to the secured creditor because either the payment was not in the ordinary course of business or the recipient was aware it was acting to the prejudice of the secured creditor or both. Here Lindsey's payment to Springs Valley (D) was not made in the ordinary course of business. The bank (D) was aware of HCC's (P) valid and perfected security interest in the proceeds of the sale of Lindsey's tractor inventory. Also, the payment was made before the debt to the bank (D) became due. The bank (D) had no reasonable expectation in being paid from the proceeds prior to HCC (P). To allow the bank (D) to retain the proceeds of the sale would constitute a windfall to the bank (D). Reversed and remanded.

EDITOR'S ANALYSIS: The court in making its determination weighed commercial policy considerations in favor of both parties. In Citizens National Bank, the court sought to alleviate the burden on secured creditors in the perfection of their interests. Conversely, *Harley-Davidson Motor Co. v. Bank of New England-Old Colony, N.A.* construed "ordinary course of business" as having a broad interpretation, thereby alleviating the burden on those recipients to determine whether they may receive those payments. The purpose of Comment 2(c) was to reconcile these conflicting considerations.

NOTES:

CHRYSLER CREDIT CORPORATION v. SUPERIOR COURT

Creditor (P) v. Debtor (D)

Cal. Ct. App., 17 Cal. App. 4th 1303 (1993).

NATURE OF CASE: Petition for writ of mandate on a denied motion to dismiss third-party claims to funds.

FACT SUMMARY: A debtor commingled funds from the sale of secured inventory with general funds, and the general funds account often had a negative balance which was covered by advances from the bank.

CONCISE RULE OF LAW: Since the U.C.C. offers no guidance as to how to trace funds deposited in a bank account after the sale of secured collateral, the common law "lowest intermediate balance rule" should be used to determine what funds in the account may be claimed by the secured creditor.

FACTS: Chrysler (P) provided financing to East County Dodge so that East County Dodge could purchase new Chrysler (P) vehicles for sale. Chrysler (P) held a security interest in each vehicle. Subsequently, East County Dodge filed for bankruptcy. The bankruptcy court authorized East County Dodge to sell vehicles and place the funds in a special cash collateral account. However, East County Dodge actually placed the funds into its general account and then placed them in the cash collateral account. Thus the sales proceeds were commingled with other funds. And the general account regularly reflected a negative balance, which the bank covered with advanced funds. Chrysler (P) filed an action to recover the funds held in the collateral account. Chrysler (P) filed a motion to dismiss third-party claims to the funds. Chrysler (P) appealed the denial of its motion.

ISSUE: Since the U.C.C. offers no guidance as to how to trace funds deposited in a bank account after the sale of secured collateral, should the common law "lowest intermediate balance rule" be used to determine what funds in the account may be claimed by the secured creditor?

HOLDING AND DECISION: (Stein, Assoc. J.) Yes. Since the U.C.C. offers no guidance as to how to trace funds deposited in a bank account after the sale of secured collateral, the common law "lowest intermediate balance rule" should be used to determine what funds in the account may be claimed by the secured creditor. In this case there is no issue as to the fact that Chrysler (P) had a perfected interest in the vehicles. The question is only whether the proceeds in the cash collateral account are identifiable proceeds from the collateral. The U.C.C. offers no guidance as to how to trace funds. The common law solution states that when a trustee depletes funds and then replaces them, the replaced funds do not return to the trust. Thus, the lowest balance will be all that is left of the trust funds, even where completely replaced. In this case, since the funds in the collateral account came from the general account, and the general account had a negative balance, the cash collateral account funds cannot be traced to the vehicle sales. Affirmed.

EDITOR'S ANALYSIS: This case is yet another situation in which secured creditors find themselves in difficulty when funds in a deposit account are sought as a security interest. Revisions of Article 9 have endorsed the use of principles of the common law, such as the lowest intermediate balance rule, to solve the problem of commingled funds. Coupled with the trend of giving banks the right to setoff, financing institutions have had to develop creative means to protect their interests, such as lock-box accounts over which the debtor has no control.

NOTES:

MCCORD v. PETLAND, INC.
Debtor (P) v. Creditor (D)
Bankr., 264 B.R. 814 (Bankr. N.D. W.Va. 2001).

NATURE OF CASE: Adversary proceeding in bankruptcy to determine priority of liens.

FACT SUMMARY: Promissory notes executed by the McCords (P) in favor of Petland, Inc. (Petland) (D) were secured by a lien on all accounts, leasehold items, fixtures, inventory, equipment, proceeds, and after-acquired collateral of stores owned by the McCords (P). Petland (D) filed financing statements covering the interests in the stores in 1997. In 1998, the I.R.S. (D) filed notices of Federal Tax Liens in the McCords' (P) county of residence covering all of the McCords' (P) property. In 1999, the McCords (P) filed for bankruptcy, and brought an adversary proceeding to determine the priority between Petland (D) and the I.R.S. (D).

CONCISE RULE OF LAW: A security interest has priority over a federal tax lien where it is perfected in property prior to the filing of the notice of the federal tax lien.

FACTS: The McCords (P) owned two pet stores in Maryland. Two promissory notes executed by the McCords (P) in favor of Petland, Inc. (Petland) (D), one for $95,000 and one for $60,646, were secured by a lien on all accounts, leasehold items, fixtures, inventory, equipment, proceeds, and after-acquired collateral of stores owned by the McCords (P). Petland (D) filed U.C.C.-1 financing statements covering the interests in the stores in 1997. On April 15, 1998, and on November 13, 1998, the I.R.S. (D) filed notices of Federal Tax Liens in the McCords' (P) county of residence in West Virginia covering all of the McCords' (P) property because they failed to pay FICA taxes. In 1999, the McCords (P) filed for bankruptcy. They claimed to have $60,000 assets in real estate and $91,803 in personal property. The entire inventory on hand on the date of the bankruptcy filing was acquired after April 14, 1998; all the leasehold items, fixtures, and equipment were purchased prior to April 14, 1998. Petland (D) claimed that its liens had priority over those of the I.R.S. (D) because it perfected its liens before the I.R.S. filed its notices of liens. The I.R.S. (D) countered that Petland's (D) liens attached after the notices were filed, and that, therefore, the I.R.S. (D) liens had priority. The McCords (P) brought an adversary proceeding to determine the priority between Petland (D) and the I.R.S. (D).

ISSUE: Does a security interest have priority over a federal tax lien where it is perfected in property prior to the filing of the notice of the federal tax lien?

HOLDING AND DECISION: (Friend, Bankr. J.) Yes. A security interest has priority over a federal tax lien where it is perfected in property prior to the filing of the notice of the federal tax lien. The U.S. Supreme Court's analysis in *United States v. McDermott*, 507 U.S. 447 (1993), holding that a federal tax lien filed before judgment debtors acquired real property had priority over the judgment creditor's previously recorded state lien, is applicable. Under that analysis, it is clear that the United States (D) has a secured claim in all of the McCord's (P) property, including the property subject to Petland's (D) interest, and it is also clear that Petland (D) has a secured interest under Maryland law. The issue, then, is when these respective interests were perfected. Petland (D) obtained an interest in all accounts, leasehold items, fixtures, inventory, equipment, proceeds, and after-acquired collateral in 1997. The liens on the relevant property already acquired by the McCords (P) were perfected when filed. However, the liens on the after-acquired property were not perfected until the McCords' (P) actual acquisition of that property. The federal tax lien notices were filed in 1998, and those liens were perfected as to property already acquired when the notices were filed. The liens on any after-acquired property were not perfected until the McCords (P) actually acquired the property. Under *McDermott*, Petland (D) has priority over the I.R.S. liens on any accounts, leasehold items, fixtures, inventory, equipment and proceeds of the pet stores acquired prior to April 15, 1998. The I.R.S. (D) has priority on any accounts, leasehold items, fixtures, inventory, equipment and proceeds of the pet stores acquired on or after April 15, 1998.

EDITOR'S ANALYSIS: Under the § 6323 of the Federal Tax Lien Act (FTLA), which is part of the Internal Revenue Code (I.R.C.), the accounts receivables and inventory would be considered "commercial financial security," and would be "qualified property" if security interests in those came into being within 45 days after the tax lien filing. As these were acquired after the April 15, 1998 tax lien notice was filed, under § 6323 Petland's (D) security interest in them would have been protected. However, the court in this case did not take these provisions into account in its opinion.

NOTES:

PLYMOUTH SAVINGS BANK v.
INTERNAL REVENUE SERVICE
Lienor (P) v. Lienor (D)
187 F.3d 203 (1st Cir. 1999).

NATURE OF CASE: Appeal from summary judgment on the priority of liens.

FACT SUMMARY: Plymouth Savings Bank (Bank) (P) and the Internal Revenue Service (I.R.S.) both held valid liens on money owed by Jordan Hospital (Hospital) to Shirley Dionne (Dionne) pursuant to a personal service contract, and each lienor claimed priority.

CONCISE RULE OF LAW: For purposes of the Federal Tax Lien Act's § 6323(c) safe harbor provisions for after-acquired property, a security interest in qualified contract rights covers the proceeds of those rights, even where such proceeds are an account receivable, and the proceeds fall within the scope of the safe harbor's protection.

FACTS: Shirley Dionne (Dionne) owed Plymouth Savings Bank (Bank) (P) $64,465 on a loan. The Bank (P) had a security interest in all of Dionne's personal property, including contract rights and all cash and non-cash proceeds resulting from the rendering of services by Dionne. Dionne had executed a $85,000 promissory note in favor of the Bank (P) on April 13, 1994. Dionne also owed money to the I.R.S. (D), which filed tax liens against Dionne's property on December 19, 1994, and February 14, 1995. On March 31, 1995, Dionne entered into a personal services contract with Jordan Hospital (Hospital). The Hospital owed Dionne a $75,000 balance on the contract, and the Bank (P) sued the Hospital in state court to recover this unpaid balance. The state court held that the Bank (P) had a secured interest in the money because it was a "proceed" of services, but instead of awarding the Bank (P) the money, it directed the Bank (P) to bring a declaratory judgment to determine whether its interest had priority over other lien-holders. The Bank (P) brought such an action. The I.R.S. (D) claimed that its liens had priority, and the federal district court granted summary judgment in its favor. The Bank (P) appealed.

ISSUE: For purposes of the Federal Tax Lien Act's safe harbor provisions for after-acquired property, does a security interest in qualified contract rights cover the proceeds of those rights, even when such proceeds are an account receivable, and the proceeds fall within the scope of the safe harbor's protections?

HOLDING AND DECISION: (Cudahy, Sr. Cir. J.) The Federal Tax Lien Act (FTLA) grants the U.S. a lien on all the property of a person who fails to pay taxes, whether acquired before or after the lien is filed. Section 6323, however, gives certain commercial liens priority over federal tax liens, including security interests in a taxpayer's property that are "in existence" before filing of the notice of the tax lien. Section 6323(c) extends the priority of these prior security interests to certain "qualified property" (the 6323(c) safe harbor) that is acquired after the notice of the tax lien. To fall within the safe harbor, a security interest must be in property covered by a "commercial transactions financing agreement." A commercial transactions financing agreement is secured by "commercial financing security," which can include paper of a kind arising in commercial transactions—which includes "contract rights"—and accounts receivable. A commercial financing security must be acquired before the 46th day after the date of the tax lien filing. Here, Dionne entered the contract with the Hospital exactly 45 days after the tax lien was filed. Thus, the issue is whether she "acquired" the right to the money owed her by the Hospital; if she did, then Bank's (P) lien trumps the I.R.S.'s (D) lien because the Dionne-Bank agreement is a commercial transactions financing agreement, the Dionne-Hospital contract is a commercial financing security, the Bank's (P) security is in qualified property, and the money is after-acquired property that falls within the safe harbor. If, conversely, Dionne did not acquire rights to the money when she signed the contract, the I.R.S.'s lien takes priority. Under I.R.S. regulations, what Dionne acquired when she signed the contract with the Hospital was a "contract right" to be paid in the future because she had not as yet performed, and, therefore, the contract, and the rights under it, is qualified property covered by the Bank's (P) security interest and protected by the safe harbor. The next issue is whether the money itself is such qualified property. Under the tax regulations, "proceeds" are whatever is received when collateral is "exchanged." Proceeds are considered acquired at the time that the qualified property is acquired. Here, therefore, the proceeds of the contract rights are considered to have been acquired by Dionne at the time she made the contract. However, the proceeds are an account receivable—the right to payment of the money upon performance. The I.R.S. (D) correctly argues that Dionne did not earn the right to payment before the 45 days from the tax lien filing. Nonetheless, it is the contract and the contract rights under it, not the account receivable, that constitutes the qualified property, and the proceeds under that qualified property are deemed acquired at the time the qualified property was acquired. This results because the regulations do not distinguish between forms of proceeds. Moreover, the account receivable is proceeds because Dionnes' performance "exchanged" her contract right into an account receivable. Here, the regulations make it clear that as long as the contract was entered into within 45 days of the

Continued on next page.

tax lien filing, the rights under that contract and all the proceeds of those rights come within the protection of § 6323's safe harbor. This result is supported by the U.C.C., the principles of which Congress intended to incorporate into the tax lien provisions. Accordingly, the Bank's (P) lien may trump the I.R.S.'s (D). Reversed and remanded.

EDITOR'S ANALYSIS: The I.R.S. argued that Dionne did not enter the contract in the "ordinary" course of her trade or business, as required by § 6323. The subject of the contract was the transfer of Dionne's business license, which, the I.R.S. argued, was not in the ordinary course of her business. However, the contract was a personal services contract, and such contracts were normally entered into in Dionne's business. The court left this issue of "ordinariness" for remand because it is a very fact-sensitive issue on which few facts had been developed, but it did note that if the I.R.S. characterized the transaction as a sale or transfer of a license, the proceeds from that transaction would clearly have entitled the Bank (P) to the money without having to "navigate § 6323(c)'s maze of definitions."

NOTES:

4

CHAPTER 4
DEFAULT AND ENFORCEMENT

QUICK REFERENCE RULES OF LAW

1. **Lender Liability.** Financing is withheld in bad faith if no reasonable loan officer in the same situation would have refused to advance funds. (K.M.C. Co., Inc. v. Irving Trust Company)

2. **Waiver and Estoppel.** Repeated acceptance of late payments by a creditor who has the contractual right to repossess collateral waives this right unless the debtor is notified that strict compliance with the contract terms will be required. (Moe v. John Deere Company)

3. **Breach of Peace.** A secured party has the right to repossess the collateral on default as long as the peace is not breached. (Williams v. Ford Motor Credit Co.)

4. **Notification Before Disposition.** A notice that fails to inform the debtor that the intended method of disposition is a private sale, that the debtor has a right to an accounting, and that the debtor will be liable for any deficiency following the sale is not sufficient to preserve the creditor's right to a deficiency claim. (In re Downing)

5. **Commercially Reasonable Disposition.** A creditor is entitled to summary judgment on damages arising from the breach of security agreements after the repossession and sale of the collateral that is the subject of the agreements where the creditor adduces evidence that it has conducted the sale of the collateral in a commercially reasonable manner. (General Electric Capital Corporation v. Stelmach Construction Company)

6. **Collection of Rights to Payment.** Under U.C.C. § 9-501, if there is a true sale of accounts, the "seller" is entitled to any surplus when the secured party collects from the account debtors only if the security agreement so provides, but if the transaction is actually a transfer of accounts to secure an indebtedness, then the transferee has a right to surplus which cannot be waived even by an express agreement. (Major's Furniture Mart, Inc. v. Castle Credit Corp.)

K.M.C. CO., INC. v. IRVING TRUST COMPANY
Corporation (P) v. Trust company (D)
757 F.2d 752 (6th Cir. 1985).

NATURE OF CASE: Appeal from judgment in an action for breach of a financing agreement.

FACT SUMMARY: Irving (D) withheld continued financing from K.M.C. (P) without notice and without a basis to believe that K.M.C. (P) was a financial risk.

CONCISE RULE OF LAW: Financing is withheld in bad faith if no reasonable loan officer in the same situation would have refused to advance funds.

FACTS: Irving (D) held a security interest in all of K.M.C.'s (P) accounts receivable. K.M.C. (P) also had a $3.5 million line of credit with Irving (D). On March 1, 1982, Irving refused to advance $800,000 requested by K.M.C. (P). K.M.C. (P) filed suit, alleging that the funds were withheld without notice, a breach of a duty of good-faith performance. The jury found for K.M.C. (P). Irving appealed a jury instruction that Irving (D) had a good-faith obligation to not withdraw financing without notice.

ISSUE: Is financing withheld in bad faith if no reasonable loan officer in the same situation would have refused to advance funds?

HOLDING AND DECISION: (Kennedy, Cir. J.) Yes. Financing is withheld in bad faith if no reasonable loan officer in the same situation would have refused to advance funds. The obligation to deal in good faith required that K.M.C. (P) be given time to locate alternative financing should Irving (D) wish to terminate its relationship. There was no basis on the record for Irving (D) to believe that K.M.C. (P) was insolvent or untenable as a business entity at the time. The jury instruction and verdict were proper. Affirmed.

EDITOR'S ANALYSIS: The U.C.C. allows creditors to include accelerate-at-will clauses in contracts. However, the use of these clauses is always tempered by a duty to act in good faith. Thus, the creditor must show that a reasonable basis exists for the belief that the ability to pay has been compromised.

NOTES:

MOE v. JOHN DEERE COMPANY
Debtor (P) v. Creditor (D)
S.D. Sup. Ct., 516 N.W.2d 332 (1994).

NATURE OF CASE: Appeal from summary judgment in an action for commercially unreasonable sale, failure to account for surplus, wrongful repossession, and fraudulent repossession.

FACT SUMMARY: John Deere (D) repeatedly accepted late payments on a tractor and then repossessed without notice.

CONCISE RULE OF LAW: Repeated acceptance of late payments by a creditor who has the contractual right to repossess collateral waives this right unless the debtor is notified that strict compliance with the contract terms will be required.

FACTS: Moe (P) bought a John Deere (D) tractor. Moe (P) was late on his first installment payment. The next year, Moe (P) was again late, and again, John Deere (D) accepted a late partial payment. In May or early June, an arrangement was made to pay the remainder of the partial payment over time, but no dates were specified. On July 30, John Deere (D) repossessed the tractor without notice. In August, John Deere (D) mailed a letter to Moe (P), stating that the tractor was to be sold. The tractor was sold, and the excess was mailed to Moe's (P) lender. Moe (P) sued John Deere (D) for wrongful repossession, fraudulent repossession, commercially unreasonable sale, and failure to account for the surplus. John Deere (D) was granted summary judgment on all issues. Moe (P) appealed.

ISSUE: Does repeated acceptance of late payments by a creditor who has the contractual right to repossess collateral waive this right?

HOLDING AND DECISION: (Moses, Cir. J.) Yes. Repeated acceptance of late payments by a creditor who has the contractual right to repossess collateral waives this right unless the debtor is notified that strict compliance with the contract terms will be required. A majority of jurisdictions adhere to the rule that when a secured party has not insisted on strict compliance in the past, notice must be given before strict compliance may be demanded. The debtor comes to rely on the fact that late payments are acceptable. The creditor is then estopped from asserting contract rights because of this reliance until notice informs the debtor that strict compliance will be enforced. In this case, John Deere (D) refrained from insisting on strict compliance for two years. Clearly, Moe (P) could have come to rely on this forbearance. Disposition of the issues on summary judgment was improper. Reversed and remanded for trial.

EDITOR'S ANALYSIS: One important goal of the U.C.C. is to increase the clarity of situations between creditors and debtors. While the holding of this case urges creditors to be more harsh with debtors, at least each party is aware of his respective position before an agreement is negotiated. If a debtor does not wish to face a default repossession without notice, he can seek to negotiate terms more favorable to himself. In any event, the rights of the parties are clarified, if not made more congenial.

NOTES:

WILLIAMS v. FORD MOTOR CREDIT CO.
Debtor (P) v. Creditor (D)
674 F.2d 717 (8th Cir. 1982).

NATURE OF CASE: Appeal from a judgment notwithstanding the verdict for conversion.

FACT SUMMARY: The trial court held the FMCC's (D) repossession of William's (P) car was not in breach of the peace and therefore was not conversion.

CONCISE RULE OF LAW: A secured party has the right to repossess the collateral on default as long as the peace is not breached.

FACTS: FMCC (D) directed S & S to repossess Williams' (P) car in which it held a security interest. S & S came at night and was stopped by Williams (P) who inquired as to what they were doing. S & S's employee politely explained and subsequently drove away without complaint from Williams (P). Williams (P) subsequently sued for conversion, contending she had objected to the repossession and thus it was accomplished through a breach of the peace. The trial court granted FMCC's (D) motion for judgment notwithstanding the verdict, and Williams (P) appealed.

ISSUE: Does a secured party have the right to peacefully repossess the collateral?

HOLDING AND DECISION: (Benson, C.J.) Yes. A secured party may take possession of the collateral as long as no breach of the peace occurs. Breach of the peace does not occur merely because the debtor fails to give express consent to the repossession. In this case, Williams (P) admitted the S & S employee was polite and that no violence was threatened. Thus the repossession was valid. Affirmed.

DISSENT: (Heaney, J.) Williams (P) did everything she could to prevent the repossession short of actual violence. Clearly the peace was broken and the repossession invalid.

EDITOR'S ANALYSIS: There is some confusion as to the appropriate measure of damages for wrongful repossession. Some commentators argue the proper measure is the value of the lost use of the collateral. This period probably would be limited to the time it would have taken to effect legal repossession.

NOTES:

IN RE DOWNING
[Parties not listed.]
Bankr., 286 B.R. 900 (W.D. Mo. 2002).

NATURE OF CASE: Objection in bankruptcy proceeding to creditor's unsecured deficiency claim.

FACT SUMMARY: Downing (debtor) (P) objected to the unsecured deficiency claim of creditor BMW Financial Services, N.A., LLC (BMW) (D) in his bankruptcy case, arguing that BMW's (D) notice was inadequate to preserve BMW's (D) right to such a claim.

CONCISE RULE OF LAW: A notice that fails to inform the debtor that the intended method of disposition is a private sale, that the debtor has a right to an accounting, and that the debtor will be liable for any deficiency following the sale is not sufficient to preserve the creditor's right to a deficiency claim.

FACTS: Downing (P) purchased a BMW auto from BMW Financial Services, N.A., LLC (BMW) (D), and granted BMW (D) a lien on the car. The following year, Downing (P) filed for bankruptcy (under Chapter 13). Under the bankruptcy plan, Downing (P) surrendered the vehicle to BMW (D). Shortly thereafter, on April 4, 2002, BMW (D) notified Downing (P) that it intended to sell the car, as allowed under state law, no sooner than 10 days after the date of the notice. On August 1, 2002, BMW (D) sold the car at a commercial auction in Milwaukee, Wisconsin. After the sale, BMW (D) filed an unsecured deficiency claim in the bankruptcy case for over $18,000. Downing (P) objected to the claim, on the grounds that BMW (D) did not provide him with proper notice of the sale as required by Missouri's version of Revised Article 9 of the U.C.C.

ISSUE: Is a notice that fails to inform the debtor that the intended method of disposition is a private sale, that the debtor has a right to an accounting, and that the debtor will be liable for any deficiency following the sale sufficient to preserve the creditor's right to a deficiency claim?

HOLDING AND DECISION: (Federman, C.J.) No. A notice that fails to inform the debtor that the intended method of disposition is a private sale, that the debtor has a right to an accounting, and that the debtor will be liable for any deficiency following the sale is not sufficient to preserve the creditor's right to a deficiency claim. In Missouri, compliance with the notice provisions of Article 9 is a prerequisite to the recovery of a deficiency following the sale of repossessed collateral. Here, BMW (D) bears the burden of proving the sufficiency of its notice. The adequacy of the notice is governed by §§ 9-613 and 9-614. Section 9-613 requires that the notice describe the debtor and the secured party; describe the collateral; state the method of intended disposition; state that debtor is entitled to an accounting of the unpaid indebtedness and state the charge, if any, for such an accounting; and state the time and place of a public sale or the time after which any other disposition is to be made. Section 9-613 applies to non-consumer goods, and § 9-614 applies those same requirements to consumer-goods dispositions. In addition, § 9-614 requires a description of any liability for a deficiency, and a telephone number for making a deficiency payment. Because an automobile is a consumer good, both sections apply. BMW (D) did not include in the notice it sent to Downing (P) the time and place of the auction. BMW (D) contended that because the auction at which the car was sold was attended only by car dealers, it was a private sale to commercial buyers, and that, therefore, it was not required to provide Downing (P) with the exact time and place of the auction. There is support for the notion that a sale that is open only to automobile dealers is closed to some aspect of the market and is, therefore, a private sale. Nevertheless, the U.C.C. clearly required BMW (D) to notify Downing (P) as to whether it would sell the car at a private or public sale. The notice did not do so. Nor did the notice inform Downing (P) that he would be responsible for any deficiency, and also failed to inform him of his right to an accounting. For these reasons, the notice did not strictly comply with the requirements of § 9-613 as applied to consumer goods by § 9-614. The notification was not sufficient, therefore, under Missouri law, and BMW (D) loses its right to a deficiency judgment—regardless of whether there was any resulting harm to the debtor from the deficient notice. Objection sustained.

EDITOR'S ANALYSIS: The court also rejected BMW's (D) contention that because the bankruptcy plan provided that the car be surrendered to BMW (D), Missouri law did not require it to advise him of his right to redeem the vehicle. The court observed that the notice did not serve only to advise Downing (P) of his redemption right, but also served to provide a debtor with the terms of a private sale so that the debtor would have an opportunity to offer better terms upon redemption. Also, if a debtor is told the time and place of a public sale, he has an opportunity to appear at the sale, directly or through an agent, and bid.

NOTES:

GENERAL ELECTRIC CAPITAL CORPORATION v. STELMACH CONSTRUCTION COMPANY

Creditor (P) v. Debtor (D)

45 U.C.C. Rep.Serv.2d 675, 57 Fed. R. Evid. Serv. 891 (D. Kan. 2001).

NATURE OF CASE: Motion for summary judgment on damages in deficiency judgment action.

FACT SUMMARY: General Electric Capital Corp. (GECC) (P) brought suit to recover a deficiency judgment against Stelmach Construction Company (Stelmach Construction) (D) on a promissory note and Stelmach (D) on his personal guaranty for a loan made by GECC (P) to Stelmach Construction (D), and sought summary judgment on damages after the repossession and sale of the collateral securing the loan at issue. The defendants challenged the commercial reasonableness of the sale of the collateral.

CONCISE RULE OF LAW: A creditor is entitled to summary judgment on damages arising from the breach of security agreements after the repossession and sale of the collateral that is the subject of the agreements where the creditor adduces evidence that it has conducted the sale of the collateral in a commercially reasonable manner.

FACTS: General Electric Capital Corp. (GECC) (P) and Stelmach Construction Company (Stelmach Construction) (D) entered into a promissory note, a master security agreement, and other related agreements (the "Agreements") for a loan made by GECC (P). Stelmach (D) provided a personal guaranty on the loan amount. After Stelmach Construction (D) failed to make required payments due under the Agreements, GECC (P) and Stelmach Construction (D) entered into a modification agreement. GECC (P) also sent Stelmach Construction (D) and Stelmach (D) (collectively "defendants") notices of default. Subsequently, GECC (P) and the defendants entered into a voluntary surrender agreement, wherein defendants voluntarily surrendered the collateral for sale by GECC (P), and wherein Stelmach Construction (D) retained all rights as a debtor, including the right to challenge the commercial reasonableness of the sale of the collateral. GECC's (P) expert, Elcor, Inc. (Elcor), valued the collateral, piece by piece, at $258,200. Stelmach Construction's (D) expert valued the collateral as one lot at $457,400. Elcor was also responsible for selling the collateral, the sale of which was advertised in two nationally recognized trade magazines and on two Internet sites known by the trade. The sale was also advertised by mass mailings to targeted potential purchasers. None of the ads specified if the collateral would be sold by the lot or individually. During the advertisement period, the collateral was available for inspection by interested bidders. All bids were made for the entire lot, ranging in price from $225,000 to $311,000. GECC (P) accepted the highest bid. GECC (P) also had $6,800 of costs for obtaining and processing the collateral, and incurred $31,100 in commission fees. At the time of sale, the principal due was $389,710; interest and delinquency charges totaled $31,355; and after the sale, interest accrued at $54.91 per diem. Net of the sale proceeds, this amount was $147,966. Under the terms of the Agreements, defendants agreed to pay GECC (P) attorneys fees and costs. The court entered summary judgment for GECC (P) on liability, finding that the defendants had breached the Agreements. Thus, the remaining issue was damages, on which GECC (P) also sought summary judgment. The parties disputed the total amount due by defendants to GECC (P), and defendants argued that the sale of the collateral conducted by GECC (P) was not commercially reasonable.

ISSUE: Is a creditor entitled to summary judgment on damages arising from the breach of security agreements after the repossession and sale of the collateral that is the subject of the agreements where the creditor adduces evidence that it has conducted the sale of the collateral in a commercially reasonable manner?

HOLDING AND DECISION: (Murguia, J.) Yes. A creditor is entitled to summary judgment on damages arising from the breach of security agreements after the repossession and sale of the collateral that is the subject of the agreements where the creditor adduces evidence that it has conducted the sale of the collateral in a commercially reasonable manner. Determination of whether a sale has been conducted in a commercially reasonable manner is a question of fact. Here, GECC (P) has the burden on this issue. To prevail on summary judgment, GECC (P) must show there is no genuine issue of material fact, and that it is entitled, as a matter of law, to $147,966. The Kansas U.C.C. provides that every aspect of the disposition of collateral, including the method, manner, time, place and terms must be commercially reasonable. In the instant case, GECC (P) gave proper notice of the sale. Defendants contend that for the sale to have been commercially reasonable, the collateral should not have been disposed of in bulk. The U.C.C. permits sale or other disposition of repossessed collateral as a unit or in parcels. Contrary to defendants' argument, potential bidders were not misled by the advertisements into believing that the collateral was available only as a lot. The ads listed each item of collateral and indicated that GECC (P) was "accepting bids." Also, an examination of the bids themselves demonstrates that the bidders placed bids on the list of equipment. For these reasons, GECC's (P) ads and its acceptance of one of six bids for the entire lot did not render the sale commercially unreasonable.

Continued on next page.

As to the reasonableness of the price received for the collateral, the fact that the sale price was $146,400 less than defendants' expert's appraisal does not by itself render the price presumptively commercially unreasonable. The fact that a better price could have been obtained by a sale at a different time or in a different method from that selected by the secured party is not itself sufficient to establish that the sale was not made in a commercially reasonable manner. Here, GECC (P) sold the collateral in the usual manner in a recognized market for the collateral, or otherwise sold in conformity with reasonable commercial practices among dealers in the type of property sold. Accordingly, it sold in a commercially reasonable manner. Defendants, however, claim that the price obtained was not the current price in the market at the time of the sale. The court finds that all other factors regarding commercial reasonableness weigh in favor of GECC (P). Therefore, even assuming the price obtained was low, that low price, on its own, does not render the sale commercially unreasonable. By hiring Elcor to prepare the collateral for sale; by choosing a private sale, which under the circumstances would yield a higher price; by advertising in multiple national trade publications and Internet sites; by conducting direct mail solicitations to targeted potential purchasers; by making the collateral available for inspection by prospective purchasers before the sale; by holding the property for a month before agreeing to a sales price; and by receiving six bids before accepting the highest bid, GECC (P) conducted the sale in a commercially reasonable manner. Accordingly, GECC (P) has met its burden. Summary judgment granted.

EDITOR'S ANALYSIS: This decision was decided under former Article 9. Under Revised Article 9, § 627(b)(3) offers a safe-harbor definition of commercial reasonableness similar to the one used in this case: "a disposition is commercially reasonable if it is 'in conformity with reasonable commercial practices among dealers in the type of property that was the subject of the disposition.'" Thus, this case would most likely have been decided the same way under Revised Article 9.

NOTES:

MAJOR'S FURNITURE MART, INC. v.
CASTLE CREDIT CORP.

Retailer (P) v. Financier (D)

602 F.2d 538 (3d Cir. 1979).

NATURE OF CASE: Appeal from summary judgment ordering accounting of surplus.

FACT SUMMARY: Major's (P) claimed that it had been involved in what was actually a transfer of accounts receivable to Castle (D) to secure an indebtedness, while Castle (D) insisted that the transaction was a sale of the accounts.

CONCISE RULE OF LAW: Under U.C.C. § 9-501, if there is a true sale of accounts, the "seller" is entitled to any surplus when the secured party collects from the account debtors only if the security agreement so provides, but if the transaction is actually a transfer of accounts to secure an indebtedness, then the transferee has a right to surplus which cannot be waived even by an express agreement.

FACTS: Major's (P), a retail seller of furniture, entered into an agreement with Castle (D), a financier for furniture dealers, for the financing of Major's (P) accounts receivable. The agreement provided that Major's (P) would from time to time "sell" accounts receivable to Castle (D), with Castle (D) having full recourse against Major's (P) as to such accounts. Major's (P) had to warrant that each account was based on a written order or contract it had fully performed; Castle (D) had the right to refuse to purchase any account at its sole discretion; Castle (D) was to pay Major's (P) an amount for each account "sold" equal to the unpaid face amount of the account exclusive of interest less a 15% "discount" and less another 10% of the unpaid face amount as a reserve against bad debts (this reserve being held by Castle (D) without interest in order to indemnify it against a customer's failure to pay the full amount of the account or against any other charges or losses Castle (D) sustained for any reason); Major's (P) was required to "repurchase" any account "sold" to Castle (D) which was in default for more than 60 days, not for the discounted amount paid to it by Castle (D) for the account but for a "repurchase" price based on the balance due by the customer, plus any costs incurred by Castle (D) upon default; in the event of bankruptcy, default under the agreement, or discontinuing business, Major's (P) was required to repurchase all outstanding accounts immediately. Eventually, Major's (P) was declared to be in default under the agreement. Thereafter, it brought an action against Castle (D) alleging that the transaction by which it had transferred its accounts to Castle (D) constituted a financing of accounts receivable, rather than a true sale of accounts receivable, and that Castle (D) had collected a surplus of monies to which Major's (D) was entitled. The district court interpreted the agreement as creating a security interest in the accounts and entered an order granting Major's (P) motion for summary

judgment and denying Castle's (D) motion for summary judgment. Castle (D) appealed, arguing that the transaction constituted a true sale of the accounts and that under U.C.C. § 9-501, when the underlying transaction is a sale of accounts, the "seller" is entitled to any surplus only if the security agreement so provides. The agreement did not so provide.

ISSUE: As U.C.C. § 9-501 operates, must one determine whether or not a transaction involving a transfer of accounts receivable was a true sale of those accounts or a transfer to secure an indebtedness in order to determine if the transferee has an unwaivable right to any surplus realized when the secured party collects from the account debtors or whether the transferee has such a right only if it is expressly provided for in the security agreement?

HOLDING AND DECISION: (Garth, Cir. J.) Yes. U.C.C. § 9-501 distinguishes between the consequences that follow on default when a transfer of accounts receivable secures an indebtedness rather than constituting a "true" sale of said accounts. It provides that the secured party must account to the debtor/transferee for any surplus realized when the secured party collects from the account debtors (that right being unwaivable) but only if the security agreement secures an indebtedness. In such a case, the right of the debtor/transferee to recover the surplus is unwaivable, but the debtor/transferee is not liable for any deficiency unless the parties have agreed otherwise. If, instead of a transfer of accounts receivable to secure an indebtedness, the underlying transaction constitutes a sale of accounts, § 9-501 provides that the debtor/seller is entitled to any surplus or is liable for any deficiency only if the security agreement so provides. The determination of whether a particular assignment constitutes a true sale or a transfer for security is left to the courts, according to Comment 4 to U.C.C. § 9-502. The presence of recourse in a sale agreement without more will not automatically convert a sale into a security interest. When recourse is present, the question for the court is whether the nature of the recourse, and the true nature of the transaction, are such that the legal rights and economic consequences of the agreement bear a greater similarity to a financing transaction or to a sale. An examination of the facts of this case reveals that none of the risks present in a true sale is present here. Additionally, neither the custom of the parties nor their relationship, as the district court held, gives rise to more than a debtor/creditor relationship in which Major's (P) debt was

Continued on next page.

secured by a transfer of Major's (P) customer accounts to Castle (D). Therefore, Castle (D) was obligated to Major's (P) for any surplus that existed, since Major's (P) had an unwaivable right thereto under U.C.C. § 9-502. Affirmed.

EDITOR'S ANALYSIS: Recognition of the difficulty in distinguishing between an outright sale of accounts and a transfer of accounts to secure an indebtedness was one of the factors which motivated the drafters of the U.C.C. to include sales of accounts and chattel paper within the coverage of Article 9, though they are not "true" secured transactions. Since accounts receivable financing has become a major means of business financing in the recent past, the ability to look to Article 9's provisions on perfection and priority has proved an important advantage of such coverage.

NOTES:

CHAPTER 5
LEASES AND CONSIGNMENTS

QUICK REFERENCE RULES OF LAW

1. **Lease With Option to Purchase or Renew.** A lease will be construed as a security interest if a debtor has obtained equity in the leased property and has an option to become the owner of the goods for a nominal additional consideration upon compliance with the lease agreement. (In re Zaleha)

2. **Lease With Option to Purchase or Renew.** An agreement where the lessee is under no obligation to make installment payments that would ultimately allow the lessee to exercise or refuse the option to own the goods is a true lease, and not an installment sale. (In re Powers)

3. **Lease Without Option to Purchase or Renew.** A security interest is created by a lease agreement expressly denying an option to purchase if there is a realistic residual value in the property at the conclusion of the contract. (In re Aspen Impressions, Inc.)

4. **Open-end Lease.** A lease is a secured transaction. (In re Tulsa Port Warehouse Co.)

5. **Knowledge of Creditors Exclusion.** Otherwise unsecured consignors do not have superior rights to a consignee/debtor in bankruptcy and the consignee/debtor's term creditors where the consignors cannot show that the consignee/debtor is generally known by his creditors to be substantially engaged in selling the goods of others. (In re Valley Media, Inc.)

IN RE ZALEHA
Lessee (D) v. Lessor (P)
Bankr., 159 B.R. 581 (D. Idaho 1993).

NATURE OF CASE: Motion to require a bankruptcy debtor to assume or reject an unexpired lease.

FACT SUMMARY: After Zaleha (D) filed for bankruptcy under Chapter 11, the Toyota Motor Credit Corporation (TMCC) (P), from whom Zaleha (D) had leased a Toyota pickup truck, moved to require Zaleha (D) to assume or reject the unexpired lease, which Zaleha (D) contended was a disguised security interest.

CONCISE RULE OF LAW: A lease will be construed as a security interest if a debtor has obtained equity in the leased property and has an option to become the owner of the goods for a nominal additional consideration upon compliance with the lease agreement.

FACTS: Zaleha (D) leased a Toyota pickup truck through the Toyota Motor Credit Corporation (TMCC) (P) for five years, with stipulated monthly payments. At the end of the lease term, Zaleha (D) could become the owner of the vehicle for $5,390, which was defined in the lease as both the "Purchase Option Price" and the "Estimated Residual Value." After Zaleha (D) filed for Chapter 11 bankruptcy, TMCC (P) moved to require Zaleha (D) to assume or reject the unexpired lease. Zaleha (D) argued that the transaction was a disguised security interest, contending that the purchase option price undervalued the vehicle, which had a current blue book value of $8,275.

ISSUE: Will a lease be construed as a security interest if a debtor has obtained equity in and has an option to become the owner of the goods for a nominal additional consideration upon compliance with the lease agreement?

HOLDING AND DECISION: (Hagan, C.J.) Yes. A lease will be construed as a security interest if a debtor has obtained equity in and has an option to become the owner of the goods for a nominal additional consideration upon compliance with the lease agreement. Under the lease agreement at issue here, the first element of the test is met. However, the consideration required to exercise the option is not nominal. Thus, the transaction does not meet the mandatory conditions of a disguised security interest, and its nature must be determined on the facts of the case. The proper standard of evaluation is whether the transaction left TMCC (P) with a meaningful residual interest in the leased property. Here, no evidence was presented to show that the estimated residual value was not a reasonable estimate of the truck's value after five years of use. Motion granted.

EDITOR'S ANALYSIS: In determining if an option price is nominal, the proper figure to compare it with is the fair market value as anticipated by the parties when the lease is signed, not the fair market value at the time the option arises. Where a security interest is deemed to exist, the lessor cannot reasonably expect to receive back anything of value at the end of the lease. While labels used by the parties are not determinative, where a transaction is denominated a lease, the burden is on the debtor to show that it is in fact a disguised security interest.

NOTES:

IN RE POWERS
Lessor (P) v. Lessee (D)
983 F.2d 88 (7th Cir. 1993).

NATURE OF CASE: Review of bankruptcy court's denial of creditor objections to a Chapter 13 plan.

FACT SUMMARY: Powers (D) rented household goods on a biweekly plan, with various discretionary options to purchase, but he filed bankruptcy before exercising any of the options.

CONCISE RULE OF LAW: An agreement where the lessee is under no obligation to make installment payments that would ultimately allow the lessee to exercise or refuse the option to own the goods is a true lease, and not an installment sale.

FACTS: Powers (D) rented used household goods from Royce (P). The rental agreements provided for an initial two-week rental with a series of optional two-week rental periods thereafter. Powers (D) could purchase the goods by paying cash immediately, by paying cash within ninety days of taking possession, by paying a sliding-scale price after ninety days, or by making all the rental payments to acquire ownership. Powers (D) filed Chapter 13 bankruptcy. At the time, he had possession of the goods and had been making payments. Royce (P) was listed on debtor schedules as partially secured and partially unsecured. Royce (P) objected and sought possession of the goods. The bankruptcy judge denied the objections. Royce (P) appealed. The district court overturned the bankruptcy decision, finding that the rental agreements were not security agreements, but rather were true leases. Powers (D) appealed.

ISSUE: Are agreements where the lessee is under no obligation to make installment payments that would ultimately allow the lessee to exercise or refuse the option to own the goods true leases, and not installment sales?

HOLDING AND DECISION: (Cummings, Cir. J.) Yes. Agreements where the lessee is under no obligation to make installment payments that would ultimately allow the lessee to exercise or refuse the option to own the goods are true leases, and not an installment sale. In characterizing an agreement as either a lease or an installment sales contract it is important to consider whether there is an obligation to buy the goods, the length of the rental periods compared to the time required to own the goods, the amount of each rental payment compared to the purchase price, and the amount of the rental payments combined compared to the purchase price. In this case, Powers (D) was under no obligation to purchase; he could walk away at any time. The rental periods were very short compared to the two years required to own most of the goods. The amount paid each rental period was very small compared to the purchase price options.

And finally, the total rental price was much greater than the purchase price. Therefore, agreements were true leases, not installment sales contracts. Affirmed.

EDITOR'S ANALYSIS: Many bankruptcy courts have been troubled by the fact that in cases such as this the debtor could have paid more in rent than the property is worth and still lose the property under a lease theory. The debtor would forfeit all the payments made as mere rentals. In these cases, the courts have often found the rental agreements to be sales with a security interest to protect the debtor from what is perceived as an unjust result.

NOTES:

IN RE ASPEN IMPRESSIONS, INC.
[Priority dispute.]
Bankr. Ct., 94 B.R. 861 (E.D. Pa. 1989).

NATURE OF CASE: Motion for determination of priority among encumbrance holders.

FACT SUMMARY: Aspen entered into an agreement to pay $700,000 over 84 months for use of a printing press that had been purchased by lessor High Tech for $410,000.

CONCISE RULE OF LAW: A security interest is created by a lease agreement expressly denying an option to purchase if there is a realistic residual value in the property at the conclusion of the contract.

FACTS: In 1986, Aspen entered into a contract with High Tech in which it agreed to pay a monthly fee of $8,355 for 84 months to lease a printing press. High Tech had purchased the printing press for $409,600. In 1988 Aspen filed for Chapter 11 bankruptcy and Aspen's secured creditor, Bucks County Bank (D), sold the press at auction. High Tech's assignee, Provident Savings Bank (P), moved for a determination of priority, arguing that the Aspen–High Tech agreement was a true lease. Bucks (D) contended that the agreement was a loan from Provident (P) to Aspen of the purchase price of the press.

ISSUE: May a security interest be created by a lease agreement expressly denying an option to purchase, if there is a realistic residual value in the property at the conclusion of the contract?

HOLDING AND DECISION: (Fox, Bankr. J.) Yes. A security interest may be created by a lease agreement expressly denying an option to purchase if there is a realistic residual value in the property at the conclusion of the contract. A lease agreement denying an option to purchase may reflect an intent to pass title with no additional consideration because the property is expected to have no market value at the end of the lease term. The crucial determination is whether there is a realistic residual value in the leased property at the end of the lease term. No evidence was introduced of the equipment's fair market value at the end of the lease term so there is no basis to conclude that no residual value would exist at that time. Judgment for Provident (P).

EDITOR'S ANALYSIS: A lease creates a security interest if its term equals or exceeds the economic life of the property. U.C.C. § 1201(37) (first a.). But Comment 37 to U.C.C. § 1-201 modifies this position, stating that a full payout lease does not automatically create a security interest.

NOTES:

IN RE TULSA PORT WAREHOUSE CO.
Lessee (P) v. Lessor (D)
690 F.2d 809 (10th Cir. 1982).

NATURE OF CASE: Appeal from finding of superiority of a security agreement.

FACT SUMMARY: In Tulsa's (P) action against General Motors Acceptance Corporation (GMAC) (D), Tulsa's (P) trustee contended that the leases which Tulsa (P) had entered into were security agreements and that, therefore, GMAC's (D) interest in the leased automobiles was subordinate to Tulsa's trustee's (P) interest.

CONCISE RULE OF LAW: A lease is a secured transaction.

FACTS: Tulsa (P) entered into four automobile lease agreements which were assigned to General Motors Acceptance Corporation (GMAC) (D). When Tulsa (P) filed for bankruptcy, Tulsa's trustee (P) disputed the priority of their respective interests in the vehicles. GMAC (D) did not comply with the requirements of Article 9 of the U.C.C. relating to the perfection of a security interest. Tulsa's trustee (P) contended that the leases which Tulsa (P) had entered into were security agreements and that, therefore, GMAC's (D) interest in the leased automobiles was subordinate to that of Tulsa's trustee (P). The bankruptcy court decided in favor of Tulsa's trustee (P), the district court affirmed, and GMAC (D) appealed.

ISSUE: Is a lease a secured transaction?

HOLDING AND DECISION: (Seymour, Cir. J.) Yes. A lease is a secured transaction. The leases at issue are open-ended, involving the sale of the vehicles to the lessee at the end of the lease. In an open-ended lease, the termination formula in the lease recognizes the equity of the lessee, here Tulsa (P), in the vehicle because the lessee is required to bear the loss or receive the gain from the adjustment between the lessee and the lessor based on the sales price of the vehicles at the termination of the lease. Also, many other factors that the lessee is required to obtain insurance in favor of the lessor; pay sales tax and licenses, registration, and title fees; pay for all maintenance and repairs; and indemnify the lessor against all loss indicate that this lease is, in reality, a secured transaction. Here, the lease agreements between Tulsa (P) and GMAC (D) were transfers of property subject to a security interest, and GMAC's (D) interest in the autos was subordinate to that of Tulsa's trustee (P). Affirmed.

EDITOR'S ANALYSIS: New cases arise constantly which question whether a lease creates a security interest. The concept of "when in doubt, file" has not yet solved the problems. Respecting consignments, the U.C.C. requires filing to protect the consignor's interest against third parties even though no security interest is created. The same is true of sales of accounts and chattel paper.

NOTES:

IN RE VALLEY MEDIA, INC.

Objecting vendors (D) v. Debtor (P)

Bankr., 279 B.R. 105 (D. Del. 2002).

NATURE OF CASE: Objection by consignors to inclusion in bankruptcy auction of debtor's inventory of inventory provided by consignors to the bankruptcy debtor.

FACT SUMMARY: Consignment vendors (D), who had provided inventory on consignment to DNA, a wholly owned, unincorporated division of Valley Media, Inc. (Valley) (P), sought to exclude from Valley's (P) bankruptcy auction sale inventory that they had provided to DNA.

CONCISE RULE OF LAW: Otherwise unsecured consignors do not have superior rights to a consignee/debtor in bankruptcy and the consignee/debtor's term creditors where the consignors cannot show that the consignee/debtor is generally known by his creditors to be substantially engaged in selling the goods of others.

FACTS: Consignment vendors (Objecting Vendors) (D) had provided inventory on consignment to DNA, a wholly owned, unincorporated division of Valley Media, Inc. (Valley) (P). Valley (P) filed for bankruptcy (under Chapter 11), and moved to sell its inventory at auction (Auction Motion). The Objecting Vendors (D) objected and sought to exclude from the sale inventory (Contested Inventory) that they had provided to DNA. Under the consignment arrangement, title in goods remained in the vendor and the goods were not paid for until sold. The Objecting Vendors argued that they had superior rights in the Contested Inventory as to both Valley's (P) primary creditor (Congress) and Valley (P), and that the sale of the Contested Inventory would be a "first sale" without the requisite permission of the Objecting Vendors (D). The parties agreed that the Objecting Vendors' (D) rights to the Contested Inventory remained the same under either the former or the revised U.C.C. provisions as enacted in California (which governed the terms of the Distribution Agreements entered into by the Objecting Vendors (D)).

ISSUE: Do otherwise unsecured consignors have superior rights to a consignee/debtor in bankruptcy and the consignee/debtor's term creditors where the consignors cannot show that the consignee/debtor is generally known by his creditors to be substantially engaged in selling the goods of others?

HOLDING AND DECISION: (Walsh, C.J.) No. Otherwise unsecured consignors do not have superior rights to a consignee/debtor in bankruptcy and the consignee/debtor's term creditors where the consignors cannot show that the consignee/debtor is generally known by his creditors to be substantially engaged in selling the goods of others. Even if the Distribution Agreements are deemed consignment contracts based on the intent of the parties, such contracts alone do not necessarily allow a consignor's ownership interests in the consigned goods to prevail over the claims of the consignee's creditors. In the instant case, under the U.C.C., either under former§ 2-326(3) or revised §§ 9-102(a)(20) & 9-319(a), the goods are deemed to be on "sale or return." This fiction enables the consignee's creditors to attach the consigned goods as if the consignee actually had title to the goods. Thus, the Objecting Vendors (D) did not lose title to the Contested Inventory by not perfecting their ownership interests. However, to be excepted from the U.C.C.'s "sale or return" provisions, the consignor must either have (1) filed a U.C.C.-1 financing statement, or (2) prove that the deliveree is generally known by his creditors to be substantially engaged in selling the goods of others. If either of these exceptions apply, the consignee's (here Valley (P)) creditor's may not reach the consigned goods in the consignee's possession. Here, none of the Objecting Vendors (D) filed U.C.C.-1 financing statements. Therefore, the key issue is whether Valley (P) was generally known by its creditors to be substantially engaged in the selling of goods of others. The Objecting Vendors (D) bear the burden on this issue, and both prongs of the test must be established—i.e., that (a) the consignee was substantially engaged in selling the goods of others, and (b) that the consignee's creditors knew this. To be "substantially engaged in selling the goods of others," the merchant must not hold less than 20% of the value of its inventory on a consignment basis. The knowledge prong of the test can be established by showing that a majority of the consignee's creditors (not just creditors making claims) were aware that consignee was substantially engaged in consignment sales. The parties disagree, however, as to whether Valley (P) or DNA should be the subject of the test. The Objecting Vendors (D) argue that DNA was the "person conducting business" or the purported "merchant." Under the definitions of "person" or "merchant," it is clear that the subject of the test must be an entity, whether legal or commercial. Valley (P) contends that DNA was not a legal entity. The Objecting Vendors (D) counter that DNA should be recognized as a commercial entity for purposes of the test. Here, a threshold question is whether DNA was an entity at all. As an unincorporated division of Valley (P), DNA had no legal existence separate from Valley (P), and there is no reason that justifies treating it as an entity for purposes of the policies underlying the test. Moreover, DNA was incapable of having creditors of its own. Therefore, DNA was not the person or merchant subject to the test, and, therefore, the Objecting Vendors (D) must prove that Valley (P) was generally known by Valley's (P) creditors to be substantially engaged in the selling of goods of others. The Objecting Vendors (D) have not met—and

Continued on next page.

cannot meet—their burden of proof on the two prongs to the test. Valley (P) had about 1,000 creditors; all that the Objecting Vendors (D) have been able to show is that they (a small fraction of the vast majority of creditors) and Congress knew that Valley was engaged in consignment sales. The policies underlying the U.C.C. would require excluding the Objecting Vendors (D) from the calculation. Even if the Objecting Vendors (D) could prevail on the first prong and show that a majority of Valley's (P) creditors knew about Valley's (P) consignment practices, the evidence showed that the percentage of consigned inventory to total inventory for Valley (P) was never more than 17.03%, which is below the 20% threshold for showing that the consignee is "substantially engaged." Therefore, the exceptions to the "sale or return" fiction are inapplicable, and the Objecting Vendors (D) may not assert ownership rights in the Contested Inventory against Valley (P), as debtor in possession, as hypothetical lien creditor of Valley (P). Judicial lien creditors may also attach consigned goods in Valley's (P) possession. Here, Valley (P) may sell the Contested Inventory since its interest in that inventory is superior to the Objecting Vendors' (D) interests. The result is that the Objecting Vendors (D) will have a pre-petition unsecured claim against the bankruptcy estate for the invoice price of the Contested Inventory.

EDITOR'S ANALYSIS: Although the opinion treats former U.C.C. law and revised U.C.C. law as the same for purposes of determining whether the goods are deemed to be on sale or return, under pre-revision U.C.C. provisions, the intent of the parties was relevant, whereas under Revised Article 9, intent is no longer a factor in the U.C.C.'s consignment provisions.

NOTES:

CHAPTER 6
SECURITY INTERESTS IN INTELLECTUAL PROPERTY

QUICK REFERENCE RULES OF LAW

1. **Copyrights.** In order to perfect a security interest in a copyright, a creditor must record that security interest with the U.S. Copyright Office. (In re Peregrine Entertainment, Ltd.)

2. **Copyrights.** State U.C.C. law rather than federal copyright law governs the perfection and priority of security interests in unregistered copyrights. (In re World Auxiliary Power Company)

3. **Trademarks.** The filing of a financing statement with the United States Patent and Trademark Office does not alone perfect a security interest in a trademark. (In re Together Development Corporation)

4. **Patents.** A holder of a security interest in a patent is not required to record that interest with the federal Patent and Trademark Office to perfect the interest as against a subsequent lien creditor. (In re Cybernetic Services, Inc.)

IN RE PEREGRINE ENTERTAINMENT, LTD.
Security interest dispute.
Bankr., 116 B.R. 194 (C. D. Cal. 1990).

NATURE OF CASE: Appeal from summary judgment award in bankruptcy court.

FACT SUMMARY: Cap Fed (D) secured a loan with NPI's (P) film library and filed U.C.C.-1 financing statements with the secretary of state, but did not record its security interest in the U.S. Copyright Office.

CONCISE RULE OF LAW: In order to perfect a security interest in a copyright, a creditor must record that security interest with the U.S. Copyright Office.

FACTS: Cap Fed (D) secured a loan to NPI (P) with NPI's (P) film library which included copyrights, distribution rights, and licenses to approximately 145 films. Cap Fed (D) filed U.C.C.-1 financing statements with the secretaries of state of California, Colorado, and Utah, but did not record its security interest in the U.S. Copyright Office. On January 30, 1989, NPI (P) filed for bankruptcy. On April 6, 1989, NPI (P) filed an amended complaint challenging the validity of Cap Fed's (D) security interest in the copyrights, as Cap Fed (D) did not record with the Copyright Office. The parties filed cross partial motions for partial summary judgment on the issue of whether Cap Fed (D) held a valid security interest in the copyrights. The bankruptcy court ruled in favor of Cap Fed (D) and NPI (P) appealed.

ISSUE: In order to perfect a security interest in a copyright, must a creditor record that security interest with the U.S. Copyright Office?

HOLDING AND DECISION: (Kozinski, Cir. J.) Yes. In order to perfect a security interest in a copyright, a creditor must record that security interest with the U.S. Copyright Office. Both federal law and state law support this conclusion. Pursuant to federal law, 17 U.S.C. § 205(a) any transfer or ownership of a copyright may be recorded in the U.S. Copyright Office. If it is clear that Congress left no room for supplementary state regulation, federal law will preempt state law. Here, the comprehensive scope of the federal copyright acts recording provisions and the unique federal interests they implicate support the view that federal law preempts state methods of perfecting security interests in copyrights and related accounts receivable. Uniform application of the federal copyright laws ensures predictability and certainty of ownership and promotes efficiency in enforcing such rights. Additionally, pursuant to U.C.C. § 9-302(3)(a), when a national system of recording exists, the U.C.C. will treat that system as tantamount to the filing of a financing statement under Article 9. Here, a national system does exist, as defined by 17 U.S.C. § 205(a), and therefore, state law respects that requirement as well. Consequently, because Cap Fed (D) did not record its

security interest in the copyrights with the Copyright Office, Cap Fed (D) did not perfect those interests. The motion for summary judgment granted in favor of Cap Fed (D) should be reversed and the case remanded for a determination of which movies in NPI's (P) library are the subject of valid copyrights and the extent to which Cap Fed's (D) security interest is unperfected. Reversed and remanded.

EDITOR'S ANALYSIS: Pursuant to 17 U.S.C. § 205(c)(1), recording a document in the Copyright Office gives notice ". . . only if the document . . . specifically identifies the work to which it pertains." Recording security agreements only gives notice with respect to the specific work involved in the agreement, even if the agreement includes after-acquired copyrights. This federal law for security interests in copyrights preempts state laws which recognize after-acquired property clauses.

NOTES:

IN RE WORLD AUXILIARY POWER COMPANY
[Parties not listed.]
303 F.3d 1120 (9th Cir. 2002).

NATURE OF CASE: Appeal from affirmance of dismissal of adversary proceeding in bankruptcy for avoidance of a security interest in unregistered copyrights and for recovery of the copyrights from subsequent transferees.

FACT SUMMARY: Aerocon Engineering (Aerocon) (P) brought an adversary proceeding in bankruptcy for avoidance of a security interest held by Silicon Valley Bank (D) in unregistered copyrights and for recovery of the copyrights from subsequent transferees, Advanced Aerospace (D), Gilsen (D), Widen (D), and Airweld (D), under the theory that the perfection and priority of the copyrights was governed by the federal Copyright Act, rather than by Article 9 of California's U.C.C. law.

CONCISE RULE OF LAW: State U.C.C. law rather than federal copyright law governs the perfection and priority of security interests in unregistered copyrights.

FACTS: Silicon Valley Bank (the "bank") (D) financed three affiliated companies (World Auxiliary Power, World Aerotechnology, and Air Refrigeration Systems) and obtained a security interest in their property, including unregistered copyrights. The bank (D) perfected its security interest in the copyrights pursuant to California's version of Article 9 of the U.C.C. by filing U.C.C.-1 financing statements and by taking possession of the materials covered by the copyrights. However, the copyrights were not registered with the United States Copyright Office, and the bank (D) did not record any document showing the transfer of a security interest with the Copyright Office. Thereafter, the three debtor companies filed for bankruptcy. Aerocon Engineering (Aerocon) (P), one of their creditors, wanted the copyrights for a planned joint venture with Advanced Aerospace (D), Gilsen (D), and Widen (D). To obtain ownership of the copyrights, Aerocon (P) worked out a deal with its prospective joint venturers to purchase from the bankruptcy trustees the debtors' assets, including the copyrights, along with the trustees' right to sue to avoid the bank's (D) security interest. The planned joint venture fell through, but through various transactions, Aerocon (P) became a tenant in common with another company, Airweld (D), with respect to the copyrights and the trustees' avoidance action. Meanwhile, Silicon Valley Bank (D) won relief from the bankruptcy court's automatic stay and, based on its security interest, foreclosed on the copyrights. Then the bank (D) sold the copyrights to Advanced Aerospace, which then sold the copyrights to Airweld (D). The result was that Aerocon (P), which had paid $90,000 for the copyrights and had owned them as a tenant in common with Airweld (D), now had a claim adverse to Airweld's (D), which purportedly owned the copyrights in fee simple. Aerocon (P) brought an adversary

proceeding in bankruptcy for avoidance of the bank's (D) security interest and for recovery of the copyrights from the subsequent transferees, Advanced Aerospace (D), Gilsen (D), Widen (D), and Airweld (D), under the theory that the perfection and priority of the copyrights was governed by the federal Copyright Act, rather than by Article 9 of California's U.C.C. law. The bankruptcy court granted the subsequent transferees' motion to dismiss Aerocon's (P) claims against them as time-barred. The bankruptcy court then granted summary judgment to Silicon Valley Bank (D) on all of Aerocon's (P) claims on the ground that the bank (D) had perfected its security interest in the copyrights under California's version of Article 9 of the Uniform Commercial Code. Aerocon (P) appealed to the Bankruptcy Appellate Panel. Silicon Valley Bank (D) objected, and the appeal was transferred to the district court, which affirmed the bankruptcy court. The appeals court granted review.

ISSUE: Does state U.C.C. law rather than federal copyright law govern the perfection and priority of security interests in unregistered copyrights?

HOLDING AND DECISION: (Kleinfeld, Cir. J.) Yes. State U.C.C. law rather than federal copyright law governs the perfection and priority of security interests in unregistered copyrights. By purchasing the bankruptcy trustees' avoidance power, Aerocon (P) became a hypothetical lien creditor. Whether Aerocon's (P) hypothetical lien would take priority over the bank's (D) lien depends on whether federal or state law governs the perfection of security interests in unregistered copyrights. The bank (D) did everything necessary to perfect its security interest under state law, so if state law governs, the bank (D) has priority and wins. The bank (D) did nothing, however, to perfect its interest under federal law, so if federal law governs, Aerocon's (P) hypothetical lien creditor arguably has priority. Under the federal Copyright Act of 1976, a copyrighted work only gets a "title or registration number" that would be revealed by a search if it is registered. Since an unregistered work does not have a title or registration number that would be "revealed by a reasonable search," recording a security interest in an unregistered copyright in the Copyright Office would not give "constructive notice" under the Copyright Act, and, because it would not, it could not preserve a creditor's priority. There just is not any way for a secured creditor to preserve a priority in an unregistered copyright by recording anything in the Copyright Office. And the secured party cannot get around this problem by registering the copyright, because the secured party is not the owner of the copyright, and the Copyright

Continued on next page.

Act states that only the owner of copyright may obtain registration of the copyright claim. Aerocon (P) argues that the Copyright Act's recordation and priority scheme exclusively controls perfection and priority of security interests in copyrights. First, Aerocon (P) argues that state law, here the California U.C.C., by its own terms "steps back" and defers to the federal scheme. Second, whether or not the U.C.C. steps back, Aerocon (P) argues that Congress has preempted the U.C.C. as it applies to copyrights.

A. U.C.C. Step Back Provisions

The U.C.C. has two "step-back" provisions. The first, more general, provision, states that Article 9 does not apply to a security interest subject to any statute of the United States to the extent that such statute governs the rights of parties to and third parties affected by transactions in particular types of property. As applied to copyrights, the relevant U.C.C. Official Comment makes it clear that this step-back clause does not exclude all security interests in copyrights from U.C.C. coverage, just those for which the federal Copyright Act "governs the rights" of relevant parties. An inspection of the Copyright Act reveals that it does not contain sufficient provisions regulating the rights of parties and third parties to exclude security interests in copyrights from the provisions of Article 9. The second step-back provision speaks directly to perfection of security interests. It exempts from U.C.C. filing requirements security interests in property subject to a statute of the United States that provides for a national registration or that specifies a place of filing different from that specified in the state statute for filing of the security interest. Compliance with such a statute is equivalent to the filing of a financing statement and a security interest in property subject to the statute can be perfected only by compliance therewith. Thus, under the U.C.C.'s two step-back provisions, there is no doubt that when a copyright has been registered, a security interest can be perfected only by recording the transfer in the Copyright Office. However, when unregistered copyrights are the subject of the security interest, the U.C.C. does not step back. That is because the Copyright Act does not provide for the rights of secured parties to unregistered copyrights—it does not provide a "national registration" for such copyrights. Thus, as a matter of state law, the U.C.C. does not step back in deference to federal law, but governs the perfection and priority of security interests in unregistered copyrights itself.

B. Federal Preemption

If, nonetheless, Congress chose to preempt state law, it wouldn't matter that state law does not step back. Federal law preempts state law under three circumstances. The first is "express preemption," where Congress explicitly preempts state law. The second is "field preemption," where Congress implicitly preempts state law by occupying the entire field, leaving no room for the operation of state law. The third is "conflict preemption," where preemption is inferred because compliance with both state and federal law would be impossible, or state law stands as an obstacle to the accomplishment and execution of the full purposes and objectives of Congress. In this regard, Aerocon (P) first argues that Congress intended to occupy the field of security interests in copyrights. However, there are not two competing filing systems for unregistered copyrights—the Copyright Act does not create one. Only the U.C.C. creates a filing system applicable to unregistered copyrights. An extension to unregistered copyrights of cases, such as *In re Peregrine Entertainment, Ltd.,* 116 B.R. 194 (C.D. Cal. 1990), which held that for registered copyrights the only proper place to file security interests is the Copyright Office, is erroneous. Such cases are rejected, not only because *Peregrine's* analysis doesn't work if it is applied to security interests in unregistered copyrights, but also because such cases would make registration of copyright a necessary prerequisite of perfecting a security interest in copyright. The implication would be that Congress intended to make unregistered copyrights practically useless as collateral— an inference that is wholly unsupported by the text and purpose of the Copyright Act, which contemplates that most copyrights will not be registered. Thus, the only reasonable inference that can be drawn is that Congress chose not to preempt the states on this issue, but instead chose not to create a federal scheme for security interest in unregistered copyrights. For similar reasons, Aerocon's (P) argument that congressional intent to preempt can be inferred from conflict between the Copyright Act and the U.C.C. is rejected. There is no conflict between the two statutes because the Copyright doesn't speak at all to security interests in unregistered copyrights. Nor does the application of state law frustrate the objectives of federal copyright law. The basic objective of federal copyright law is to "promote the Progress of Science and useful Arts" by "establishing a marketable right to the use of one's expression" and supplying "the economic incentive to create and disseminate ideas." Aerocon (P) argues that allowing perfection under state law would frustrate this objective by injecting uncertainty in secured transactions involving copyrights. Aerocon (P) conjures up the image of a double-crossing debtor who, having gotten financing based on unregistered copyrights, registers them, thus triggering federal law, and gets financing from a second creditor, who then records its interest with the Copyright Office and takes priority. It is not up to this court to prevent this fraud by drawing the unreasonable inference that Congress intended to render copyrights useless as collateral unless registered. Prudent creditors will always demand that debtors disclose any copyright registrations and perfect under federal law and will protect themselves against subsequent creditors gaining priority by means of covenants and policing mechanisms. Aerocon's (P) argument also ignores the special problem of copyrights as after-acquired (or after-created) collateral, as in the software industry, which in many instances will

Continued on next page.

have to use its unregistered after-created software as collateral for financing. If, e.g., after-created software had to be registered, creditors would not tolerate a gap between the software's creation and the registration of the copyright. Thus, the court's reading of the law "promote[s] the Progress of Science and useful Arts" by preserving the collateral value of unregistered copyrights, which is to say, the vast majority of copyrights. Aerocon's (P) reading of the law—which would force producers engaged in the ongoing creation of copyrightable material to constantly register and update the registrations of their works before obtaining credit—does not. Affirmed.

EDITOR'S ANALYSIS: It is clear that whether filing is the exclusive manner of perfecting a security interest is answered differently with respect to each federal statute, on a statute-by-statute basis. This case clarifies the law on security interests in unregistered copyrights, but as the case itself points out, the result is different where registered copyrights are involved. Thus, even where the same federal statute is involved, the outcome as to whether the U.C.C. or the federal statute governs can turn on the type of collateral involved.

NOTES:

IN RE TOGETHER DEVELOPMENT CORPORATION

Secured creditor (P) v. Debtor (D)

Bankr., 227 B.R. 439 (D. Mass. 1998).

NATURE OF CASE: Evidentiary hearing to determine the validity and perfection of a security interest.

FACT SUMMARY: Trimarchi (P) sought to enforce a security interest in the trademark of Together Development (D), which it claimed to have perfected by filing a financing statement with the United States Patent and Trademark Office.

CONCISE RULE OF LAW: The filing of a financing statement with the United States Patent and Trademark Office does not alone perfect a security interest in a trademark.

FACTS: Trimarchi (P) is a former shareholder of Together (D). Together (D) purchased all its shares owned by Trimarchi (P) and two other shareholders pursuant to a written agreement in 1986. The price for the shares was $200,000 as evidenced by a promissory note providing for 10% interest per annum payable in 780 weekly installments of $500. Together (D) also gave Trimarchi (P) a promissory note for $30,372.12 providing for the same 10% interest per annum and 780 weekly installments. The notes were both secured by Together's (D) accounts receivable. Those accounts consisted of Together's (D) trademark, franchise fees, and royalties. Together (D) executed a separate assignment describing the assigned property as its trademark and goodwill. Together (D) also gave Trimarchi (P) a signed U.C.C.-1 financing statement describing Together's (D) fixtures, accounts receivable, franchise fees, royalties, license fees, franchise agreements, license agreements and its trademark. Trimarchi (P) did not record its interest with the state; rather, he filed the financing statement with the United States Patent and Trademark Office (PTO). By previous order, the court authorized Together (D) to sell substantially all its assets free of Trimarchi's (P) security interest. The security interest was attached to the proceeds of the sale. An evidentiary hearing was ordered to determine the validity and perfection of Trimarchi's (P) security interest.

ISSUE: Does the filing of a financing statement with the United States Patent and Trademark Office alone perfect a security interest in a trademark?

HOLDING AND DECISION: (Queenan, Bankr. J.) No. The filing of a financing statement with the United States Patent and Trademark Office does not alone perfect a security interest in a trademark. The agreement here provided that it was to be governed by New York law. New York law defers to the federal law in respect to the filing requirements for certain collateral, including the filing of a security interest in compliance with a statute or treaty providing for national registration or which "specifies a place of filing different from that specified in this Article for filing of the security interest." (Section 9-302(3).) The Lanham Act governs trademarks. The Lanham Act provides that a registered mark is assignable with the goodwill of the business in which the mark is used. The assignment is void against any subsequent purchaser for value without notice, unless it is recorded in the PTO within three months after the date thereof or prior to the subsequent purchase (15 U.S.C.S. section 1060). The issue is whether this statute specifies a place of filing different from that specified by New York law for the filling of the security interest. First, it must be determined whether the term assignment under federal law includes the grant of a security interest. Both the legislative history of the Lanham Act and case law indicate that the term assignment does not include such an interest. Thus, Trimarchi's (P) interest in the trademark was unperfected and was subordinate to a person who becomes a lien creditor before the security interest was perfected. As a debtor in possession, Together (D) had the rights and powers of the trustee to avoid any transfer of the property of the debtor that is voidable by a lien creditor. Thus, Trimarchi's (P) security interest was subordinate to that of Together (D) and Together (D) may avoid Trimarchi's (P) security interest. Order issued declaring Trimarchi's (P) security interest in the trademark invalid for lack of perfection.

EDITOR'S ANALYSIS: The court refers to several reasons why the term "assignment" as used in the Lanham Act does not include security interest filings. In the copyright context, Congress has specifically included consensual liens, including security interests, in the copyright recording system. Moreover, in *In re Peregrine Entertainment, Ltd.*, 116 B.R. 194 (C.D.Cal. 1990), the court stated that the proper method of perfection of security interests in copyrights was by filing with the United States Copyright Office. No similar provision was included in respect to trademarks. The court declined to interpret the statute otherwise.

NOTES:

IN RE CYBERNETIC SERVICES, INC.

Holder of security interest (D) v. Bankruptcy trustee (P)

252 F.3d 1039 (9th Cir. 2001).

NATURE OF CASE: Appeal from affirmance of a grant of relief from an automatic stay in bankruptcy for the purpose of foreclosing on a security interest in a patent.

FACT SUMMARY: Matsco, Inc., and Matsco Financial Corporation (Petitioners) (D), which corporations had a security interest in a patent developed by Cybernetic Services, Inc. (Debtor) (P), moved for relief from an automatic stay in the bankruptcy proceedings of Debtor (P) so they could foreclose on the security interest. The bankruptcy Trustee (P) opposed the motion, arguing that Petitioners (D) had failed to perfect their interest because they had not recorded it with the federal Patent and Trademark Office (PTO).

CONCISE RULE OF LAW: A holder of a security interest in a patent is not required to record that interest with the federal Patent and Trademark Office to perfect the interest as against a subsequent lien creditor.

FACTS: Matsco, Inc., and Matsco Financial Corporation (Petitioners) (D) had a security interest in a patent developed by Cybernetic Services, Inc. (Debtor) (P). Petitioners' (D) security interest in the patent was "properly prepared, executed by the Debtor and timely filed with the Secretary of State of the State of California," in accordance with the California Commercial Code. Petitioners did not record their interest with the federal Patent and Trademark Office (PTO). After Petitioners (D) had recorded their security interest with the State of California, certain creditors filed an involuntary Chapter 7 bankruptcy petition against Debtor (P), and an order of relief was granted. The primary asset of Debtor's (P) estate was the patent. Petitioners (D) then filed a motion for relief from the automatic stay so that they could foreclose on their interest in the patent. The bankruptcy Trustee (P) opposed the motion, arguing that Petitioners (D) had failed to perfect their interest because they did not record it with the PTO. The bankruptcy court ruled that Petitioners (D) had properly perfected their security interest in the patent by following the provisions of Article 9. The court also ruled that because Petitioners (D) had perfected their security interest before the filing of the bankruptcy petition, Petitioners (D) had priority over the Trustee's (P) claim in the patent and deserved relief from the stay. Accordingly, the bankruptcy court granted Petitioners' (D) motion. The Bankruptcy Appellate Panel affirmed, and the Ninth Circuit Court of Appeals granted review.

ISSUE: Is a holder of a security interest in a patent required to record that interest with the federal Patent and Trademark Office to perfect the interest as against a subsequent lien creditor?

HOLDING AND DECISION: (Graber, Cir. J.) No. A holder of a security interest in a patent is not required to record that interest with the federal Patent and Trademark Office to perfect the interest as against a subsequent lien creditor. Article 9 of the U.C.C., as adopted in California, governs the method for perfecting a security interest in personal property including "general intangibles," a term that includes intellectual property. The parties do not dispute that Petitioners (D) complied with Article 9's general filing requirements. The narrower question in this case is whether Petitioners' (D) actions were sufficient to perfect their interest when the "general intangible" to which the lien attached is a patent. The parties also do not dispute that if Petitioners (D) were required to file notice of their security interest in the patent with the PTO, then the Trustee (P), as a hypothetical lien creditor, has a superior right to the patent. The Trustee (P) argues that (1) the federal Patent Act preempts Article 9's filing requirements; and (2) that Article 9 itself provides that a security interest in a patent can be perfected only by filing it with the PTO.

A. Preemption

The Trustee (P) argues that the recording provision found in 35 U.S.C. § 261 (the federal Patent Act) requires that the holder of a security interest in a patent record that interest with the PTO in order to perfect as to a subsequent lien creditor. That statute provides in pertinent part that "[a]n assignment, grant or conveyance shall be void as against any subsequent purchaser or mortgagee for a valuable consideration, without notice, unless it is recorded in the Patent and Trademark Office...." If this section of the Patent Act expressly specifies the place a party must go to acquire notice and certainty about liens on patents, then state law, such as California's Article 9, that requires the public to look elsewhere would be preempted. Thus, the question becomes whether § 261 required Petitioners (D) to record their interest with the PTO. To resolve this issue requires a determination of whether Congress intended to include a security interest such as that held by Petitioners (D) within § 261's scope. Based on the language of § 261, its context, and its structure, it is clear that Petitioners' (D) transaction with Debtor (P) was not a type of "assignment, grant or conveyance," as that phrase concerns transfers of ownership interests only. Petitioners (D) held a "mere license," which, therefore, did not have to be recorded with the PTO. It is also clear that the Trustee (P), who has the status of a hypothetical lien creditor, is not a "subsequent purchaser or mortgagee." The historical meaning of "purchaser or mortgagee" proves that Congress intended for the recording provision to give

Continued on next page.

constructive notice only to subsequent holders of an ownership interest—as does the structure of § 261 and Supreme Court precedent. Here, the Trustee (P) is not a subsequent "mortgagee," as that term is used in § 261 because the holder of a patent mortgage holds title to the patent itself. Instead, the Trustee (P) is a hypothetical lien creditor. The Patent Act does not require parties to record documents in order to provide constructive notice to subsequent lien creditors who do not hold title to the patent. Finally, even if the Trustee (P) is correct that requiring lien creditors to record their interests with the PTO is in line with general policy behind recording statutes, such policies cannot override the text of the Patent Act, which, as demonstrated, is concerned with patent ownership. The recording provision of § 261 is in line with the policy behind that section if the section is read to include ownership interests only. The Patent Act must be interpreted as Congress wrote it, and it is not for the Court to modify it. Because the Patent Act does not cover security interests or lien creditors at all, there is no conflict between the Patent Act and Article 9. Therefore, Petitioners (D) did not have to file with the PTO to perfect their security interest as to a subsequent lien creditor.

B. Article 9 Step-Back Provision

The Trustee's (P) second major argument is that Article 9 itself requires that a creditor file notice of a secured transaction with the PTO in order to perfect a security interest. California Commercial Code § 9302(3)(a) states that the filing of a financing statement pursuant to Article 9 "is not necessary or effective to perfect a security interest in property subject to . . . [a] statute . . . which provides for a national or international registration . . . or which specifies a place of filing different from that specified in" Article 9. If § 9302(3)(a) applies, then a party must use the federal registration system in order to perfect its security interest. The question, then, is whether the Patent Act is such a statute. The Patent Act is clearly a statute that provides for a national registration. But that begs the more focused question: a national registration of what? Courts have tended to use the context of the statute to amplify the bare text and to answer the focused question: a national registration of security interests. Under that more restrictive definition, it is clear that the Patent Act is outside the scope of § 9302(3)(a). As previously explained, a transaction that grants a party a security interest in a patent but does not effect a transfer of title is not the type of "assignment, grant or conveyance" that is referred to in § 261. The transaction in this case did not transfer an ownership interest. Therefore, § 9302(3)(a) does not require that Petitioners (D) record their security interest with the PTO. The Comments to Article 9 of the U.C.C. support this view, as they provide examples of statutes that are the "type of federal statutes" referred to in § 9302(3). Each of the statutes listed in the Comments refers expressly to security interests; however, the Patent Act is not among them. Affirmed.

EDITOR'S ANALYSIS: The Comments to Article 9 instruct that "17 U.S.C. § 28, 30 (copyrights), 49 U.S.C. § 1403 (aircraft), [and]

49 U.S.C. § 20(c) (railroads)" are examples of the "type of federal statutes" referred to in § 9302(3). Thus, it is clear that whether filing is the exclusive manner of perfecting a security interest is answered differently with respect to each federal statute, on a statute-by-statute basis.

NOTES:

CHAPTER 7
SECURITY INTERESTS IN INVESTMENT SECURITIES

QUICK REFERENCE RULES OF LAW

1. **What Is A Security?** A franchise share certificate is not a "certificated security" for purposes of U.C.C. Article 8. (In re Turley)

2. **Certificate in Possession of Securities Intermediary.** A securities intermediary (broker) does not owe a duty to a holder of an unperfected security interest in a collateral brokerage account maintained by the intermediary. (First Nat. Bank of Palmerton v. Donaldson, Lufkin & Jenrette Securities Corp.)

3. **Uncertificated Securities.** A secured creditor has perfected its security interest in uncertificated securities where it is the only party who can release the uncertificated securities in a frozen loan collateral account, where it does not need to obtain the owner's permission to do so, and where the owner has granted the secured creditor the right to sell the securities upon default. (In re Pfautz)

IN RE TURLEY
[Priority dispute.]
172 F.3d 671 (9th Cir. 1999).

NATURE OF CASE: Appeal from affirmance of summary judgment in bankruptcy proceeding involving interpleaded funds.

FACT SUMMARY: Turley (debtor) pledged a franchise share certificate to Farmers and Merchants Bank of Long Beach (Bank). Thompson Sports held a perfected interest in Turley's general intangibles. When Turley declared bankruptcy, he had to redeem his franchise share certificate, and the franchise, Championship Auto Racing Teams (CART) (P), interpleaded the funds that it otherwise would have owed to Turley. Both the Bank and Thompson Sports lay claim to the funds.

CONCISE RULE OF LAW: A franchise share certificate is not a "certificated security" for purposes of U.C.C. Article 8.

FACTS: Turley (debtor), a racecar driver, was a member of the Championship Auto Racing Teams (CART) (P) franchise. As a franchise member, he owned one share of CART (P). Turley pledged the share to Farmers and Merchants Bank of Long Beach (Bank). In addition, Thompson Sports held a perfected interest in Turley's general intangibles. Turley declared bankruptcy, and had to redeem his share in CART (P). CART (P) valued debtor's share at $220,000. Additionally, Turley was entitled to a $29,394 payment from CART (P). Given the competing claims to the funds, CART (P) filed a complaint in interpleader, and both the Bank and Thompson Sports lay claim to the funds. On cross-motions for summary judgment, the bankruptcy court entered summary judgment in favor of the Bank. The district court affirmed, and the Court of Appeals granted review.

ISSUE: Is a franchise share certificate a "certificated security" for purposes of U.C.C. Article 8?

HOLDING AND DECISION: (Rymer, Cir. J.) No. A franchise share certificate is not a "certificated security" for purposes of U.C.C. Article 8. The resolution of this priority dispute turns on the characterization of the proceeds. The Bank argues that it is entitled to the funds because the proceeds stem from the redemption of a certificated security, governed by Article 8. Thompson Sports argues that it has priority to the funds because they represent proceeds from a general intangible—a franchise agreement between the debtor and CART (P)—governed by Article 9. Whether Turley's CART (P) share is a certificated security turns on whether it is "of a type" that is generally traded in markets and exchanges, because a certificated security is defined as being of such a type. The Bank argues that the share

in CART (P) is nothing more than a share in a closely held corporation, and that CART (P) transfer restrictions, being typical of such corporations, do not remove the share from Article 8 purview. The Bank, however, is incorrect in this assertion. As a franchise member, Turley was required to purchase one share of CART (P) stock, and, upon termination of his franchise membership, he was compelled to return the share certificate. To maintain his membership, Turley was also required to participate in racing events. Therefore, with these requirements, the CART (P) share is definitely not "of a type commonly dealt in on securities exchanges or markets...." It is also not the kind of security commonly recognized as a medium for investment. Accordingly, it is not an Article 8 certificated security. Instead, it is an interest of the kind governed by Article 9's "general intangible" provisions. As a security interest in a general intangible may only be perfected by filing, possession of the share certificate is inconsequential—the Bank can have nothing more than an unperfected security interest in the share. Judgment must, therefore, be entered for Thompson Sports. Reversed and remanded.

EDITOR'S ANALYSIS: Revised Article 8 was written to address the problems raised both by indirect holdings of securities by securities intermediaries and by uncertificated securities. As the court points out in the opinion, Article 8's "of a type" test is intended to ensure that the Article 8 rules do not apply to interests or obligations in circumstances so unconnected with the securities markets that parties are unlikely to have thought of the possibility that Article 8 might apply.

NOTES:

FIRST NAT. BANK OF PALMERTON v. DONALDSON, LUFKIN & JENRETTE SECURITIES CORP.

Secured creditor (P) v. Securities intermediary (D)

38 U.C.C. Rep.Serv.2d 564, 1999 WL 163606 (E.D. Pa. 1999).

NATURE OF CASE: Action for negligence, breach of fiduciary duty, and fraud involving a security interest in marketable securities.

FACT SUMMARY: First National Bank of Palmerton ("the bank") (P) held an unperfected security interest in Patel's brokerage account that was maintained by Donaldson, Lufkin & Jenrette Securities Corp. (DLJ) (D). The bank (P), which had informed DLJ (D) that it held a security interest in Patel's security entitlements, claimed that DLJ (D) was negligent, breached fiduciary duties, and committed fraud by allowing Patel to liquidate the account without the bank's (P) consent.

CONCISE RULE OF LAW: A securities intermediary (broker) does not owe a duty to a holder of an unperfected security interest in a collateral brokerage account maintained by the intermediary.

FACTS: First National Bank of Palmerton ("the bank") (P) entered a loan agreement with Kadam and Patel, whereby the bank (P) was granted a security interest in marketable securities registered in Patel's name that were held by Donaldson, Lufkin & Jenrette Securities Corp. (DLJ) (D), a securities broker. Pursuant to an acceptance and acknowledgment, which explained that Patel agreed for the bank (P) to perfect its security interest, DLJ (D) forwarded the stock certificates for the subject securities to the bank (P). Subsequently, in 1996, Patel requested that the stocks be returned to her brokerage account so she could trade them, and the bank (P) agreed. The certificates were returned to DLJ (D) with a transmittal letter from the bank (P) explaining that the principal in Patel's account should be maintained. DLJ (D) did not respond to this letter. Then, in 1997, Patel individually executed a second promissory note, the collateral for which was her brokerage account with DLJ (D). Patel signed a security agreement and collateral pledge agreement that granted the bank (P) an assignment and security interest in the account. The bank (P) sent a copy of the pledge agreement to DLJ (D), and requested that DLJ (D) sign and return an acknowledgment form whereby it would agree that the bank (P), as the secured party, would have the sole right to make withdrawals from the collateral. DLJ (D) neither signed nor returned this form. Several months later, Patel and Kadam defaulted on the first loan, and Patel defaulted on her second loan. When the bank (P) tried to liquidate the securities in the collateral brokerage account, it learned that Patel had already done so, without the bank's (P) written consent. To recover its loss, the bank (P) sued DLJ (D), claiming that by allowing Patel to liquidate the brokerage account, DLJ (D) was

negligent, breached its fiduciary duties, and committed fraud. DLJ (D) defended by asserting that it owed no duty to the bank (P).

ISSUE: Does a securities intermediary (broker) owe a duty to a holder of an unperfected security interest in a collateral brokerage account maintained by the intermediary?

HOLDING AND DECISION: (Yohn, J.) No. A securities intermediary (broker) does not owe a duty to a holder of an unperfected security interest in a collateral brokerage account maintained by the intermediary. To prevail, the bank (P) must allege the existence of a duty owed it by DLJ (D). DLJ (D) claims that the bank (P) did not perfect its security interest in the collateral securities, and, therefore, DLJ (D) owed it no duty. The apposite U.C.C. articles are Revised Articles 8 and 9. Under the U.C.C., the collateral at issue here is characterized as investment property, and is further defined as "security entitlements"—"the rights and property interest of a person who holds securities or other financial assets through a securities intermediary." DLJ (D) is a "securities intermediary," and Patel was the "entitlement holder." The mere granting by Patel of a security interest in her security entitlements to the bank (P) by itself created no duty between DLJ (D) and the bank (P). The U.C.C. drafters have stated that a securities intermediary owes no duties to the secured party, unless the intermediary has entered into a control agreement in which it agrees to act on entitlement orders originated by the secured party. DLJ (D) did not expressly enter into such a written control agreement in favor of the bank (P). The bank (P) could also have gained control over the securities entitlements by becoming the entitlement holder. To do so, the bank (P) would have had to establish a separate account to which DLJ (D) would credit Patel's securities. This, too, did not occur. Nonetheless, the bank (P) maintains that DLJ (D) entered into a control agreement by its conduct, rather than through a written agreement. Although a securities intermediary must be a party to a control agreement, the U.C.C. does not require that the securities intermediary agree in writing. The bank claimed that it "clearly thought" that DLJ's (D) forwarding of the stock certificates in connection with the first loan's security agreement was a manifestation of implicit agreement to the terms of the security arrangement generally. However, there is no allegation that DLJ (D) possessed or had knowledge of the security agreement such that it could have agreed with all or any of its terms. Furthermore, DLJ's (D) conduct evidenced only that it complied with Patel's

Continued on next page.

explicit authorization. The fact that DLJ (D) accepted the returned certificates also does not evidence an agreement between the bank (P) and DLJ (D) whereby DLJ (D) agreed to maintain the balance in the account. In fact, DLJ (D) did not sign or return the transmittal letter's acknowledgment form. Also, there was no other kind of unconditional and absolute manifestation by DLJ (D) that it had accepted the terms of the acknowledgment form. Moreover, no control agreement was already in place at the time the bank (P) negotiated the second loan, so the bank (P) cannot argue that when DLJ (D) accepted the returned certificates, the bank (P) perfected its interest in the account. Thus, neither DLJ's (D) individual actions, nor the pattern of dealings between the parties, served to create a control agreement. As no agreement existed, no duty arose between DLJ (D) and the bank (P). DLJ's (D) motion to dismiss with prejudice is granted, and the bank's (P) complaint is dismissed with prejudice.

EDITOR'S ANALYSIS: As a matter of practice, typical control agreements are detailed documents that spell out the securities intermediary's obligations, including an agreement by the securities intermediary not to agree to comply with entitlement orders by third parties without the secured creditor's consent. Such agreements usually also include a subordination of specific existing and after-acquired liens in favor of the securities intermediary, specification of the conditions under which the secured creditor can exercise control and the way the creditor can do so, and the indemnification of the securities intermediary against liability arising from its compliance with the control agreement.

NOTES:

IN RE PFAUTZ
Bankruptcy trustee (P) v. Secured creditor (D)
264 B.R. 551 (W.D. Mo. 2001).

NATURE OF CASE: Motion in bankruptcy proceeding to compel secured creditor to turn over uncertificated securities.

FACT SUMMARY: The bankruptcy trustee (the Trustee) (P) for the bankruptcy estate of the Pfautzes (debtors) moved to compel Liberty Bank (D) to turn over uncertificated securities—shares in a mutual fund—owned by the debtors in which Liberty Bank (D) claimed a security interest, and which were held in a loan collateral account administered by a transfer agent who would release the securities only to Liberty Bank (D).

CONCISE RULE OF LAW: A secured creditor has perfected its security interest in uncertificated securities where it is the only party who can release the uncertificated securities in a frozen loan collateral account, where it does not need to obtain the owner's permission to do so, and where the owner has granted the secured creditor the right to sell the securities upon default.

FACTS: The Pfautzes (debtors) acquired shares of Guardian Park Avenue Fund-A (Guardian), a mutual fund, in the form of uncertificated securities. Thereafter, debtors executed a Third Party Pledge Agreement in which they granted Liberty Bank (D) a security interest in the uncertificated securities. Liberty Bank (D) and the debtors established a loan collateral account with State Street Bank and Trust Co. (State Street), as the transfer agent for Guardian, to hold the securities. Pursuant to the request establishing the loan collateral account, State Street would only release the securities upon instructions from Liberty Bank (D); the debtors' signatures were not required to release the securities. Close to three years later, debtors filed for bankruptcy, and Liberty Bank (D) moved to lift the automatic stay so it could foreclose on its security interest. The bankruptcy trustee (the Trustee) (P) for the bankruptcy estate opposed the motion, claiming that Liberty Bank (D) had failed to perfect its interest, and moved to compel Liberty Bank (D) to turn over the uncertificated securities.

ISSUE: Has a secured creditor perfected its security interest in uncertificated securities where it is the only party who can release the uncertificated securities in a frozen loan collateral account, where it does not need to obtain the owner's permission to do so, and where the owners have granted the secured creditor the right to sell the securities upon default?

HOLDING AND DECISION: (Federman, C.J.) Yes. A secured creditor has perfected its security interest in uncertificated securities where it is the only party who can release the

uncertificated securities in a frozen loan collateral account, where it does not need to obtain the owner's permission to do so, and where the owner has granted the secured creditor the right to sell the securities upon default. To perfect a security interest in uncertificated securities, a form of "investment property" under state law (here, Missouri), the secured party must exercise control over the securities. Control is defined as having the power to sell the securities without the consent of the owners. Control may be obtained by obtaining delivery, or by having an issuer agree that it will comply with the instruction originated by the purchaser without further consent by the registered owner. Here, the Third Party Pledge Agreement granted Liberty Bank (D) the authority to dispose of the securities in the event of default, but did not specifically say that Liberty Bank (D) could sell the securities without the consent of the debtors. The evidence showed that State Street, through a subsidiary, National Financial Data Services (NFDS), froze the assets in the loan collateral account pursuant to a stop transfer contained in the parties' agreement. NFDS would act only upon instructions from Liberty Bank (D) to release the collateral. The release did not require the signature of the debtors. Liberty Bank (D) does not contend that it accepted delivery of the uncertificated securities by becoming their registered owner. Thus, if it obtained control over the securities, it could do so only if it could demand that Guardian, or its transfer agent (State Street), redeem or dispose of the securities without regard to the Pfautzes' wishes. Here, the language in the Third Party Pledge Agreement authorized the secured party to dispose of the collateral in the event of default. By signing the Agreement, the debtors agreed to allow Liberty Bank (D) to sell the uncertificated securities without their consent. Thus, Liberty Bank (D) properly perfected its security interest. The Trustee's (P) motion for turnover is denied.

EDITOR'S ANALYSIS: This case illustrates the rule that to perfect a security interest in uncertificated securities, where the securities are not to be delivered to the secured creditor, both the registered owners and the secured party must request the establishment of a loan collateral account. The case also highlights that for a security interest to be perfected via this route, the agreements governing the loan collateral account must be clear, and the transfer agent must follow procedures that ensure compliance with those agreements.

CHAPTER 8
SECURITY INTERESTS IN FIXTURES

QUICK REFERENCE RULES OF LAW

1. **Manufactured Homes.** A properly recorded mortgage does not perfect a security interest in a mobile home where a statute specifically provides an alternative means of doing so. (In re Kroskie)

2. **Enforcement.** A first mortagee is entitled to priority over a fixture financier in the funds realized from a foreclosure sale of the mortgaged premises. (Maplewood Bank and Trust v. Sears, Roebuck and Co.)

IN RE KROSKIE

Bankruptcy trustee (P) v. Unperfected creditor (D)

315 F.3d 644 (6th Cir. 2003).

NATURE OF CASE: Appeal from reversal of summary judgment granting bankruptcy trustee the power to avoid a lien on a mobile home.

FACT SUMMARY: Chase Manhattan Mortgage Corporation (Chase Manhattan) (D) held a properly recorded mortgage in the Kroskies' mobile home. After the Kroskies declared bankruptcy, the bankruptcy trustee (Trustee) (P) moved to avoid Chase Manhattan's (D) purported lien in the mobile home.

CONCISE RULE OF LAW: A properly recorded mortgage does not perfect a security interest in a mobile home where a statute specifically provides an alternative means of doing so.

FACTS: The Kroskies owned a mobile home located on their own land. When they refinanced their real estate and mobile home, their lender, R-B Financial Mortgages, Inc. (R-B Financial), secured the debt by recording a traditional mortgage with the county register of deeds. Simultaneously, the mortgage was assigned to Chase Manhattan Mortgage Corporation (Chase Manhattan) (D). Neither R-B Financial nor Chase Manhattan (D) filed anything with the state's Mobile Home Commission. The Kroskies filed for bankruptcy, and the bankruptcy trustee (Trustee) (P) moved to avoid Chase Manhattan's (D) purported lien in the mobile home. The parties agreed that the mobile home was legally a fixture to the real estate. The bankruptcy court held that Michigan's Mobile Home Commission Act (MHCA) provided the exclusive method for perfecting a security interest in mobile homes. It reached this conclusion based upon the MHCA provision that made every mobile home located in the state subject to its certificate of title provisions and the requirement that "an owner named in a certificate of title . . . shall immediately execute an application in the form prescribed by the department showing the name and address of the holder of the security interest." The MHCA created a Mobile Home Commission with which all certificates of title and security interests are to be filed. Because neither R-B Financial nor Chase Manhattan (D) filed anything with the Mobile Home Commission, the bankruptcy court concluded that Chase Manhattan (D) was an unsecured creditor with regard to the Kroskies' mobile home. The bankruptcy court therefore granted the Trustee's (P) motion for summary judgment. On appeal, the district court reversed, holding that Chase Manhattan (D) had perfected its security interest in the affixed mobile home when it recorded its mortgage. The Court of Appeals granted review.

ISSUE: Does a properly recorded mortgage perfect a security interest in a mobile home where a statute specifically provides an alternative means of doing so?

HOLDING AND DECISION: (Gilman, Cir. J.) No. A properly recorded mortgage does not perfect a security interest in a mobile home where a statute specifically provides an alternative means of doing so. Under general real property principles, the recording of Chase Manhattan's (D) mortgage would have sufficed to perfect its interest in all fixtures on the Kroskie's land. However, the MHCA conflicts with those principles. Invoking the principle that a specific statute trumps a more general one when statutes conflict, the bankruptcy court held that the MHCA was the sole method of perfecting a security interest in a mobile home, regardless of its fixture status. Because the MHCA specifically applies to mobile homes that are permanently affixed to real property, much of Chase Manhattan's (D) argument about the fixtures status of the mobile home is irrelevant. In other words, the general rule that a security interest in a fixture can be perfected through a properly recorded mortgage on real estate does not govern where, as here, there is a specific statute dealing with mobile home security interests. Chase Manhattan (D), on the other hand, attempts to read parts of Michigan's U.C.C. Article 9 dealing with fixtures as being in harmony with the MHCA's provisions. This attempt falters, however, because all security interests in fixtures do not have to be perfected under Article 9 as do all security interests in mobile homes under the MHCA. The specific MHCA provisions govern over the more general provisions of the U.C.C. The district court, on the other hand, reasoned that just because filing under the MHCA was sufficient to perfect a security interest in a mobile home did not mean that it was the exclusive means of perfecting such an interest. Therefore, it determined that the U.C.C. provided an alternative route for perfecting a mobile home security interest. The district court's reasoning was erroneous, however, because it disregarded the MHCA's mandate that it terms be complied with, and because the U.C.C. itself, in Article 9, provided that a mobile home security interest could only be perfected through compliance with the MHCA. For these reasons, Chase Manhattan (D) did not perfect its security interest in the Kroskies' mobile home. Accordingly, its interest is avoidable because the Trustee's (P) interest as a statutory judgment lien creditor is superior to that of an unperfected creditor. Reversed and remanded.

EDITOR'S ANALYSIS: A dissenting opinion by Judge Merritt concluded that the procedures required under the MHCA did not preclude the securing of an interest in a mobile home as a fixture on real property through the recording of a mortgage. The dissent found convincing that the MHCA itself did not purport to be the

Continued on next page.

exclusive means of recording a security interest in a fixture on real property. Instead, the dissent argued that the MHCA provides the means by which mobile home security interests are perfected, whether or not the mobile home is a fixture, and that no part of the statute suggests that it was intended to override ordinary real estate law. According to the dissent, the MHCA itself provides only that a filing under the Act "is equivalent to the filing of a financing statement with respect to the security interest under Article 9" and that financing statements generally do not provide the exclusive means of perfecting a security interest in goods, including fixtures.

NOTES:

MAPLEWOOD BANK AND TRUST v. SEARS, ROEBUCK AND CO.

First mortgagee (P) v. Fixture financier (D)

Sup. Ct. N.J., 265 N.J.Super. 25, 625 A.2d 537;
aff'd, 135 N.J. 97, 638 A.2d 140 (1994).

NATURE OF CASE: Appeal from the dismissal of a counterclaim in an action to determine priority interests in a foreclosure sale.

FACT SUMMARY: Sears (D) took a security interest in certain kitchen fixtures it installed on the Capers' (D) property on which Maplewood (P) had previously taken a purchase-money mortgage.

CONCISE RULE OF LAW: A first mortgagee is entitled to priority over a fixture financier in the funds realized from a foreclosure sale of the mortgaged premises.

FACTS: Maplewood Bank and Trust (P) was the holder of a first purchase-money mortgage dated September 20, 1988, and recorded on October 5, 1988, on the Capers' (D) property. On May 31, 1989, Sears, Roebuck and Company (D) filed a financing statement covering kitchen fixtures it installed on the mortgaged premises. When the Capers (D) defaulted on their loans, Maplewood (P) filed a complaint for foreclosure. Sears (D) filed an answer and counterclaim stating that it was entitled to priority over Maplewood (P) for the sums received in the foreclosure sale because of its fixture filing pursuant to U.C.C. § 9-313, and that it was entitled to the difference between the price of the home with and without the new kitchen. Sears's (D) answer and counterclaim were stricken and an unopposed foreclosure sale ensued. Sears (D) appealed the dismissal of the counterclaim.

ISSUE: Is a first mortgagee entitled to priority over a fixture financier in the funds realized from a foreclosure sale of the mortgaged premises?

HOLDING AND DECISION: (Coleman, J.) Yes. A first mortgagee is entitled to priority over a fixture financier in the funds realized from a foreclosure sale of the mortgaged premises. Here, U.C.C. § 9-313 does not give Sears (D) priority over Maplewood (P) on the proceeds from the foreclosure sale. Sears's (D) perfected security interest was in the goods and chattels that became fixtures, and such interest attached to those goods before they became fixtures. Therefore, Sears's (D) superiority pursuant to U.C.C. § 9-313 applies only to those goods that became fixtures, and not the premises at large. Pursuant to U.C.C. § 9-313(8) as adopted in New Jersey, Sears's (D) remedy is to remove the goods from the premises and reimburse Maplewood (P) for any damage caused by the removal. In entering into this security agreement, Sears (D) knew of the risk it was taking and the remedy offered by state law. If the law is to be changed to allow creditors such as Sears (D) to have priority in similar foreclosure

sale funds, that is to be determined by the state legislature. Summary judgment in favor of Maplewood (P) is affirmed.

EDITOR'S ANALYSIS: Draft § 9-604(b), formerly § 9-501(g), states that "if a security agreement covers goods that are or become fixtures, a secured party, subject to subsection (c), may proceed under this part or in accordance with the rights and remedies with respect to real [estate] [property], in which case the other provisions of this part do not apply." This subsection is intended to clarify the notion that a security interest in fixtures may be enforced under any of the applicable provisions of Part 5. The subsection also serves to overrule cases holding that a secured party's only remedy after default is the removal of the fixtures from the real estate.

NOTES:

9

CHAPTER 9
SECURITY INTERESTS IN BANKRUPTCY

QUICK REFERENCE RULES OF LAW

1. **Consumer Debtors—In Chapter 13.** A secured creditor who repossesses property and obtains a transfer title for the property pursuant to state law, but does not sell the property prior to the debtor's filing for bankruptcy in Chapter 13, does not obtain ownership of the property so as to take the property out of the bankruptcy estate. (In re Robinson)

2. **Valuing Collateral in Bankruptcy.** Under § 506(a) of the Bankruptcy Code, the value of property retained because the debtor has exercised Chapter 13's "cram down" option is the cost the debtor would incur to obtain a like asset for the same proposed use (i.e., replacement value). (Associates Commercial Corporation v. Rash)

3. **Ordinary Course Payments.** Pursuant to Bankruptcy Code § 547(c)(2)(C), a creditor asserting the "ordinary business terms" exception to voidable preference law must show that the "ordinary business terms" in question fall within the range of terms encompassed by the practices in which similar firms engage. (Matter of Tolona Pizza Products Corp.)

4. **False Preferences: Delayed Perfection of Security Interests.** The transfer of a security interest is perfected under 11 U.S.C. section 547(c)(3)(B) on the date the secured party has completed the necessary steps to perfect its interest, and a creditor may invoke the enabling loan exception only by satisfying state law perfection requirements within the 20-day period provided by federal law. (Fidelity Financial Services, Inc. v. Fink)

IN RE ROBINSON
Debtor (P) v. Holder of security interest (D)
Bankr., 285 B.R. 732 (W.D. Okla. 2002).

NATURE OF CASE: Motion to reconsider grant of motion for turnover in bankruptcy proceeding.

FACT SUMMARY: Eldorado (D) repossessed Debtor's (P) car, in which Eldorado (D) had a security interest. Debtor filed for bankruptcy the day before Eldorado (D) was to sell the car, and moved for turnover of the vehicle, which Eldorado (D) refused. Debtor (P) claimed that Eldorado's (D) repossession title did not convey ownership to Eldorado (D), so that the vehicle remained part of the Debtor's (P) bankruptcy estate, subject to an automatic stay.

CONCISE RULE OF LAW: A secured creditor who repossesses property and obtains a transfer title for the property pursuant to state law, but does not sell the property prior to the debtor's filing for bankruptcy in Chapter 13, does not obtain ownership of the property so as to take the property out of the bankruptcy estate.

FACTS: Eldorado (D) financed Debtor's (P) purchase of an automobile (hereinafter the "Vehicle") in return for which Debtor (P) granted to Eldorado (D) a security interest therein. When Debtor (P) became delinquent on payments under the note, Eldorado (D) exercised its right to self-help repossess the Vehicle. Thereafter, Eldorado (D) sent to Debtor (D) a document entitled "Notice After Repossession or Voluntary Surrender," which stated, inter alia, that Eldorado (D) had obtained Debtor's (P) Vehicle by repossession and would be offering it for private sale beginning August 13, 2002. Further, the Notice of Sale informed Debtor (P) she could still redeem her Vehicle by paying in full the amount due under the contract up until the time the Vehicle was actually sold. In contemplation of the disposition sale of Debtor's (P) Vehicle, Eldorado (D) applied for and obtained a "Repossession Title." This Repossession Title was in Eldorado's (D) name and did not reflect any liens on the Vehicle. On August 12, 2002, Debtor (P) filed for bankruptcy. That same day, Debtor's (P) attorney notified Eldorado (D) of the bankruptcy filing, and the next day requested return of the Vehicle, which Eldorado (D) refused to surrender. Debtor (P) filed, inter alia, a motion for turnover and motion for determination of willful violation of automatic stay, seeking return of her vehicle. The bankruptcy court granted the motion, and Eldorado (D) requested reconsideration, which the court also granted.

ISSUE: Does a secured creditor who repossesses property and obtains a transfer title for the property pursuant to state law, but does not sell the property prior to the debtor's filing for bankruptcy in Chapter 13, obtain ownership of the property so as to take the property out of the bankruptcy estate?

HOLDING AND DECISION: (Jackson, Bankr. J.) No. A secured creditor who repossesses property and obtains a transfer title for the property pursuant to state law, but does not sell the property prior to the debtor's filing for bankruptcy in Chapter 13, does not obtain ownership of the property so as to take the property out of the bankruptcy estate. Eldorado (D) argued that the fact it (D) had obtained a Repossession Title meant that ownership of the Vehicle had been transferred to Eldorado (D). Based upon this argument, Eldorado (D) asserted the Vehicle could not be property of Debtor's (P) bankruptcy estate subject to the automatic stay. According to Eldorado (D), the nature and extent of Debtor's (P) interest in the Vehicle at the time of bankruptcy filing was limited to the right to redeem under state law. While Debtor (P) conceded that Eldorado's (D) pre-petition repossession was legal and proper, Debtor (P) argued that so long as the Vehicle had not been sold prior to Debtor's (P) bankruptcy filing, it had to be returned to Debtor (P) upon the filing of bankruptcy. Debtor (P) pointed out that if the court sustained Eldorado's (D) position, then every creditor who repossessed a vehicle would immediately obtain a Repossession Title and thereby defeat all rights of debtors to bring their vehicles back into the bankruptcy estate. In addition, Debtor (P) argued that the title held by Eldorado (P) was simply for the purpose of facilitating the transfer at a subsequent disposition sale. In *United States v. Whiting Pool, Inc.*, 462 U.S. 198 (1983), the U.S. Supreme Court held that property of a debtor that has been seized by a creditor pre-bankruptcy filing is included in the bankruptcy estate, and remains the debtor's property until sold to a bona fide purchaser. *Whiting Pools* is applicable here. The issue then becomes whether under state law—U.C.C. Article 9—the Repossession Title obtained by Eldorado (D) transferred legal ownership of the Vehicle from Debtor (P) to Eldorado (D). Under Article 9's repossession procedures in § 9-619(c), "[a] transfer of of the record or legal title to collateral to a secured party…is not of itself a disposition of collateral under this article and does not of itself relieve the secured party of its duties under this article." Eldorado's (D) interest in the Vehicle, as of the petition date, was, therefore, limited to enforcement of its security interest or lien, and Debtor (P) retained an interest in the Vehicle subject to that lien. Thus, this interest was includable in the property of the bankruptcy estate as of the date of the bankruptcy petition. This is supported by the fact that clearly Debtor's (P) right of redemption was the bankruptcy estate's property. Even though under state law, Debtor's (P) sole right was the right of

Continued on next page.

66

redemption, federal bankruptcy law gave her the right to cure default and reinstate the accelerated note. This federal right cannot be frustrated by the law of any state. Accordingly, the order granting Debtor's (P) motion for turnover is reaffirmed.

EDITOR'S ANALYSIS: This case demonstrates the interplay between state U.C.C. law and federal bankruptcy law, and illustrates the importance for creditors to understand the concept of the bankruptcy estate, and that federal bankruptcy law can "trump" state U.C.C. law. By allowing debtors to cure defaults in cases in which there is still a right of redemption under state law, the bankruptcy law furthers the intent of Chapter 13, which is to facilitate debtor rehabilitation while protecting the rights of creditors.

NOTES:

ASSOCIATES COMMERCIAL CORPORATION v. RASH

Secured creditor (D) v. Debtor (P)

520 U.S. 953 (1997).

NATURE OF CASE: Appeal from affirmances in Chapter 13 bankruptcy proceedings of using the replacement-value approach to valuing collateral retained by a debtor under the Bankruptcy Code's "cram down" provisions.

FACT SUMMARY: The Rashes (P) exercised their "cram down" option in their Chapter 13 bankruptcy proceeding which permitted them to retain collateral. Associates Commercial Corporation (ACC) (D), which held a secured interest in the Rashes' (P) truck, argued that the value of the truck should be calculated by a replacement-value approach, whereby the asset is valued at the cost the debtor would incur to obtain a like asset for the same proposed use. The Rashes (P) urged that the truck's value be calculated under a foreclosure-value approach, whereby the asset is valued at the net amount the creditor would realize upon foreclosure and sale of the collateral.

CONCISE RULE OF LAW: Under § 506(a) of the Bankruptcy Code, the value of property retained because the debtor has exercised Chapter 13's "cram down" option is the cost the debtor would incur to obtain a like asset for the same proposed use (i.e., replacement value).

FACTS: Associates Commercial Corporation (ACC) (D) holds a loan and lien on a tractor truck purchased by Rash (P). Rash (P) and his wife (P) filed a joint petition and repayment plan under Chapter 13 of the Bankruptcy Code (Code), listing ACC (D) as a secured creditor. Under the Code, ACC's (D) claim for the $41,171 balance owed on the truck was secured only to the extent of the value of the collateral; its claim over and above that value was unsecured. The Rashes (P) could gain confirmation of their Chapter 13 plan only if ACC (D) accepted it, if the Rashes (P) surrendered the truck to ACC (D), or if the Rashes (P) invoked the Bankruptcy Code's "cram down" provision, which allows the debtor to keep the collateral over the objection of the creditor; the creditor retains the lien securing the claim, and the debtor is required to provide the creditor with payments, over the life of the plan, that will total the present value of the collateral, as per § 1325(a)(5)(B)(ii) of the Code. The value of the allowed secured claim is governed by § 506(a) of the Code. The Rashes (P) invoked the cram down power, proposing to keep the truck for use in their freight-hauling business. ACC (D) objected to the plan, sought to repossess the truck, and disputed the value the Rashes (P) had assigned to the truck. ACC (D) maintained that the proper valuation was the price the Rashes (P) would have to pay to purchase a like vehicle (the replacement-value standard), estimated to be $41,000. The Rashes (P), however, maintained that the proper valuation was the net amount ACC (D) would realize upon foreclosure and sale of the collateral (the

foreclosure-value standard), estimated to be $31,875. The bankruptcy court adopted the Rashes' (P) valuation figure and approved the plan. The district court affirmed, and court of appeals affirmed on rehearing. The U.S. Supreme Court granted review.

ISSUE: Under § 506(a) of the Bankruptcy Code, is the value of property retained because the debtor has exercised Chapter 13's "cram down" option the cost the debtor would incur to obtain a like asset for the same proposed use (i.e., replacement value)?

HOLDING AND DECISION: (Ginsburg, J.) Yes. Under § 506(a) of the Bankruptcy Code, the value of property retained because the debtor has exercised Chapter 13's "cram down" option is the cost the debtor would incur to obtain a like asset for the same proposed use (i.e., replacement value). The words "the creditor's interest in the estate's interest in such property" contained in the first sentence of § 506(a) do not call for the foreclosure-value standard adopted by the Court of Appeals. Even read in isolation, the phrase imparts no valuation standard. The first sentence, read as a whole, instructs that a secured creditor's claim is to be divided into secured and unsecured portions. The sentence tells a court what it must evaluate, but it is not enlightening on how to value collateral. Section 506(a)'s second sentence, however, speaks to the *how* question, providing that "[s]uch value shall be determined in light of the purpose of the valuation and of the proposed disposition or use of such property." By deriving a foreclosure-value standard from § 506(a)'s first sentence, the Court of Appeals rendered inconsequential the sentence that expressly addresses how "value shall be determined." The "proposed disposition or use" of the collateral is of paramount importance to the valuation question. Such "disposition or use" turns on which alternative the debtor chooses when a secured creditor refuses to accept the debtor's Chapter 13 plan, as ACC (D) did here—in one case the collateral will be surrendered to the creditor, and in the other, the collateral will be retained and used by the debtor. Applying a foreclosure-value standard attributes no significance to the different consequences of the debtor's choice. A replacement-value standard, on the other hand, distinguishes retention from surrender and renders meaningful the key statutory words "disposition or use." Surrender and retention are not equivalent acts. When a debtor surrenders the property, a creditor obtains it immediately, and is free to sell it and reinvest the proceeds. If a debtor keeps the property and continues to use it, the creditor obtains at once neither the property nor its value,

Continued on next page.

and is exposed to double risks against which the Bankruptcy Code affords incomplete protection: the debtor may again default and the property may deteriorate from extended use. Of prime significance, the replacement-value standard accurately gauges the debtor's "use" of the property. Here, the Rashes (P) chose to use the collateral to generate an income stream by using the truck in their business. That actual use, rather than a foreclosure sale that will not take place, is, therefore, the proper guide under a prescription hinged to the property's "disposition or use." The Court of Appeals also considered the replacement-value standard disrespectful of state law, which permits the secured creditor to sell the collateral, thereby obtaining only its net foreclosure. In allowing Chapter 13 debtors to retain and use collateral over the objection of secured creditors, however, the Bankruptcy Code has reshaped debtor and creditor rights in marked departure from state law. It no more disrupts state law to make "disposition or use" the guide for valuation than to authorize the rearrangement of rights that the cram down power entails. There is also no support in the Bankruptcy Code for a valuation standard that uses the midpoint between foreclosure and replacement values. Reversed and remanded.

EDITOR'S ANALYSIS: In a dissenting opinion, Justice Stevens favored the foreclosure-value approach on policy grounds, stating that the foreclosure-value approach "…best comports with economic reality. Allowing any more than the foreclosure value simply grants a general windfall to undersecured creditors at the expense of unsecured creditors." This is clearly an area where vying interests are involved, and amendments to Bankruptcy Code § 506(a) continue to be proposed. For example, the National Bankruptcy Review Commission has recommended that in situations such as those presented in this case, the measure of value of personal property should be its wholesale price, and the value of real property should be its fair market value, less the hypothetical costs of the sale. Other proposed amendments would value the property of consumer debtors at its retail price.

NOTES:

MATTER OF TOLONA PIZZA PRODUCTS CORP.
Company (P) v. Supplier (D)
3 F.3d 1029 (7th Cir. 1993).

NATURE OF CASE: Appeal in a bankruptcy matter alleging preferential transfer.

FACT SUMMARY: Tolona Pizza Products Corp. (Tolona) (P) issued eight checks to Rose (D), its sausage supplier, less than ninety days before Tolona (P) was thrown into bankruptcy by its creditors.

CONCISE RULE OF LAW: Pursuant to Bankruptcy Code § 547(c)(2)(C), a creditor asserting the "ordinary business terms" exception to voidable preference law must show that the "ordinary business terms" in question fall within the range of terms encompassed by the practices in which similar firms engage.

FACTS: Tolona (P) issued eight checks to Rose (D), who supplied Tolona's (P) sausage. The checks were issued less than ninety days before Tolona (P) was thrown into bankruptcy. The checks totaled $46,000 and were paid in full; however, other creditors stood to receive only thirteen cents on the dollar. It was the custom between the two parties to allow Tolona (P) to pay late, even though Rose's (D) invoice required payment within seven days. Other sausage makers for pizza companies allowed similar time delays with respect to their pizza makers. Tolona (P) brought an adversary proceeding against Rose (D) to recover the payments as voidable preferences. Rose (D) claimed an exception to the voidable preference law on ordinary course of business grounds, pursuant to § 547(c)(2). The bankruptcy court ruled for Tolona (P), but the district court reversed. Tolona (P) appealed.

ISSUE: Pursuant to Bankruptcy Code § 547(c)(2)(C), must a creditor asserting the "ordinary business terms" exception to voidable preference law show that the "ordinary business terms" in question fall within the range of terms encompassed by the practices in which similar firms engage?

HOLDING AND DECISION: (Posner, Cir. J.) Yes. Pursuant to Bankruptcy Code § 547(c)(2)(C), a creditor asserting the "ordinary business terms" exception to voidable preference law must show that the "ordinary business terms" in question fall within the range of terms encompassed by the practices in which similar firms engage. The question presented here involves the third prong of the ordinary course of business test, as recited in § 547(c)(2)(C) — what are "ordinary business terms"? The first two prongs of the § 547(c)(2) test are satisfied because the debt was incurred in the ordinary course of business between Tolona (P) and Rose (D), and the payments had been received in the ordinary course of business between the parties. Here, the payments satisfy the "ordinary business terms" prong because the delays that Rose (D) allowed Tolona (P) to take in paying its loans are consistent not only with the history between the parties, but also with the customs of similar companies in similar situations. The delay was well within the industry norm and therefore falls within the § 547(c)(2) exception to voidable preferences. The decision of the district court is affirmed.

EDITOR'S ANALYSIS: Preference law rests on the policy of treating creditors equally. The idea of taking something away from a creditor who has acted unfairly dates back to the sixteenth century. This policy also takes into consideration the type of creditor, and treats insiders who behave poorly differently from other creditors, as shown in the shorter, ninety-day time limit.

NOTES:

FIDELITY FINANCIAL SERVICES, INC. v. FINK

Creditor (D) v. Bankruptcy trustee (P)

522 U.S. 211 (1998).

NATURE OF CASE: Appeal from circuit court judgment setting aside a lien as a voidable preference.

FACT SUMMARY: The bankruptcy trustee (P) sought to set aside a lien held by Fidelity (D) as a voidable preference due to Fidelity's (D) failure to perfect its interest within the 20 days required by federal law.

CONCISE RULE OF LAW: The transfer of a security interest is perfected under 11 U.S.C. section 547(c)(3)(B) on the date the secured party has completed the necessary steps to perfect its interest, and a creditor may invoke the enabling loan exception only by satisfying state law perfection requirements within the 20-day period provided by federal law.

FACTS: Beasley purchased a 1994 Ford and gave Fidelity (D) a promissory note for the purchase price, secured by the car. Fidelity (D) mailed the application for perfection of its security interest in the car 21 days later. Two months later, Beasley filed bankruptcy. The bankruptcy trustee (P) moved to set aside Fidelity's (D) security interest, claiming the lien was a voidable preference. Furthermore, the trustee (P) argued that the enabling loan exception did not apply because Fidelity (D) failed to perfect its interest within 20 days pursuant to 11 U.S.C. section 547(c)(3)(B). Fidelity (D) claimed that the security interest was perfected under state law on the date of its creation, so long as the creditor filed the required documents within 30 days after the debtor takes possession. The bankruptcy court set aside the lien as a voidable preference, and concluded that the state statute could not extend the 20-day perfection period established by federal law. Fidelity (D) appealed. The district court and Court of Appeals for the Eight Circuit affirmed. Certiorari was granted to resolve conflicting views among the circuits courts regarding the issue of when a transfer is perfected under section 547(c)(3)(B).

ISSUE: Is the transfer of a security interest perfected under 11 U.S.C. section 547(c)(3)(B) on the date the secured party has completed the necessary steps to perfect its interest, and may a creditor invoke the enabling loan exception only by satisfying state law perfection requirements within the 20-day period provided by federal law?

HOLDING AND DECISION: (Souter, J.) Yes. The transfer of a security interest is perfected under 11 U.S.C. section 547(c)(3)(B) on the date the secured party has completed the necessary steps to perfect its interest, and a creditor may invoke the enabling loan exception only by satisfying state law perfection requirements within the 20-day period provided by federal law. Perfection is accomplished when a creditor cannot require a judicial lien superior to that of the transferee. Fidelity (D) argued that the

federal law provided for the state law relation-back period so that its lien should be treated as being perfected on the date of its creation, since it was delivered within 30 days in compliance with the state statute, thus enabling Fidelity to invoke the enabling loan exception of section 547(c)(3). The statute states that a transfer is perfected when a contract creditor cannot acquire a superior lien. This is accomplished when the secured party performs the last act necessary to prevent other creditors from obtaining superior liens. The terms of section 547(e)(1)(B), however, imply that the security interest is perfected only when the secured party has done all the acts required to perfect its interest, not at the moment when state law may retroactively deem perfection to be effective. Affirmed.

EDITOR'S ANALYSIS: The Court stated several reasons to support its conclusion that Congress did not intend for state law relation back-provisions or grace periods to affect the trustee's power to avoid a preferential transfer. The Bankruptcy Code expressly limits other avoidance powers of the trustee under other provisions of the code, but does not include section 547 among those provisions. Moreover, a 1994 amendment to the code extended the period for perfection under section 547 from 10 to 20 days. Had Congress intended the section to be read together with state law as Fidelity (D) contended, the 1994 amendment would have been meaningless.

NOTES:

10

CHAPTER 10
LETTERS OF CREDIT

QUICK REFERENCE RULES OF LAW

1. **Formal Requirements.** Where the substantive provisions of an instrument require the issuer to deal in facts relating to the performance of a separate contract, rather than dealing in documents alone, that instrument is a guaranty contract and not a letter of credit. (Wichita Eagle and Beacon Publishing Company, Inc. v. Pacific National Bank of San Francisco)

2. **The Strict Compliance Standard.** Discrepancies between a letter of credit and presentation documents that are technical or typographical in nature do not warrant the rejection of the documents where the whole of the documents obviously relate to the transaction on their face. (Voest-Alpine Trading USA Corp. v. Bank of China)

3. **Notice of Discrepancies: Waiver and Preclusion.** An issuing bank is required to tell the beneficiary of a letter of credit, at the time the bank notifies the beneficiary that it will dishonor a letter of credit, the discrepancies in the documentation that led to the bank's decision to dishonor the letter of credit. (Esso Petroleum Canada v. Security Pacific Bank)

4. **Subrogation, Restitution and Breach of Warranty.** Equitable subrogation is available to both the issuer and applicant on a standby letter of credit. (Ochoco Lumber Co. v. Fibrex & Shipping Co., Inc.)

5. **Forgery and Fraud.** A party seeking an injunction against the honoring of a letter of credit must prove that the beneficiary has no bona fide claim to payment for the underlying transaction. (Intraworld Industries, Inc. v. Girard Trust Bank)

6. **Letters of Credit in Bankruptcy.** Where a bankrupt party purchased a letter of credit within 90 days of filing bankruptcy, payment on the letter is not a voidable preference if it was issued contemporaneously with a new extension of credit, but payment is voidable if the letter secured a preexisting unsecured debt. (Matter of Compton Corp.)

WICHITA EAGLE AND BEACON PUBLISHING COMPANY, INC. v. PACIFIC NATIONAL BANK OF SAN FRANCISCO

Assignee (P) v. Bank (D)

493 F.2d 1285 (9th Cir. 1974).

NATURE OF CASE: Appeal from district court determination that an instrument is a letter of credit.

FACT SUMMARY: Circular Ramp Garages, as a lessee, obtained a document purported to be a letter of credit from Pacific National Bank of San Francisco (D), guaranteeing payment of $250,000 to the original lessors if Circular failed to build a contracted parking lot.

CONCISE RULE OF LAW: Where the substantive provisions of an instrument require the issuer to deal in facts relating to the performance of a separate contract, rather than dealing in documents alone, that instrument is a guaranty contract and not a letter of credit.

FACTS: Circular, as a lessee, obtained a document claiming to be a letter of credit from Pacific (D), which guarantied payment of $250,000 to the original lessors if Circular failed to build a contracted parking lot. The document was entitled "Letter of Credit No. 17084." The document stated that it was available for drafts drawn at sight, providing that certain factual conditions involving Circular's failure to perform were met. Circular failed to obtain financing and the original lessor's assignee, Wichita Eagle and Beacon Publishing Company, Inc. (P), presented the alleged letter of credit to Pacific (D). Pacific (D) denied payment and Wichita (P) brought suit. The district court ruled that the document was a letter of credit and Pacific (D) appealed.

ISSUE: Where the substantive provisions of an instrument require the issuer to deal in facts relating to the performance of a separate contract, rather than dealing in documents alone, is that instrument a letter of credit?

HOLDING AND DECISION: (Per curiam) No. Where the substantive provisions of an instrument require the issuer to deal in facts relating to the performance of a separate contract, rather than dealing in documents alone, that instrument is not a letter of credit, but rather, it is an ordinary guaranty contract. Upon presentation of the "Letter of Credit No. 17084," Wichita (P) had to prove that Circular failed to perform the terms of the lease, that Wichita (P) had given notice to Circular specifying how it failed to perform, and that Circular failed to cure any defaults within thirty days. These are facts that are usually the subject of litigation. The purpose of a letter of credit is to avoid litigation. Because payment on the instrument was conditioned on the proving of the above-referenced facts, the instrument was not a letter of credit, but rather an ordinary guaranty contract. Letters of credit must be strictly and tightly drafted to limit the liability of the issuer since the mere presentation of the requisite documents will require

payment. Pacific (D) is liable for $250,000, plus interest to Wichita (P) as guarantor, but the district court's ruling that the instrument was a letter of credit is reversed.

EDITOR'S ANALYSIS: This case highlights the importance of having the correct form when issuing a letter of credit. The primary thrust of a letter of credit is that the credit provided is independent of the underlying contract. Because the issuer is required to pay independently of the performance of the contract, the letter of credit must make clear that the duty to pay is not contingent on debatable facts, and the issuer's liability should be narrowly defined.

NOTES:

VOEST-ALPINE TRADING USA CORP. v. BANK OF CHINA
Beneficiary of credit (P) v. Issuer (D)
167 F. Supp. 2d 940 (S.D. Tex. 2000).

NATURE OF CASE: Action for payment on letter of credit.

FACT SUMMARY: Bank of China (D) issued a letter of credit for the benefit of Voest-Alpine (P). On the basis of several discrepancies between the letter of credit and documents submitted by Voest-Alpine (P), the Bank of China (D) refused to honor the letter of credit. Voest-Alpine (P) claimed that Bank of China (D) had not provided adequate notice of refusal and that the discrepancies were technical and typographical in nature and did not warrant dishonor.

CONCISE RULES OF LAW: Discrepancies between a letter of credit and presentation documents that are technical or typographical in nature do not warrant the rejection of the documents where the whole of the documents obviously relate to the transaction on their face.

FACTS: Voest-Alpine Trading USA Corp. (Voest-Alpine) (P) entered into a contract with Jiangyin Foreign Trade Corp. (JFTC) to sell to JFTC styrene monomer for $1.2 million. JFTC applied for a letter of credit for the benefit of Voest-Alpine (P) from the Bank of China (D). The letter of credit provided for payment once the goods had arrived at Zhangjiagang, China, and Voest-Alpine (P) had presented the documents called for in the letter of credit. The letter of credit had numerous typographical errors in it, including that "Trading USA" in Voest-Alpine's (P) name was inverted and the destination port's name omitted the final "a." The letter of credit clearly stated that it was subject to the 1993 Uniform Customs and Practice, International Chamber of Commerce Publication Number 500 (UCP 500). The goods shipped on July 18, 1995, and on August 1, 1995, Voest-Alpine (P) presented the required documents to Texas Commerce Bank, the presenting bank, which found the discrepancies and alerted Voest-Alpine (P). Voest-Alpine (P) decided the discrepancies would not warrant refusal to pay, and the documents were sent on August 3, 1995, and received by Bank of China (D) on August 9, 1995. On August 11, 1995, Bank of China (D) sent a telex to Texas Commerce Bank that informed of seven discrepancies and that indicated that Bank of China (D) would contact the applicant about the discrepancies. On August 15, 1995, Texas Commerce Bank faxed Bank of China (D) indicating that the discrepancies were not an adequate basis to refuse to pay the letter of credit and requesting honor and payment. Finally, on August 19, 1995, Bank of China (D) sent a telex to Texas Commerce Bank indicating that the discrepancies "may have us refuse to take up the documents . . . ." Bank of China (D) returned the document and did not honor the letter of credit. Voest-Alpine (P) sued for payment.

ISSUES: Do discrepancies between a letter of credit and presentation documents that are technical or typographical in

nature warrant the rejection of the documents where the whole of the documents obviously relate to the transaction on their face?

HOLDING AND DECISION: (Gilmore, Dist. J.) No. Voest-Alpine (P) claims the discrepancies were technical and typographical in nature that do not warrant the rejection of the documents and urges that a "functional standard" of compliance be used to measure the discrepancies. Although there is a wide range of standards that are used to examine presentation documents for compliance—from strict compliance, to strict compliance where there is risk to the issuer, to strict compliance where there is risk to the applicant, to a mirror image approach—the UCP 500 itself contains a moderate standard that requires "consistency" between the letter of credit and the documents. This standard requires that "the whole of the documents must obviously relate to the same transaction…on its face." This is a common-sense, case-by-case approach that permits minor typographical deviations because the standard is whether the documents bear a rational link to one another. Here, the discrepancies pointed to by Bank of China (D) do not warrant rejection of the documents. Six of the seven discrepancies are at issue. The first, the inversion of "Trading USA" in Voest-Alpine's (P) name, was not a complete misspelling or an omission, and did not signify a different corporate entity, and thus bore an obvious link to the documents. The second, the stamping of the set of originals of the bill of lading as "original," "duplicate," and "triplicate" instead of "original," also did not warrant rejection because it was clear from the face of these documents that they were all originals. Third, the failure to stamp the packing list documents as "original" was also insufficient to reject these documents because they, too, were clearly originals on their face. Fourth, the date of the survey report was after the bill of lading, but it was clear from the plain language of the report that the survey was conducted before the ship departed. Fifth, the letter of credit number had an extra numeral in it on the beneficiary's certified copy of fax. However, adding the letter of credit number to this document was gratuitous and the document checker could have looked to any other document to verify the letter of credit number or looked to the balance of the information in the document and found that, as a whole, it bore an obvious relationship to the transaction. Finally, the fact that the destination port was misspelled by omitting its last "a" also did not warrant rejection of the documents because it was an obvious misspelling (there are no ports in China with the misspelled name) and the other information contained in the document demonstrated linkage to the transaction on its face.

EDITOR'S ANALYSIS: The U.C.C.'s standard for examining presentation documents is strict compliance. This requires an issuer to honor a presentation that "appear on its face strictly to comply with the terms and conditions of the letter of credit." Thus, application of the U.C.C. standard in the instant case could have led to a different result.

ESSO PETROLEUM CANADA v. SECURITY PACIFIC BANK

Holder of letter of credit (P) v. Bank (D)

710 F. Supp. 275 (D. Or. 1989).

NATURE OF CASE: Cross-motions for summary judgment in action arising from a refusal to honor a letter of credit.

FACT SUMMARY: Security Pacific Bank (D) dishonored Esso Petroleum Canada's (P) letter of credit but failed to state the discrepancies that caused rejection or notify Esso of the discrepancies in a timely manner.

CONCISE RULE OF LAW: An issuing bank is required to tell the beneficiary of a letter of credit, at the time the bank notifies the beneficiary that it will dishonor a letter of credit, the discrepancies in the documentation that led to the bank's decision to dishonor the letter of credit.

FACTS: Prior to October 22, 1987, Esso (P) entered into a contract with Valley Oil Co. ("Valley") to sell aviation gasoline to Valley for $1,196,580. Esso (P) required Valley to obtain a standby letter of credit from the Bank (D), naming Esso (P) as beneficiary. The Bank (D) further required Valley to obtain a backup letter of credit from Western Pioneer, Inc., d.b.a. Delta Western ("Delta"). On October 21, 1987, Delta transferred by wire $1,288,140 to the Bank (D) for deposit to Valley's account. On October 22, 1987, the Bank (D) delivered to Esso (P) an executed, irrevocable standby letter of credit. The letter of credit provided that it was subject to the Uniform Customs and Practices for Documentary Credits (1983 Revision) International Chamber of Commerce (Publication 400) (the "U.C.P."). At 1:00 p.m. on Friday, November 13, 1987, Esso (P) presented its letter of credit and documentation to the Bank (D) and demanded immediate payment. At 5:15 p.m. on Friday, November 13, 1987, the Bank (D) refused to honor Esso's (P) letter of credit, claiming certain discrepancies in the documentation, but not detailing them at the time to Esso (P). The Bank (D) told Esso (P) that Esso (P) would have to wait for a written response detailing the discrepancies, which would be available on Monday, November 16, 1987. The Bank (D) sent Esso (P) a list of discrepancies on November 16, 1987. Esso (P) attempted to fix the problems, but the Bank (D) continued to dishonor the letter of credit. On February 10, 1988, Esso (P) filed action against the Bank (D), claiming money damages in the amount of the letter of credit, plus interest and punitive damages. The Bank (D) filed a motion for summary judgment and Esso (P) filed a cross-motion for relief.

ISSUE: Is an issuing bank required to tell the beneficiary of a letter of credit, at the time the bank notifies the beneficiary that it will dishonor a letter of credit, the discrepancies in the documentation that led to the bank's decision to dishonor the letter of credit?

HOLDING AND DECISION: (Frye, Dist. J.) Yes. An issuing bank is required to tell the beneficiary of a letter of credit, at the time the

bank notifies the beneficiary that it will dishonor a letter of credit, the discrepancies in the documentation that led to the bank's decision to dishonor the letter of credit. Both parties concede that they are bound by the U.C.P. which, in Article 16, paragraph d requires the issuing bank to give timely notice of its decision to dishonor a letter of credit. The U.C.P. also requires that such notice must state the discrepancies in respect of which the issuing bank refuses the documents, and whether it is holding the documents or returning them to the presenter. Furthermore, paragraph e of the U.C.P. states that if the issuing bank fails to act in accordance with these provisions, the bank shall be precluded from claiming that the documents are not in accordance with the terms and conditions of the letter of credit. Here, once the Bank (D) notified Esso (P) on November 13, 1987, that it was dishonoring the letter of credit, it was required to inform Esso (P) of the discrepancies at the time of the notice. Because the Bank (D) waited three days to explain the discrepancies to Esso (P), the Bank (D) is precluded from claiming that Esso's (P) documentation is not in accordance with the letter of credit. Therefore, Esso's (P) motion for summary judgment is granted.

EDITOR'S ANALYSIS: This case highlights differences between the U.C.P. and the former Article 5 governing letters of credit. Under the former version of Article 5, there was no requirement that an issuing bank which dishonors a letter of credit notify the beneficiary of discrepancies in the documentation in a timely manner. The revised version has adopted many of the approaches of the U.C.P.

NOTES:

OCHOCO LUMBER CO. v. FIBREX & SHIPPING COMPANY, INC.

Applicant on standby letter of credit (P) v. Borrower (D)

Or. App. Ct., 994 P.2d 793 (2000).

NATURE OF CASE: Appeal from dismissal of equitable subrogation claims.

FACT SUMMARY: Ochoco Lumber Co. (Ochoco) (P) was the applicant on a standby letter of credit that was made for the benefit of West One Idaho Bank (West One) and served as security for a loan from West One to Fibrex & Shipping Co., Inc. (Fibrex) (D). When Fibrex (D) defaulted on the loan and refused to reimburse Ochoco (P) on its payment of the standby letter of credit, Ochoco (P) claimed that it was equitably subrogated to West One's rights against Fibrex (D).

CONCISE RULE OF LAW: Equitable subrogation is available to both the issuer and applicant on a standby letter of credit.

FACTS: Fibrex & Shipping, Co., Inc. (Fibrex) (D) obtained a $3,900,000 loan from West One Idaho Bank (West One) for the purchase of timber. Fibrex's (D) sole shareholder and his wife personally guaranteed the loan. As further security, Fibrex (D) obtained a standby letter of credit that was applied for by Ochoco Lumber Co. (Ochoco) (P) and issued by First Interstate Bank (First Interstate). Ochoco (P) had agreed to purchase timber logs from Fibrex (D). When Fibrex defaulted on the loan, West One drew $2 million on the letter of credit from First Interstate. Ochoco (P) reimbursed First Interstate and demanded repayment from Fibrex (D). When Fibrex (D) refused, Ochoco notified West One that it was subrogated to West One's rights against Fibrex (D), but West One refused to acknowledge Ochoco's (P) equitable subrogation rights. The trial court ruled that neither an applicant nor the issuer on a standby letter of credit can be subrogated to the beneficiary's claims, and Ochoco (P) appealed.

ISSUE: Is equitable subrogation available to both the issuer and applicant on a standby letter of credit?

HOLDING AND DECISION: (Kistler, J.) Yes. The defendants argue that equitable subrogation is available only to persons who are secondarily liable for a debt, and that an issuer of a standby letter of credit is primarily liable on the debt. When the standby letter of credit was issued, the statutes that governed letters of credit did not address whether equitable subrogation was available on a standby letter of credit. The fact that a subsequent legislature amended the statute to provide for subrogation for standby letters of credit does not reflect a judgment as to the law that preceded the amendment. Therefore, the court must decide the issue under common-law principles. As a general rule, courts have required that the party seeking subrogation must have paid a debt for which it was secondarily liable. The majority of courts to address this issue have held that although the issuer's obligation on a standby letter of credit is secondary in the sense that it does not arise until the applicant has defaulted, the issuer is not comparable to a guarantor. The minority position is that the issuer is akin to a surety, and that once the issuer has honored the letter of credit, denying subrogation is an insistence on pointless formalism (i.e., the difference between letters of credits and suretyships and guarantees pursuant to the independence principle). The minority view is more persuasive. Here, that view recognizes that First Interstate was a de facto surety for Fibrex's (D) obligations and is consistent with the view that the standby letter of credit issuer's obligation only arises upon default. More importantly, it is consistent with the equitable recognition that having paid the beneficiary, the issuer (or the applicant if it has reimbursed the issuer) should be able to step into the beneficiary's shoes and assert its rights. Reversed and remanded.

EDITOR'S ANALYSIS: The independence principle discussed by the court states that a letter of credit imposes an independent obligation on the issuer to pay. The majority view, based on this principle, is that the issuer is satisfying its own absolute and primary obligation to pay rather than satisfying a secondary obligation, and, therefore, the issuer is primarily liable. In the minority view, once the issuer has honored the letter of credit, the purpose of the independence principle—to ensure prompt payment on the credit—is satisfied and should not be a reason to deny equitable subrogation.

NOTES:

INTRAWORLD INDUSTRIES, INC. v. GIRARD TRUST BANK

Hotel lessee (P) v. Issuer of letters of credit (D)
Sup. Ct. Pa., 461 Pa. 343, 336 A.2d 316 (1975).

NATURE OF CASE: Appeal from denial of a preliminary injunction to present the honoring of a letter of credit.

FACT SUMMARY: Paulette Cymbalista ("Cymbalista") (D) demanded payment from Girard Trust Bank ("Girard") (D) for letters of credit given on behalf of Intraworld Industries, Inc. ("Intraworld") (P), to guarantee payment under a lease.

CONCISE RULE OF LAW: A party seeking an injunction against the honoring of a letter of credit must prove that the beneficiary has no bona fide claim to payment for the underlying transaction.

FACTS: On February 11, 1972, Intraworld (P) executed a lease with Cymbalista (D) to rent a luxury hotel from Cymbalista (D) in Switzerland. Intraworld (P) initially had to provide a performance bond to guarantee payment of the rent. On May 1, 1972, Intraworld (P) entered into possession of the hotel. Later, Intraworld (P) and Cymbalista (D) added an addendum to the lease (the "Nachtrag") which canceled Intraworld's (P) performance bonds and substituted a duty to provide letters of credit issued by Girard (D) in order to guarantee rental payments up to one year in advance. Two $100,000 letters of credit were required, maturing November 1973 and May 1974. After each rental payment, Intraworld (P) was required to provide similar letters of credit. If Cymbalista (D) terminated the lease because of Intraworld's (P) failure to fulfill its obligations, Cymbalista (D) was entitled to the full year's guarantied rent. On September 5, 1972, Girard (D) issued the two letters of credit. Intraworld's (P) and Cymbalista's (D) relationship deteriorated in the summer of 1973 and Cymbalista (D) claimed Intraworld (P) was running the hotel into the ground and attempted to contact Intraworld (P) to no avail. On August 20, 1973, Cymbalista's (D) counsel notified Intraworld's (P) counsel that if the problems with the management of the hotel were not remedied, the lease would be terminated. On September 18, 1973, Cymbalista's (D) counsel sent another letter terminating the lease. In subsequent correspondences, Cymbalista (D) demanded the November rent from Intraworld (P) and Intraworld (P) contested the termination of the lease. In both November 1973 and May 1974 the rent was not paid and Cymbalista (D) made a demand on Girard (D). Girard (D) notified Intraworld (P) each time that it intended to honor the letters of credit and Intraworld (P) sought a preliminary injunction to prevent Girard (D) from honoring the letters of credit. Intraworld (P) claimed that there was fraud not apparent on the face of the documents and as such was entitled to an injunction under § 5-114(2)(b). The trial court denied the preliminary injunction and Intraworld (P) appealed.

ISSUE: Must a party seeking an injunction against the honoring of a letter of credit prove that the beneficiary has no bona fide claim to payment for the underlying transaction?

HOLDING AND DECISION: (Roberts, J.) Yes. A party seeking an injunction against the honoring of a letter of credit must prove that the beneficiary has no bona fide claim to payment for the underlying transaction. Here, Intraworld (P) contends that because of fraud not apparent on the face of the documents presented by Cymbalista (D), Cymbalista (D) does not have a bona fide claim in the lease. However, the circumstances that will justify an injunction against honor must be narrowly limited to situations of fraud in which the wrongdoing of the beneficiary has so vitiated the entire transaction that the legitimate purposes of the independence of the issuer's obligation would no longer be served. That is not the case here. We cannot conclude that Intraworld (P) has established that Cymbalista (D) has no bona fide claim to pay, or that the documents have no basis in fact. Intraworld's (P) contention that the lease was terminated is contested by its own statements to Cymbalista (D) challenging the termination. Intraworld (P) did not persuasively argue that Cymbalista (D) fraudulently concealed the termination from Girard (D). Therefore, the denial of the preliminary injunction is affirmed.

EDITOR'S ANALYSIS: This case highlights the challenges courts face in trying to limit the independence principle in letters of credit cases. The "fraud in the transaction principle" before the Intraworld case allowed courts to look outside the documents presented to determine whether the issuer must honor the letter of credit, thereby potentially limiting the independence principle. Intraworld has since become the leading case in point.

NOTES:

MATTER OF COMPTON CORP.
Bankruptcy trustee (P) v. Supplier (D)
831 F.2d 586 (5th Cir. 1987).

NATURE OF CASE: Appeal of summary judgment denying claim to void preferential transfer.

FACT SUMMARY: The bankruptcy trustee (P) sought to void MBank's payment to Blue Quail (D) on a letter of credit purchased by Compton.

CONCISE RULE OF LAW: Where a bankrupt party purchased a letter of credit within 90 days of filing bankruptcy, payment on the letter is not a voidable preference if it was issued contemporaneously with a new extension of credit, but payment is voidable if the letter secured a preexisting unsecured debt.

FACTS: Blue Quail (D) delivered oil to Compton, but Compton did not make timely payment. On May 6, Compton paid MBank to issue a standby letter of credit payable to Blue Quail (D), if Compton did not pay its outstanding debt to Blue Quail (D) by June 22. To secure the letter MBank perfected an interest in some of Compton's assets. On May 7, creditors filed an involuntary bankruptcy petition against Compton. On June 22, MBank paid Blue Quail (D) on the letter. The bankruptcy trustee (P) claimed payment on the latter was a voidable preference under Bankruptcy Code § 547, so Blue Quail (D) should be required to turn the payment over to Compton's estate. The bankruptcy court granted summary judgment for Blue Quail (D). The district court affirmed, finding no voidable preference since money paid by MBank to Blue Quail (D) was never property of the Compton's estate, and since Compton's transfer of assets to MBank to secure the letter solely benefited MBank and not Blue Quail (D). The trustee (P) appealed.

ISSUE: Is payment on a letter of credit which secures a preexisting debt subject to a voidable preference attack in bankruptcy?

HOLDING AND DECISION: (Williams, Cir. J.) Yes. Where a bankrupt party purchased a letter of credit within 90 days of filing bankruptcy, payment on the letter is not a voidable preference if it was issued contemporaneously with a new extension of credit. However, payment is voidable if the letter secured a preexisting unsecured debt. Where a debtor pledges assets to secure a letter of credit, there is a direct transfer to the issuer and an indirect transfer to the creditor/beneficiary. If the letter is issued in exchange for new credit, the creditor has given new value for the indirect benefit and, as a secured creditor, is not subject to a preference attack. But, if (as here) the letter secures a preexisting unsecured debt, the unsecured creditor (Blue Quail (D)) substitutes in a secured creditor (MBank) to guaranty an unsecured debt. In this way, Blue Quail (D) sought full payment of an unsecured debt, to the detriment of Compton's other unsecured creditors who would receive less. This indirect benefit was a voidable preference. [The court ordered Blue Quail (D) to give the payment to Compton's estate, to be divided pro rata among all unsecured creditors, including Blue Quail (D).] Reversed.

EDITOR'S ANALYSIS: For a standby letter of credit to function as a guaranty, it must still be payable if the debtor goes bankrupt. In *In re Page*, 18 B.R. 713 (D.D.C. 1982), the court held that the automatic stay of § 362(a) does not restrain the creditor from drawing on the note from the issuer if the creditor goes bankrupt.

NOTES:

CHAPTER 11
NEGOTIABILITY AND HOLDERS IN DUE COURSE

QUICK REFERENCE RULES OF LAW

1. **Formal Requisites of Negotiable Instruments.** A note is a contract, not a negotiable instrument, if computation of the amount payable must be made with reference to a source other than the note itself. (Taylor v. Roeder)

2. **Good Faith and Notice.** Unless a holder of an instrument is a holder in due course, he takes the instrument subject to the defenses of want or failure of consideration, nonperformance of any condition precedent, nondelivery, or delivery for a special purpose. (Kaw Valley State Bank & Trust Co. v. Riddle)

3. **Good Faith and Notice.** In determining whether a party is a holder in due course, the jury must determine whether the party acted in good faith through honesty and fact and the observance of reasonable commercial standards of fair dealing. (Maine Family Federal Credit Union v. Sun Life Assurance Co.)

4. **Negotiability in Consumer Transactions.** A consumer financer is a holder in due course of a promissory note where there is no evidence that at the time of purchasing the note the financer had reason to know, or had actual knowledge of, the payee's fraud. (Universal C.I.T. Credit Corp. v. Ingel)

5. **The Legislative Response—New Subsection 3-305(e).** (1) For purposes of a state home improvement installment contract act, a mortgage obtained by a contractor for a consumer transaction, where the mortgage company pays the contractor directly and where loan origination fees are part of the cost of the loan to the consumer, is not a "direct loan" that excepts the loan from the act's provisions. (2) A direct lender of a loan used for financing home improvements by a contractor is liable under the Federal Trade Commission's (FTC's) Holder Rule for claims the issuer could assert against the contractor, even though the loan documents do not contain a Notice of Preservation of Claims and Defenses as required by the FTC. (Gonzalez v. Old Kent Mortgage Company)

6. **Transactions With Fiduciaries.** A purchaser of a negotiable instrument is not a holder in due course if the purchaser has knowledge that a fiduciary is transferring the instrument for the fiduciary's own benefit or otherwise in breach of duty. (Smith v. Olympic Bank)

7. **Article 9 Security Interest as Value.** A bank which accepts a check for deposit and applies it to debts owed to it by the depositor is not liable to the party who gave the check to the depositor even though that party never received the consideration for which the instrument was given. (Bowling Green, Inc. v. State Street Bank & Trust Co.)

TAYLOR v. ROEDER
Purchaser of property (P) v. Trustee (D)
Va. Sup. Ct., 234 Va. 99, 360 S.E.2d 191 (1987).

NATURE OF CASE: Appeal of denial of injunction against foreclosures.

FACT SUMMARY: Two notes securing deeds of trust provided for interest payments at 3% over Chase Manhattan Bank's prime rate.

CONCISE RULE OF LAW: A note is a contract, not a negotiable instrument, if computation of the amount payable must be made with reference to a source other than the note itself.

FACTS: VMC made real estate loans to two investors. Each investor gave VMC a note for its debt, secured by a deed of trust on the land. The notes provided for interest payments of 3% above Chase Manhattan Bank's prime rate. The notes and deeds were transferred by VMC to Pruitt. Both properties were sold by the investors to Taylor (P) and other purchasers, who paid VMC the outstanding balances on the notes but never received the canceled notes or the deeds. Taylor (P) never had notice that one Pruitt held the notes. VMC never informed Pruitt of Taylor's (P) payments. VMC defaulted on its debt to Pruitt. Pruitt, as holder of the notes, demanded payment from Taylor (P). They refused, since they already had paid VMC. Roeder (D), whom Pruitt had made trustee for the deeds of trust, moved to foreclose on the properties. The chancellor issued preliminary injunctions against foreclosure but dissolved the injunctions after a hearing. Taylor (P) appealed, arguing that the notes were not actually negotiable instruments, but rather contracts.

ISSUE: Is a note a negotiable instrument if computation of the amount payable must be made with reference to an outside source?

HOLDING AND DECISION: (Russell, J.) No. A note is a contract, not a negotiable instrument, if computation of the amount payable must be made with reference to a source other than the note itself. Where a note is a negotiable instrument, payment to a party not in possession of the note does not discharge the obligation to the holder. Lack of notice of transfer is irrelevant. However, if a note is a contract, a debtor without notice of transfer may pay his original creditor and extinguish his obligation. To be a negotiable instrument a note must be for a "sum certain" [a "fixed amount of money" under the revised U.C.C. Article 3]. Payment may include interest, but the amount must be calculable within the "four corners" of the note. Here, the amount could only be determined by reference to Chase Manhattan's prime rate. Thus, the note was a contract, not a negotiable instrument, and Taylor's (P) debt was discharged by payments to VMC. Permanent injunction against foreclosure issued; reversed.

DISSENT: (Compton, J.) The U.C.C. should be interpreted to permit expansion of commercial practices by custom, usage, and agreement and to make possible development of law in light of unforeseen and new practices. Interest rates met by reference to prime lending rates have become common. The amount payable is a "sum certain," easily determinable with a call to the bank or from a published list.

EDITOR'S ANALYSIS: Only "orders" or "promises" can be negotiable instruments. An order is a signed, written instruction to pay money (e.g., a check). U.C.C. § 3-103(a)(6). A promise is a signed, written undertaking to pay money (e.g., a note for a debt). § 3-103(a)(9). Under § 3-104, a negotiable instrument must be "unconditional" (§ 3-106), payable on demand or at a definite time (§ 3-109), and for a fixed amount of money (§ 3-112).

NOTES:

KAW VALLEY STATE BANK & TRUST CO. v. RIDDLE
Holder of note (P) v. Buyer (D)
Kan. Sup. Ct., 219 Kan. 550, 549 P.2d 927 (1976).

NATURE OF CASE: Appeal from denial of damages for nonpayment of a note.

FACT SUMMARY: Kaw Valley (P), a bank and trust, sought to recover against Riddle (D), a purchaser of heavy machinery, for nonpayment of a note.

CONCISE RULE OF LAW: Unless a holder of an instrument is a holder in due course, he takes the instrument subject to the defenses of want or failure of consideration, nonperformance of any condition precedent, nondelivery, or delivery for a special purpose.

FACTS: Over a 10-year period, Riddle (D) made several credit purchases of heavy machinery from Co-Mac, a dealer, who sold discounted notes and security agreements on these purchases to Kaw Valley (P), and bank and trust. On May 11, 1971, Riddle (D) purchased from Co-Mac two tractors and a dozer and executed a signed note and security agreement therefor. Ten days later, Riddle (D) called Co-Mac to change his order which had not yet been delivered. Co-Mac agreed to sell two different pieces of equipment to Riddle (P) in place of the original order and promised to destroy the May 11th papers. A new note and security agreement were executed and the substitute order was delivered. However, the May 11th papers, rather than having been destroyed, were discounted and assigned to Kaw Valley (P). On February 24, 1972, Riddle (D), Co-Mac, and Kaw Valley (P) representatives met to consolidate Riddle's (P) indebtedness on several notes, and during this meeting the May 11th papers were never mentioned. On March 12, 1972, Kaw Valley (P) advised Riddle (D) that it held the May 11th papers which Riddle (D) explained were to have been destroyed by Co-Mac. Co-Mac, however, had been on shaky financial ground, had continued to make payments on the May 11th transaction, and had been taken over by a receiver a week before Kaw Valley (P) gave notice to Riddle (D). Kaw Valley (P) brought suit against Riddle (D) for payment of the May 11th transaction arguing that it was a holder in due course of the note. The trial court found that there had been no consideration for the transaction as Riddle (D) never received delivery of the original equipment. Kaw Valley (P) appealed.

ISSUE: Unless a holder of an instrument is a holder in due course, does he take the instrument subject to the defenses of want or failure of consideration, nonperformance of any condition precedent, nondelivery, or delivery for a special purpose?

HOLDING AND DECISION: (Fromme, J.) Yes. Unless a holder of an instrument is a holder in due course, he takes the instrument subject to the defenses of want or failure of consideration, nonperformance of any condition precedent, nondelivery, or

nondelivery for a special purpose. While a holder in due course is one who takes an instrument (1) for value, (2) in good faith, and (3) without any notice of any defense, and it appeared that Kaw Valley (P) took the May 11th papers for value, it did not take wholly in good faith and without notice of any defense. While there is little evidence of lack of good faith, it seemed that Kaw Valley (P) had reason to know of a defense. Kaw Valley (P) acted cooperatively and closely with Co-Mac for 10 years, recognized Co-Mac's authority to act for it, and met with Co-Mac and Riddle (D) to consolidate the latter's debts. During the consolidation meeting, Kaw Valley (P) for some reason omitted mention of the May 11th papers, and Kaw Valley (P) knew that Co-Mac and not Riddle (D) were making the payments on the transaction in question. Kaw Valley (P) had the burden of showing it was a holder in due course after Riddle (D) raised his defense, and it failed to sustain this burden. Affirmed.

EDITOR'S ANALYSIS: There are four categories of cases where a "reason to know a defense exists" arises, as follows: (1) where it is established the instrument holder had information from the transferor or obligor which disclosed the existence of a defense; (2) where the defense appears in an accompanying document delivered to the holder with the note; (3) where information appears in the written instrument indicating the existence of a defense, such as where the note shows that the due date has passed or the note bears evidence of alteration or forgery or is clearly incomplete; and (4) where the holder is precluded from assuming holder in due course status because of knowledge of business practices of his transferor or when he is so closely aligned with the transferor that the transferor may be considered to be the holder's agent. Kaw Valley is an example of this last circumstance.

NOTES:

MAINE FAMILY FEDERAL CREDIT UNION v. SUN LIFE ASSURANCE CO.

Credit union (P) v. Insurance company (D)
Me. Sup. Jud Ct., 727 A.2d 335 (1999).

NATURE OF CASE: Suit to recover amount of dishonored checks.

FACT SUMMARY: The credit union (P) brought suit against Sun (D) to recover the amount of dishonored life insurance premium checks.

CONCISE RULE OF LAW: In determining whether a party is a holder in due course, the jury must determine whether the party acted in good faith through honesty and fact and the observance of reasonable commercial standards of fair dealing.

FACTS: Elden Guerrette purchased a life insurance policy from Sun Life (D), naming his children as beneficiaries. Upon his death, Sun Life (D) issued three checks to each of the children, which were given to Hall, Sun Life's agent, for delivery. Hall and Richard, an associate of Hall, then fraudulently induced the children to endorse the checks and transfer them to Hall and Richard purportedly to be invested in "HER, Inc." The children sought to stop payment on the checks, which were returned to the credit union (P). The credit union (P) received notice that the checks had been dishonored; however, by that time Richard had withdrawn the funds from his account. The credit union (P) filed a complaint against Sun (D) alleging it was liable as drawer of the instruments and that Sun (D) had been unjustly enriched. The jury found that the credit union (P) had not acted in good faith and therefore was not a holder in due course. Judgment was entered in favor of Sun (D) and the credit union (P) appealed.

ISSUE: In determining whether a party is a holder in due course, must the jury determine whether the party acted in good faith through honesty and fact and the observance of reasonable commercial standards of fair dealing?

HOLDING AND DECISION: (Saufley, J.) Yes. In determining whether a party is a holder in due course, the jury must determine whether the party acted in good faith through honesty and fact and the observance of reasonable commercial standards of fair dealing. The credit union (P) argues that the court erred in failing to find that it was a holder in due course as a matter of law. First it must be determined whether the credit union (P) acted in good faith. "Good faith" is defined in Article 3 of the Maine U.C.C. as "honesty in fact and the observance of reasonable commercial standards of fair dealing." It has both a subjective and an objective component. Courts in interpreting this language have held banks to be holders in due course, notwithstanding the failure to investigate or hold otherwise negotiable instruments, when they took the instruments with no knowledge of any defects, defenses or stop payment orders. Application of the standard here shows that the credit union (P) acted with honesty in fact, having no knowledge that the checks had been obtained by fraud or were subject to a stop payment order. The objective prong requires the holder to prove conduct meeting "reasonable commercial standards of fair dealing." The fact finder must first determine whether the conduct of the holder comported with industry or commercial standards applicable to the transaction and, second, whether those standards were reasonable and intended to result in fair dealing. The record here allowed the jury to rationally conclude that the reasonable commercial standard of fair dealing would require the placing of a hold on the uncollected funds for a reasonable period of time and that the credit union (P) did not act according to commercial standards reasonably structured to result in fair dealing.

EDITOR'S ANALYSIS: Where a party is not a holder in due course, its right to enforce the obligations of a drawer and indorsers of a negotiable instrument becomes subject to various defenses, including ordinary contract defenses. Where a party establishes itself as a holder in due course, then it is only subject to the defenses specified in U.C.C. § 3-305(a)(1).

NOTES:

UNIVERSAL C.I.T. CREDIT CORP. v. INGEL
Consumer financer (P) v. Consumer debtor (D)
Mass. Sup. Jud. Ct., 196 N.E.2d 847 (1964).

NATURE OF CASE: Appeal from directed verdict in action on a promissory note.

FACT SUMMARY: The Ingels (D) claimed that Universal C.I.T. Credit Corp. (P) was not a holder in due course of a promissory note the Ingels (D) had made in favor of Allied Aluminum Associates, Inc. (Allied) because, they claimed, plaintiff (P) had financed the transaction and was aware of Allied's fraudulent consumer practices used in obtaining such notes.

CONCISE RULE OF LAW: A consumer financer is a holder in due course of a promissory note where there is no evidence that at the time of purchasing the note the financer had reason to know, or had actual knowledge of, the payee's fraud.

FACTS: The Ingels (D) made a promissory note in favor of Allied Aluminum Associates, Inc. (Allied) to finance some type of home repair/improvement. Universal C.I.T. Credit Corp. (plaintiff) (P), which regularly purchased installment contracts, purchased the Ingel's (D) note as assignee. Plaintiff (P) brought an action of contract on the promissory note. The trial court (district court) found for the plaintiff (P) on remand. The trial court also disallowed evidence that plaintiff (P) knew that Allied was engaged in fraudulent consumer practices and that plaintiff (P) had worked with Allied on various aspects of the financing. The case was transferred to the Superior Court for trial by jury, at the conclusion of which, the court granted plaintiff's (P) motion for a directed verdict. The state's highest court (Supreme Judicial Court) granted review.

ISSUE: Is a consumer financer a holder in due course of a promissory note where there is no evidence that at the time of purchasing the note the financer had reason to know, or had actual knowledge of, the payee's fraud?

HOLDING AND DECISION: (Spiegel, J.) Yes. A consumer financer is a holder in due course of a promissory note where there is no evidence that at the time of purchasing the note the financer had reason to know, or had actual knowledge of, the payee's fraud. The evidence that the Ingels (D) wanted to introduce was properly excluded because the trial court found a prima facie case that the plaintiff (P) took the note for value and without notice, and the burden was on the Ingels (D) to rebut this prima facie case. There was nothing in the Ingels' (D) evidence that would have shown that the plaintiff (P) had reason to know of any fraud at the time it purchased the note. Any evidence that might have shown that plaintiff (P) may have found out about

Allied's alleged fraudulent conduct after it purchased the note was immaterial. Exceptions overruled (affirmed).

EDITOR'S ANALYSIS: Since this case was decided, all courts have denied a consumer financer the status of holder in due course, and the courts have allowed consumers with valid defenses to assert those defenses, even if those defenses are purportedly cut off by assignment. Revised Article 3 of the U.C.C. also greatly restricts the use of the holder-in-due-course doctrine in consumer transactions. Furthermore, the advent of the credit card also replaced promissory notes in all but the largest consumer purchases, thus effectively rendering the negotiability issue in consumer transactions largely moot.

NOTES:

GONZALEZ v. OLD KENT MORTGAGE COMPANY

Consumer debtor (P) v. Consumer financer (D)

2000 WL 1469313 (E.D. Pa. 2000).

NATURE OF CASE: Motion to dismiss action for, inter alia, violation of state installment contract act and breach of contract.

FACT SUMMARY: Gonzalez (P) entered into a consumer credit transaction with Old Kent Mortgage Company (Old Kent) (D) whereby Gonzalez (P) gave Old Kent (D) a mortgage on her home, which included various fees and costs, to finance home improvements by Quality Builders. Gonzalez (P) brought suit claiming that the loan she entered was in reality a home improvement installment contract that violated the terms of the state's Home Improvement Finance Act (HIFA) and that Old Kent (D), by virtue of the Federal Trade Commission's Holder Rule, was liable for claims Gonzalez (P) had against Quality Builders.

CONCISE RULE OF LAW: (1) For purposes of a state home improvement installment contract act, a mortgage obtained by a contractor for a consumer transaction, where the mortgage company pays the contractor directly and where loan origination fees are part of the cost of the loan to the consumer, is not a "direct loan" that excepts the loan from the act's provisions. (2) A direct lender of a loan used for financing home improvements by a contractor is liable under the Federal Trade Commission's (FTC's) Holder Rule for claims the issuer could assert against the contractor, even though the loan documents do not contain a Notice of Preservation of Claims and Defenses as required by the FTC.

FACTS: Gonzalez (P) contacted Quality Builders (Quality), a contractor, for home improvements. Quality arranged, through Accelerated Mortgages, for financing with Old Kent Mortgage Company (Old Kent) (D). Instead of entering into a contract, Gonzalez (P) entered into a consumer credit transaction giving Old Kent (D) a mortgage on her home. The loan, which consolidated other debt, was at 11.75% interest for 360 months and included various fees and origination costs. Old Kent (D) paid Quality directly and paid Accelerated Mortgage a loan origination commission, which was included in the cost to Gonzalez (P). Gonzalez (P) brought suit, contending that the loan was in fact a "home improvement installment contract" governed by the Home Improvement Finance Act (HIFA), and that inclusion of fees, costs, and commissions violated HIFA. She sought as damages three times the excess charges, the remedy for such a HIFA violation. Old Kent (D) countered that the loan was not a "home improvement installment contract" because it was a direct loan between the retail buyer and the lender. HIFA contained an exception for direct loans. Gonzalez (P) also claimed that pursuant to the FTC Holder Rule, Old Kent (D) was liable for the claims that she had against Quality. Old Kent (D) argued that

there was no contract between itself and Gonzalez (P) that would permit Gonzalez (P) to hold it liable for damages caused by Quality's conduct; that the FTC Holder Rule would not apply; and that even if the Holder Rule did apply, it would not authorize the type of damages sought by Gonzalez (P).

ISSUE: (1) For purposes of a state home improvement installment contract act, is a mortgage obtained by a contractor for a consumer transaction a "direct loan" that excepts the loan from the act's provisions, where the mortgage company pays the contractor directly and where loan origination fees are part of the cost of the loan to the consumer? (2) Is a direct lender of a loan used for financing home improvements by a contractor liable under the Federal Trade Commission's (FTC's) Holder Rule for claims the issuer could assert against the contractor, even though the loan documents do not contain a Notice of Preservation of Claims and Defenses as required by the FTC?

HOLDING AND DECISION: (Hart, Mag. J.) (1) No. For purposes of a state home improvement installment contract act, a mortgage obtained by a contractor for a consumer transaction, where the mortgage company pays the contractor directly and where loan origination fees are part of the cost of the loan to the consumer, is not a "direct loan" that excepts the loan from the act's provisions. It is difficult to call the loan at issue a direct loan. "The 'direct loan' exception would be superfluous if the basic definition did not cover any home improvement financing payable to an independent lender." Other courts have held that similar loans, where the contractor does all the arranging of the loan, are not direct loans and fall within the definition of a home improvement installment contract. To hold otherwise would provide a gaping loophole that would allow lenders and contractors to choose when they wished to allow the HIFA to apply to a transaction. (2) Yes. A direct lender of a loan used for financing home improvements by a contractor is liable under the Federal Trade Commission's (FTC's) Holder Rule for claims the issuer could assert against the contractor, even though the loan documents do not contain a Notice of Preservation of Claims and Defenses as required by the FTC. The arguments that Old Kent (D) makes against the existence of a contract between itself and Gonzalez (P) that would render Old Kent (D) liable for any claims that Gonzalez (P) has against Quality, are incorrect. First, there is a contract here that consists of the loan agreement and the promissory note. Presumably, Old Kent (D) failed to include in the promissory note the Notice of Preservation of Claims and

Continued on next page.

Defenses required by the FTC (the FTC Holder Rule). Such failure is a per se unfair or deceptive practice. The notice would have stated that any holder of the "consumer credit contract" would be subject to all claims and defenses which the debtor could assert against the seller of the goods or services obtained pursuant to the contract or with the proceeds thereof. Old Kent (D) argues that the absence of this language negated the necessary elements of a breach of contract. Gonzalez (P) counters that contract terms may be implied where public policy so requires, and that the court should read the Holder Rule into the agreements. Gonzalez (P) is correct. Assuming that Old Kent (D) should have included the notice somewhere in its loan documents, and that this notice would have given Gonzalez (P) at least the right to offset against monies claimed by Old Kent (D) the value of any claims Gonzalez (P) may have had against Quality, it would turn the law on its head to allow Old Kent (D) to avoid the consequences of the Holder Rule through its own failure to include it in the loan documents. Old Kent (D) is also incorrect that even if the Holder Rule appeared in the note, it would be inapplicable in this case because the rule simply limits when a defendant, as assignee of the contract, may rely on the holder-in-due-course defense. Contrary to Old Kent's (D) assertion, the rule is used (in cases such as this one) to preserve the claims against the seller to defeat a creditor's right to be paid under the note. Finally, Old Kent (D) is wrong that even if the Holder Rule Notice was present and applied to these facts, it would not support a claim for affirmative relief. This argument misses the point: Gonzalez (P) is not using the Holder Rule as an affirmative defense, but, rather, is simply using her claims against Quality as an offset against any attempt by Old Kent (D) to collect on the note. Motion to dismiss denied as to these claims.

EDITOR'S ANALYSIS: In 2002, U.C.C. § 3-305 was amended to include a provision that provided that in a consumer transaction, if law other than the U.C.C. itself (e.g., FTC law) requires that an instrument include a statement to the effect that the rights of a holder or transferee are subject to claims or defenses that the issuer could assert against the original payee, and the instrument does not include such a statement, the instrument has the same effect as if the instrument contained such a statement. Thus, the U.C.C. now codifies the result of this case, and others like it.

NOTES:

SMITH v. OLYMPIC BANK
Guardian (P) v. Bank (D)
Wash. Sup. Ct., 103 Wash. 2d 418, 693 P.2d 92 (1985).

NATURE OF CASE: Appeal of reversal of summary judgment in action for damages for breach of fiduciary duty.

FACT SUMMARY: Olympic Bank (D) allowed a father to open a personal account with a check made out to the father as guardian for his son, and to use the funds for personal benefit.

CONCISE RULE OF LAW: A purchaser of a negotiable instrument is not a holder in due course if the purchaser has knowledge that a fiduciary is transferring the instrument for the fiduciary's own benefit or otherwise in breach of duty.

FACTS: Charles Alcombrack was appointed guardian for his son Chad, the beneficiary of his grandfather's life insurance policy. The insurer issued a $30,000 check payable to Charles as guardian for Chad. These facts were printed on the back of the check where Charles endorsed it. Olympic (D) allowed Charles to place the funds in new accounts in Charles' name. That day, the attorney for Chad's estate called Olympic's (D) trust officer to ask about fees Olympic (D) charged on trust accounts. The officer replied in a letter which mentioned the "Estate of Chad Alcombrack." Charles wrote $16,000 in checks for personal use and used $3,000 to pay off a loan from Olympic (D). Olympic (D) directly took $12,500 to make payments on other loans to Charles. Only $300 of the insurance money remained. Smith (P) was appointed new guardian of Chad's estate. Smith (P) received judgment against Charles for breach of fiduciary duty. Smith (P) also sued Olympic (D) for the spent funds. The trial court dismissed, the court of appeals reversed, and Olympic (D) appealed.

ISSUE: Is a purchaser of a negotiable instrument a holder in due course if the purchaser knows that a fiduciary is transferring the instrument for personal benefit or otherwise in breach of duty?

HOLDING AND DECISION: (Dore, J.) No. A purchaser of a negotiable instrument in not a holder in due course if the purchaser has knowledge that a fiduciary is transferring the instrument for the fiduciary's own benefit or otherwise in breach of duty. Olympic (D) knew Charles was breaching his fiduciary duty when it allowed him to deposit the check into his own account. The check was payable to Charles as guardian, Charles endorsed it in that capacity, Chad's attorney contacted Olympic (D) about the funds, and the trust officer referred to Chad's estate. Reasonable commercial practices dictate that when the funds were deposited into Charles' account Olympic (D) knew Charles had breached his duty. To protect wards, banks and guardians must be required to place a check payable to an individual as guardian into a guardianship account. If Chad's funds had been in

a guardianship account, neither Charles nor Olympic (D) could have removed the funds as they did. Olympic (D) was not a holder in due course and became liable for the misappropriated funds. Affirmed.

EDITOR'S ANALYSIS: The opposite conclusion was reached in *Matter of Knox*, 64 N.Y.2d 434, 488 N.Y.S.2d 146, 477 N.E.2d 448 (1985). The court held that mere knowledge that the father was a fiduciary and was putting the funds in his personal account was not enough. A bank cannot be charged with misappropriation unless it had notice that the fiduciary intended to, or did, use the funds for improper purposes.

NOTES:

BOWLING GREEN, INC. v. STATE STREET BANK & TRUST CO.

Buyer (P) v. Seller's bank (D)

425 F.2d 81 (1st Cir. 1970).

NATURE OF CASE: Action to recover the amount of a check.

FACT SUMMARY: Bowling Green (P) gave Bowl-Mor a government check as payment for goods which were never received. When Bowl-Mor became insolvent, its bank (D) applied the check to debts owed to it by Bowl-Mor.

CONCISE RULE OF LAW: A bank which accepts a check for deposit and applies it to debts owed to it by the depositor is not liable to the party who gave the check to the depositor even though that party never received the consideration for which the instrument was given.

FACTS: Bowl-Mor, Inc. agreed to sell pinsetting machines to Bowling Green, Inc. (P). On September 26, 1966, Bowling Green (P) negotiated to Bowl-Mor a $15,306 federal government check which Bowling Green (P) had acquired through a Small Business Administration loan. Although Bowling Green (P) never received the equipment for which it paid, the check was deposited by Bowl-Mor on September 27th at State Street Bank and Trust Co. (D). Immediately, State Street (D) credited $5,024.85 of the check against an overdraft in Bowl-Mor's account. That same day, upon learning that Bowl-Mor had petitioned for reorganization under Chapter 10 of the Bankruptcy Act, State Street (D) transferred $233.61 of Bowl-Mor's money to another account and applied the remaining $10,047.54 against debts which Bowl-Mor owed to State Street (D). Subsequently, Bowl-Mor's Chapter 10 petition was dismissed and the company was adjudicated a bankrupt. Bowling Green (P) sued State Street (D) to recover the amount of the check, alleging that State Street (D) had had intimate knowledge of Bowl-Mor's financial situation and had realized the sales contract with Bowling Green (P) would not be performed. On the basis of this averment, Bowling Green (P) argued that State Street (D) should be deemed the constructive trustee of Bowling Green (D) for the amount of the check. The district court disagreed, concluding that State Street (D) was a holder in due course of the check, and thus was not subject to personal defenses. Bowling Green (P) then appealed.

ISSUE: Is a bank which applies a depositor's check to debts which the depositor owes to it liable to the party who gave the depositor the check if that party did not receive the promised consideration for the instrument?

HOLDING AND DECISION: (Coffin, Cir. J.) No. A bank which accepts a check for deposit and applies it to debts owed to it by the depositor is not liable to the party who gave the check to the depositor even though that party never received the consideration for which the instrument was given. Bowling Green

(P) argued that State Street (D) was not a "holder" of the check because it was unendorsed, and thus was not taken by State Street (D) as an instrument endorsed to it, to bearer, or in blank, as § 1-201(20) of the Uniform Commercial Code requires. But State Street (D) has met the burden of proving that it was a holder. Bowl-Mor was a holder, and the transferee of a negotiable instrument acquires the rights and status of the transferor. Banks commonly accept unendorsed checks and merely stamp them appropriately upon receipt. It is doubtful that banks were even intended to be bound by the § 1-201(20) definition of "holder" because a restrictive definition would undermine Article 4 of the U.C.C., which is designed to simplify and expedite bank collection practices. Even if State Street (D) was a holder, however, Bowling Green (P) argued that the Bank's (D) intimacy with Bowl-Mor precludes a finding that it acted in good faith. It is true that a State Street (D) loan officer was a Bowl-Mor director, and that the bank (D) had absorbed $1,000,000 of Bowl-Mor's past debts. And State Street (P) was apparently familiar with some details of Bowl-Mor's transaction with Bowling Green (P). However, the Bank (D) evidently did not know of Bowl-Mor's anticipated Chapter 10 filing. Section 1-201(19) of the Code makes "good faith" synonymous with "honesty in fact," and contemplates a subjective test. State Street (P) had no actual notice of Bowl-Mor's imminent collapse. In fact, the Chapter 10 petition was apparently precipitated by another financier's withdrawal of suppose. Bowling Green (P) cites *Jones v. Approved Bancredit Corp.* and erroneously argued that that case mandates an objective test vitiating good faith when a bank and its depositor are intimately affiliated. Bowling Green (P) misreads Jones, and the rule contended for is particularly inappropriate when checks, rather than consumer notes, are involved. Parties rely upon the ready negotiability of a check, and commerce would suffer immeasurably if banks were deemed constructive trustees for every drawer who tendered a check to a depositor who showed some signs of insolvency. As its final argument, Bowling Green (P) argued that State Street (D) could not have been a holder in due course of the $10,047.54 which was applied to Bowl-Mor's account because State Street (D) did not give value for that portion of the check. But § 4-209 states that a collecting bank gives value to the extent that it acquires a "security interest." The trial court deemed that section satisfied by the fact that an existing security agreement gave State Street (D) a floating lien against all Bowl-Mor's chattel paper. This conclusion, which compels the finding that State Street (D) gave value for the entire amount of

Continued on next page.

the check, seems proper. It is consistent with the rule that a holder gives value when he accepts a negotiable instrument as security for an antecedent debt. In this case, both Bowling Green (P) and State Street (D) elected to deal with Bowl-Mor despite its precarious financial footing. At least the Bank (D) arranged for some security, and if Bowling Green (P) lacked the prudence to do likewise, it is fitting that it should bear the burden of its loss.

EDITOR'S ANALYSIS: At least one case has followed the holding of *Bowling Green*, but the court's resolution of the issue relating to the qualifications of a holder was rejected in *United Overseas Bank v. Veneers, Inc.*, 375 F. Supp. 596 (D. Md. 1974). That case concluded that a bank cannot claim the status of holder unless it actually supplies the missing endorsement to a check. As a precaution, many banks refuse to accept a check for deposit unless it has been endorsed, while others will accept an unendorsed check for deposit although they will refuse to cash it, even for the payee.

NOTES:

12

CHAPTER 12
LIABILITY OF PARTIES TO NEGOTIABLE INSTRUMENTS

QUICK REFERENCE RULES OF LAW

1. **Issuing Bank's Right to Raise Own Claims or Defenses.** (1) A bank is justified in placing a stop payment order on a cashier's check that it has mistakenly issued. (2) A presenting bank is not immune from an issuing bank's defenses to payment of a cashier's check where the presenting bank has transferred no value for the cashier's check. (3) A presenting bank cannot recover attorneys' fees and costs when it prevails in an action to enforce a right to a check where the obligated bank had reasonable grounds to believe it had a claim or defense. (State Bank & Trust v. First State Bank of Texas)

2. **Lost Cashier's, Teller's or Certified Checks under Section 3-312.** Security must be posted by the payee before a court will order payment on a lost negotiable instrument. (Diaz v. Manufacturers Hanover Trust Co.)

3. **Accommodated Party Is Business Organization.** A shareholder/officer of a corporation is an accommodation party on an instrument issued for value to the corporation where the shareholder signs the instrument in both his corporate capacity and individually without being a direct beneficiary of the value given for the instrument. (Plein v. Lackey)

4. **Liability of Agent on Checks.** A corporate agent who does not place his title on a check drawn on the corporation's account is not personally liable on the check where the corporation is identified on the check and the agent's signature is authorized. (Medina v. Wyche)

5. **Accord and Satisfaction.** For purposes of effecting an accord and satisfaction of a disputed claim, a letter accompanying a check that states that the check constitutes "final payment on the contract" is a sufficiently conspicuous statement to the effect that the check has been tendered as full satisfaction of the claim. (Gelles & Sons, Inc. v. Jeffrey Stack, Inc.)

STATE BANK & TRUST v. FIRST STATE BANK OF TEXAS

Issuing bank (P) v. Presenting bank (D)

242 F.3d 390 (10th Cir. 2000).

NATURE OF CASE: Appeal from judgment absolving counterclaim defendant from liability in action to recover amount of a cashier's check and documentary drafts.

FACT SUMMARY: First State Bank of Texas (Bank of Texas) (D) claimed that State Bank & Trust, N.A. (State Bank) (P) could not put a stop payment order on a cashier's check that State Bank (P) had issued, and that it was immune from any defenses to payment of the cashier's check that State Bank (P) may have had.

CONCISE RULE OF LAW: (1) A bank is justified in placing a stop payment order on a cashier's check that it has mistakenly issued. (2) A presenting bank is not immune from an issuing bank's defenses to payment of a cashier's check where the presenting bank has transferred no value for the cashier's check. (3) A presenting bank cannot recover attorneys' fees and costs when it prevails in an action to enforce a right to a check where the obligated bank had reasonable grounds to believe it had a claim or defense.

FACTS: First State Bank of Texas (Bank of Texas) (D) presented to State Bank & Trust, N.A. (State Bank) (P) documentary drafts that on their face were drawn on Ventura's account at State Bank (P) that had been forged by Speer, a customer of Bank of Texas (D). Because the drafts were not verified by Ventura, State Bank (P) returned the drafts to Bank of Texas (D) unpaid. Bank of Texas (D) resubmitted the drafts, claiming the return was untimely, and an employee of State Bank (P) mistakenly issued a cashier's check to pay for the drafts, having been unaware that the drafts had not been verified. The check was mailed before State Bank's (P) Vice President was made aware of the issuance of the check. Therefore, the check could not be retrieved from the mail. The next day, State Bank (P) notified that it was placing a stop payment order on the cashier's check due to mistake. Bank of Texas (D) claimed that it had submitted the check for payment before it received the notice of the stop payment order. State Bank (P) then sued Bank of Texas (D) to recover an amount of a cashier's check issued by Bank of Texas (D) and documentary drafts issued by Speer. Bank of Texas (D) counterclaimed for recovery of the amount of the cashier's check issued by State Bank (P) and the documentary drafts that appeared to have been issued by Ventura. The trial court granted summary judgment to State Bank (P) on its claims and in a non-jury trial held that State Bank (P) was not liable on any of Bank of Texas's (D) counterclaims. The trial court also denied State Bank (P) attorneys' fees and costs. Bank of Texas (D) appealed on the merits of its counterclaims, and State Bank (P) appealed the denial of attorneys' fees and costs.

ISSUE: (1) Is a bank justified in placing a stop payment order on a cashier's check that it has mistakenly issued? (2) Is a presenting bank immune from an issuing bank's defenses to payment of a cashier's check where the presenting bank has transferred no value for the cashier's check? (3) Can a presenting bank recover attorneys' fees and costs when it prevails in an action to enforce a right to a check where the obligated bank had reasonable grounds to believe it had a claim or defense?

HOLDING AND DECISION: (Lucero, J.) (1) Yes. A bank is justified in placing a stop payment order on a cashier's check that it has mistakenly issued. Under U.C.C. § 3-305(a)(2), an obligated party may assert a defense "stated in another section of this article" or a defense that would be available if the person entitled to enforce the instrument were enforcing a right to payment under a simple contract. State Bank (P) argues, among other things, that it properly stopped payment due to the fact that the check was issued by mistake. This defense to payment is sufficient because under state U.C.C. (Oklahoma) law, § 3-418(b), if an instrument has been paid by mistake, the paying party may, to the extent permitted by the law of mistake and restitution, revoke the acceptance. Here, State Bank (P) had accepted the cashier's check. State Bank's (P) employee mistakenly believed State Bank (P) was authorized by its customer to issue the cashier's check, so that check was mistakenly issued. The fact that State Bank (P) attempted to retrieve the check from the mail and immediately placed a stop payment order on it shows that State Bank (P) had mistakenly issued the check. Because of this mistake, State Bank (P) had a viable defense to payment of the check and was able to revoke its acceptance. Therefore, State Bank (P) was justified in stopping payment on the check. (2) No. A presenting bank is not immune from an issuing bank's defenses to payment of a cashier's check where the presenting bank has transferred no value for the cashier's check. State Bank (P) cannot successfully invoke mistake as a defense to the payment of the cashier's check if Bank of Texas (D) took it for value. It can also not assert a common law contract defense or other defense listed in Article 3 if Bank of Texas (D) was a holder in due course, i.e., one has taken an instrument for value. Because State Bank (P) issued the check to pay for the drafts—which were worthless because Ventura refused to authorize payment—and not in response to Bank of Texas's (D) claim of late return, Bank of Texas (D) transferred no value for the cashier's check. Therefore, Bank of Texas (D) was not immune under § 3-418 to State Bank's (P) defense of mistaken payment of the check—it was not a holder in due course. (3) No. A presenting bank cannot recover attorneys' fees and costs when it prevails in an action to enforce a right to a check where the obligated bank had reasonable grounds to believe it had a claim or defense. Section 3.411(b) of the Tex. Bus. & Com.Code Ann. provides that a person who enforces a right to a check "is entitled to compensation for expenses and loss of interest resulting from…nonpayment and may recover consequential damages." However, § 3.411(c) provides that such damages are not recoverable if the obligated bank refused to pay because it had reasonable grounds to believe it had a claim or defense against the person entitled to enforce the instrument. The trial court was correct in concluding that Bank of Texas (D) had a reasonable basis for asserting the positions it took, despite the court's ultimate finding that Bank of Texas (D) had no viable defense. Therefore, State Bank's (P) position is frivolous. Affirmed as to these claims.

EDITOR'S ANALYSIS: Some commentators have urged that cashier's checks be treated as cash equivalents, given that the commercial world treats them as such. Under such treatment, an issuing bank could never stop payment on such an instrument because they would be prohibited from raising any defenses to payment even against non-holders in due course. This cash equivalent theory, however, was not incorporated into Revised Article 3. Moreover, as this case illustrates, the issuing bank may refuse payment if it asserts a claim or defense that it has reasonable grounds to believe is available against the person entitled to enforce the instrument.

NOTES:

DIAZ v. MANUFACTURERS HANOVER TRUST CO.
Payee on lost checks (P) v. Bank (D)
N.Y. Sup. Ct., 92 Misc. 2d 802, 401 N.Y.S.2d 952 (1977).

NATURE OF CASE: Order to show cause or to issue negotiable instrument.

FACT SUMMARY: Diaz (P) sought payment or replacement of certified checks given to her for posting of bond and which were lost or stolen from her.

CONCISE RULE OF LAW: Security must be posted by the payee before a court will order payment on a lost negotiable instrument.

FACTS: Diaz (P) posted bond for a criminal defendant with one Newman. After the criminal action concluded, Diaz (P) sought recovery of her security from Newman. Diaz (P) received from Newman two certified checks for the amount drawn on Manufacturers Hanover Trust ("Trust") (D). Diaz (P) lost the checks or they were stolen. Diaz (P) told Newman, who notified Trust (D) to stop payment. Trust (D) told Diaz (P) it would refuse to honor Newman's (D) replacement checks unless an indemnity bond in twice the amount was posted with Trust (D). Diaz (P) sought payment of the security by Trust (D) or an order that Newman (D) issue a new negotiable instrument to her in the same amount.

ISSUE: Can a court order payment on a lost negotiable instrument without requiring the payee to post security?

HOLDING AND DECISION: (Rodell, J.) No. Security must be posted by the payee before a court will order payment on a lost negotiable instrument. U.C.C. § 3-804 makes the provision for security discretionary, using the word "may." The New York version of § 3-804 makes furnishing security mandatory by use of the word "shall" and set the amount at twice the amount allegedly unpaid. Although Diaz (P) was deprived of her life savings and Trust (D) gained no benefit from holding frozen funds, it is for the state legislature to fix this gap in the law. Affirmed.

EDITOR'S ANALYSIS: U.C.C. § 3-309, the successor to U.C.C. § 3-804, requires that the court find that the party required to pay the lost instrument is adequately protected from future loss due to a claim by another party to enforce the instrument. Under U.C.C. § 3-804, the rights to an instrument were vested in the "owner," whereas § 3-309 vests the rights in "a person entitled to enforce the instrument." See Uniform Commercial Code (12th ed. 1990), § 3-309, comment, p. 389.

NOTES:

PLEIN v. LACKEY
Subordinate creditor (P) v. Attorney for superior creditor (D)
Wash. Sup. Ct., 149 Wash.2d 214, 67 P.3d 1061 (2003).

NATURE OF CASE: Appeal from reversal of summary judgment in favor of secured party claiming to be entitled to foreclosure of deed of trust.

FACT SUMMARY: Cameron (D) signed a promissory note both in his corporate capacity and individually, secured by a deed of trust, to purchase property from Sunset Investments (Sunset) for his corporation, Alpen Group, Inc. (Alpen). Later, Cameron (D) paid off the Sunset note. He then sought to enforce the instrument and foreclose the deed of trust when Alpen defaulted, claiming he signed the note as an accommodation party and was therefore entitled to foreclose. Subordinate creditors, including Plein (P), claimed the deed of trust was void because the underlying debt had been paid, so there could be no default.

CONCISE RULE OF LAW: A shareholder/officer of a corporation is an accommodation party on an instrument issued for value to the corporation where the shareholder signs the instrument in both his corporate capacity and individually without being a direct beneficiary of the value given for the instrument.

FACTS: Cameron (D) signed a promissory note both in his capacity as secretary-treasurer/shareholder of Alpen Group, Inc. (Alpen) and individually, secured by a deed of trust, to purchase real property from Sunset Investments (Sunset) for Alpen. Alpen then borrowed money from other sources and commenced constructing a log home on the lot. At some point thereafter, after various loans had been made to Alpen, the creditors, in order of their secured interests in the log home property, were (1) Columbia State Bank (Columbia), (2) Sunset, (3) unpaid trade creditors, (4) Cameron (D), and (5) Plein (P), who was Alpen's former president. Subsequently, Cameron (D) paid the amount due to Columbia with his personal funds and Columbia endorsed the note to Cameron (D). In addition, Columbia assigned the beneficial interest in its deed of trust to Cameron (D). Then, Cameron (D) paid the amount due Sunset, Sunset endorsed the promissory note for this loan to Cameron (D), and Sunset assigned its beneficial interest in its deed of trust to him. By these two transactions, Cameron (D), as beneficiary of the two deeds of trust originally issued to Columbia and Sunset, claimed secured interests in the property superior to all other secured interests. Cameron (D), as assignee of the Sunset note, hired attorney Lackey to begin nonjudicial foreclosure proceedings as a result of Alpen's default on the Sunset note. All of the secured creditors received notice of the foreclosure. Plein (P) and the trade creditors (P) brought suit against Cameron (D) and Lackey (D), seeking a permanent injunction barring the trustee's sale and a declaration that the deed of trust was void because the underlying debt had been paid, i.e., there was no default on the underlying debt. Plein (P) did not seek a preliminary injunction or any other order restraining the sale, but did seek an order declaring that his and the trade creditors' (P) security interests were superior to Cameron's (D). The sale went forward and Cameron (D) bought the property. The trial court granted summary judgment for Cameron (D) and dismissed Plein's (P) suit. The appellate court reversed, and the state's highest court granted review.

ISSUE: Is a shareholder/officer of a corporation an accommodation party on an instrument issued for value to the corporation where the shareholder signs the instrument in both his corporate capacity and individually without being a direct beneficiary of the value given for the instrument?

HOLDING AND DECISION: (Madsen, J.) Yes. A shareholder/officer of a corporation is an accommodation party on an instrument issued for value to the corporation where the shareholder signs the instrument in both his corporate capacity and individually without being a direct beneficiary of the value given for the instrument. Application of U.C.C. § 3-419(1) resolves the issue of whether Cameron (D) signed the Sunset note as an accommodation party. That section provides that "[i]f an instrument is issued for value given for the benefit of a party to the instrument ('accommodated party') and another party to the instrument ('accommodation party') signs the instrument for the purpose of incurring liability on the instrument without being a direct beneficiary of the value given for the instrument, the instrument is signed by the accommodation party 'for accommodation.'" Thus, the question is an issue of fact, and the party asserting accommodation status bears the burden of proof on this issue. Here, the direct beneficiary of the loan was Alpen. As Alpen's stockholder, any benefit obtained by Cameron (D) was derivative and indirect. In addition to the direct/indirect benefit inquiry, another factor that serves to establish accommodation party status is that the lender would not have made the loan in the absence of the party's signature on the note giving rise to liability. Here, Plein's (P) complaint itself asserted that Sunset would not have loaned the money to Alpen, which had no assets, unless the corporate officers signed individually, thus incurring personal liability. Because there are no disputed material questions of fact, as a matter of law, Cameron (D) signed the note as an accommodation party. Reversed.

EDITOR'S ANALYSIS: As the court points out, under § 3-419(b), an accommodation party may be a maker, a drawer, an acceptor, or an indorser. He or she is liable on the note in the capacity in which he or she signed, usually as a maker or indorser. However, the nature of the liability on the note does not dictate whether the signing party was an accommodation party. Instead, the absence of direct benefit, and the fact that value would not have been given without individual liability on the part of the signer dictate that the signer signed as an accommodation party.

MEDINA v. WYCHE

Corporate agent (D) v. Landlord (P)

Fla. Ct. App., 796 So.2d 622 (2001).

NATURE OF CASE: Appeal from judgment of personal liability on a corporate check.

FACT SUMMARY: Wyche (P) claimed that Medina (D) was personally liable on a "bounced" check drawn on the corporate account of First Delta Financial because Medina (D) had not placed his title before his signature.

CONCISE RULE OF LAW: A corporate agent who does not place his title on a check drawn on the corporation's account is not personally liable on the check where the corporation is identified on the check and the agent's signature is authorized.

FACTS: Medina (D) and Allied Transportation Resources, Inc. (Allied) (D) were found to be liable to Wyche (P) for rent. After a non-jury trial, the trial court entered judgment against Medina (D) and Allied (D) on account of a check for insufficient funds. The check indicated on its face that it was written on the account of First Delta Financial, a corporation. Median (D) signed the check, and his corporate title did not appear before his signature on the check. Medina (D) appealed, and the state court of appeals granted review.

ISSUE: Is a corporate agent who does not place his title on a check drawn on the corporation's account personally liable on the check where the corporation is identified on the check and the agent's signature is authorized?

HOLDING AND DECISION: (Cope, J.) No. A corporate agent who does not place his title on a check drawn on the corporation's account is not personally liable on the check where the corporation is identified on the check and the agent's signature is authorized. Wyche (P) claimed Medina (D) was personally liable on account of the check because he had not placed his corporate title before his signature. However, under Revised Article 3 of the U.C.C., if a representative signs, as Medina (D) did here, without indicating his corporate status, and the entity is identified on the check, the signer is not liable on the check if his signature is an authorized signature. This U.C.C. modification gives legal approval on the obvious intent of the transaction, i.e., that the company's check binds only the company, even if the agent signs in his or her own name. Reversed as to this issue.

EDITOR'S ANALYSIS: The official comment to this section of Revised Article 3 makes it clear that if the check identifies the "represented person" (e.g., a corporation), the agent who signs on the signature line does not to indicate agency status. This reflects contemporary commercial practice insofar as virtually all checks use today are in personalized form that identifies the person on whose account the check is drawn. Thus, nobody is deceived into thinking that the person signing the check is meant to be liable.

NOTES:

GELLES & SONS, INC. v. JEFFREY STACK, INC.
Contracting party (P) v. Contracting party (D)
Va. Sup. Ct., 569 S.E.2d 406 (2002).

NATURE OF CASE: Appeal from judgment holding that a claim for monies due under a contract was barred by an accord and satisfaction.

FACT SUMMARY: Gelles & Sons General Contracting, Inc. (Gelles) (P) claimed that Jeffrey Stack, Inc. (JSI) (D) owed it additional monies under a contract. JSI (D) maintained that Gelles's (P) claim was barred by an accord and satisfaction that occurred when Gelles (P) cashed a check sent by JSI (D) that was accompanied by a letter stating that the check represented "final payment on the contract."

CONCISE RULE OF LAW: For purposes of effecting an accord and satisfaction of a disputed claim, a letter accompanying a check that states that the check constitutes "final payment on the contract" is a sufficiently conspicuous statement to the effect that the check has been tendered as full satisfaction of the claim.

FACTS: Gelles & Sons General Contracting, Inc. (Gelles) (P) claimed that Jeffrey Stack, Inc. (JSI) (D) owed it additional monies under a contract for brick laying work Gelles (P) performed on JSI's (D) construction project. Gelles (P) claimed that around $26,000 was stilled owed, but JSI (D) maintained that only about $13,500 remained as a balance. Gelles (P) disagreed with JSI's (D) statement of account. Eventually, JSI (D) sent Gelles (P) a letter detailing deficiencies in Gelles's (P) work, along with a check for the amount JSI (D) maintained it still owed. The final letter's final paragraph stated "JSI...stands by its final amounts....Enclosed please find a check...representing final payment on the contract." Gelles (P) negotiated the check. Then Gelles (P) brought suit for what it claimed was the entire unpaid balance. JSI (D) asserted that Gelles's (P) claim was barred by an accord and satisfaction that occurred when Gelles (P) cashed the check sent by JSI (D). The trial court found an accord and satisfaction, and the state's highest court granted review.

ISSUE: For purposes of effecting an accord and satisfaction of a disputed claim, is a letter accompanying a check that states that the check constitutes "final payment on the contract" a sufficiently conspicuous statement to the effect that the check has been tendered as full satisfaction of the claim?

HOLDING AND DECISION: (Lacy, J.) Yes. For purposes of effecting an accord and satisfaction of a disputed claim, a letter accompanying a check that states that the check constitutes "final payment on the contract" is a sufficiently conspicuous statement to the effect that the check has been tendered as full satisfaction of the claim. The resolution of this case lies in § 8.3A-311, which provides that if a person against whom a claim is asserted proves that (i) that person in good faith tendered an instrument to the claimant as full satisfaction of the claim, (ii) the amount of the claim was unliquidated or subject to a bona fide dispute, and (iii) the claimant obtained payment of the instrument, the claim is discharged if the person against whom it is asserted proves that the instrument or an accompanying written communication contained a conspicuous statement to the effect that the instrument was tendered as full satisfaction of the claim. Conspicuous, as statutorily defined, means a term or clause that a reasonable person "ought to have noticed." This definition describes a physical attribute of the statement, not the content or meaning conveyed by the statement. There is no statutory requirement that the term or clause must be displayed in specific type or in any other distinguishing manner. Thus, the issue becomes whether the statement adequately relayed JSI's (D) intent to tender the check in full satisfaction of Gelles's (P) claim. The crux of Gelles's (P) argument is that the language at issue would not clearly inform a reasonable person that the check was being offered in full satisfaction of the claim. As § 8.3A-311 follows the common law, those principles are instructive. Under the common law, an accord and satisfaction requires both that the debtor intend that the proffered amount be given in full satisfaction of the disputed claim and that the claimant accept that amount in accordance with the debtor's intent. The acceptance need not be express, but may be implied, as where the instrument is accepted with intelligent appreciation of its possible consequences, coupled with knowledge of all relevant facts. Unlike the common law, however, the statute requires the claimant to overcome the presumption by satisfying an objective rather than a subjective test, that is, would a reasonable person have considered that the instrument was tendered as full satisfaction of the claim? Applying these principles here, it is clear that the statute itself, by describing the required statement as one "to the effect" that the tender will satisfy the debt, necessarily contemplates that no specific language is required and that each case must be considered on its own merits. The trial court concluded that the evidence presented a prima facie case of accord and satisfaction under the statute in light of the parties' course of conduct and communications between them. The court found that a reasonable person could not have considered the language at issue was anything other than an expression of JSI's (D) intent that the check and letter was, in effect, "a drop-dead letter that says, 'This is it. This is what we're going to pay you.'" Therefore, the trial court's findings were not clearly erroneous.

Continued on next page.

JSI's (D) letters to Gelles (P) made it clear that JSI (D) would pay no more under the contract than the amount of the check it offered. Affirmed.

EDITOR'S ANALYSIS: Revised Section 3-311 of the U.C.C. codifies the common law rule of accord and satisfaction. The inclusion of these principles was supported both by consumer groups and large businesses—a rare show of consensus in the commercial arena. The consumers believed the provisions would help consumers settle disputes without having to incur the expenses of litigation, whereas insurance companies and other businesses saw the provisions as a means for inducing their customers to settle claims by sending the customers checks in full satisfaction of the businesses' obligations on the theory that the customers would be enticed into cashing the checks on the belief that "something" was better than "nothing."

NOTES:

13

CHAPTER 13
PAYMENT SYSTEMS: CHECKS AND CREDIT CARDS

QUICK REFERENCE RULES OF LAW

1. **Time Check Is Paid by Payor Bank—The Midnight Deadline.** Under U.C.C. § 4-302, if a payor bank misses its midnight deadline, the bank is accountable for the face amount of a check presented for payment. (Blake v. Woodford Bank & Trust Co.)

2. **Check Kiting.** A depository bank has no good-faith obligation to disclose a suspected kite or to refrain from attempting to shift the kite loss, except in cases where there is a fiduciary or contractual relationship, a duty created by law, or fraud or misrepresentation by the defendant bank. (First National Bank in Harvey v. Colonial Bank)

3. **Effect of Regulation CC on the Midnight Deadline.** A federal reserve bank's banking day is that part of the day that the bank's check-processing department is open for the receipt of checks. (Oak Brook Bank v. Northern Trust Company)

4. **Right of Collecting Bank to Revoke Settlement on Dishonored Check.** A collecting bank retains the right to revoke or charge back funds that are provisionally credited to a customer until the collecting bank's settlement with the payor bank becomes final. (Essex Construction Corporation v. Industrial Bank of Washington, Inc.)

5. **Check Encoding.** A collecting bank must account to its customer for final payment on an item that the customer coded incorrectly where the final payment amount is greater than the encoded amount but the payor bank has suffered no loss. (First Union National Bank v. Bank One, N.A.)

6. **When Is Use Authorized?** A cardholder's failure to examine credit card statements that would reveal fraudulent use of the card constitutes a negligent omission that creates apparent authority for charges that would otherwise be unauthorized. (Minskoff v. American Express Travel Related Services Company, Inc.)

7. **Assertion of Cardholder Defenses.** A "no refund" policy is not a determinative factor per se in applying 15 U.S.C. § 1666i. (Izraelewitz v. Manufacturers Hanover Trust Co.)

BLAKE v. WOODFORD BANK & TRUST CO.
Account holder (P) v. Bank (D)
Ky. Ct. App., 555 S.W.2d 589 (1977).

NATURE OF CASE: Appeal from dismissal of action for accountability on a check.

FACT SUMMARY: In Blake's (P) action against Woodford Bank (D), Blake (P) alleged that Woodford (D) was accountable for the amount of two checks Blake (P) deposited at Woodford (D), but which were not processed in time to meet Woodford's (D) midnight deadline, causing Blake's (P) bank to return the checks for insufficient funds.

CONCISE RULE OF LAW: Under U.C.C. § 4-302, if a payor bank misses its midnight deadline, the bank is accountable for the face amount of a check presented for payment.

FACTS: On December 6, 1973, Blake (P) deposited a check to his account at his bank. The check was payable to Blake (P) and drawn on the K and K Farm Account at Woodford Bank (D). The check was dated December 3, 1973. On December 19, 1973, Blake (P) deposited a second check in his account at his bank. This check was also drawn on the K and K Farm Account at Woodford Bank (D). The check was dated December 17, 1973. When Blake (P) deposited the second check, he was told by his bank that the first check had been dishonored and returned for insufficient funds. Blake (P) asked his bank to re-present the first check along with the second check to Woodford (D) for payment. The two checks were received by Woodford (D) on December 24, 1973, but not returned until December 27, 1973. Woodford's (D) midnight deadline was December 26, 1973 and as Woodford (D) retained the checks beyond its deadline, Blake (P) asserted that Woodford (D) was accountable for the amount of the two checks. At trial, Woodford (D) was excused from meeting its deadline because its posting machine had broken and an employee was ill, preventing Woodford (D) from meeting the deadline. Blake (P) appealed.

ISSUE: Under U.C.C. § 4-302, if a payor bank misses its midnight deadline, is the bank accountable for the face amount of a check presented for payment?

HOLDING AND DECISION: (Park, J.) Yes. Under U.C.C. § 4-302, if a payor bank misses its midnight deadline, the bank is accountable for the face amount of a check presented for payment. A payor bank may give provisional credit for a check on the business day it was received and may then revoke credit at any time before midnight of the bank's next business day following receipt. If the bank does not meet its midnight deadline, its liability for the check, under the U.C.C., is explicit. The lower court here excused Woodford (D) from its midnight deadline because of the cumulative effects of the heavy volume of Christmas transactions, machine breakdown, and absence of a regular bookkeeper. However, the increased volume of business at Woodford (D) was clearly foreseeable the day after Christmas. Also, it should have been foreseeable to the responsible officers of the bank that the bookkeepers would be delayed in completing posting of the checks on December 26. However, no arrangements were made for return of "bad" items which might be discovered by the bookkeepers and no instructions had been left for employees to cover the handling of "bad" checks. Woodford (D) could have returned the checks by the midnight deadline by simply depositing the checks in the mail rather than waiting for the courier to pick them up the next day. The circumstances for timely return of the checks were not out of Woodford's (D) control, and Woodford (D) should not have been excused from meeting its midnight deadline. Reversed.

EDITOR'S ANALYSIS: Concerning payees and subsequent holders, the check-payment system has defects. Several days may pass before the payee or the holder obtains use of the drawer's money. Also, the drawer may have no money in the account or may stop payment on the check. In both cases, the payee or holder must proceed against the drawer because the holder has no rights against the drawee bank on which the check was written.

NOTES:

FIRST NATIONAL BANK IN HARVEY v. COLONIAL BANK

Depository bank (P) v. Issuing bank (D)

898 F. Supp. 1220 (N.D. Ill. 1995).

NATURE OF CASE: Cross-motions for summary judgment in case involving check kiting.

FACT SUMMARY: First National (P), one of several banks victimized by a check-kiting scheme, filed suit against Colonial (D) after Colonial (D) missed a midnight deadline to return the suspect checks.

CONCISE RULE OF LAW: A depository bank has no good-faith obligation to disclose a suspected kite or to refrain from attempting to shift the kite loss, except in cases where there is a fiduciary or contractual relationship, a duty created by law, or fraud or misrepresentation by the defendant bank.

FACTS: Shelly International Marketing opened a checking account at First National (P) in December 1989. The principals at Shelly opened several other checking accounts over the next two years, including one at Colonial Bank (D) in the name of World Commodities, Inc. Beginning in early 1991, the principals of Shelly and World Commodities began operating a check-kiting scheme among the various accounts. When an officer with First National's (P) holding company began to suspect that a kite was operating, he presented his findings to First National's (P) president and chief lending officer. The three agreed that further investigation was necessary and decided to return the suspect checks to Colonial (D). Pursuant to federal regulations, First National (P) notified Colonial (D) of the return, and Colonial (D) began to investigate the matter with the knowledge that there was a midnight deadline to return the checks and thereby protect Colonial (D) from liability. The loan officer in charge of the World Commodities account was assured by corporate officers that the checks were good. Colonial (D) decided not to return the checks that day, but instead to meet the next morning to discuss the matter. At the conclusion of the meeting Colonial (D) decided to return the checks to First National (P) and sent the checks back through the Reserve Bank. Upon learning of this, First National (P) challenged the return based on the fact that Colonial (D) had missed the midnight deadline. First National (P) submitted to the Reserve Bank a "Sender's Claim of Late Return" form. The form was processed, First National's (P) Reserve Bank account was credited, and Colonial's (D) Reserve Bank account was debited. Colonial (D) then filed a "Paying Bank's Response to Claim of Late Return" form, arguing that First National's (P) actions had forced it to miss the midnight deadline, and, consequently, the Reserve Bank (D) reversed the credits and debits. First National (P) filed suit against Colonial (D) and the Reserve Bank (D), alleging that Colonial (D) had wrongfully returned the Colonial (D) checks after the midnight deadline in breach of U.C.C. § 4-302, and that the Reserve Bank (D) had wrongfully accepted the late return. The parties moved for summary judgment.

ISSUE: Does a depository bank have a good-faith obligation to disclose a suspected kite or to refrain from attempting to shift the kite loss?

HOLDING AND DECISION: (Grady, Dist. J.) No. A depository bank has no good-faith obligation to disclose a suspected kite or to refrain from attempting to shift the kite loss, except in cases where there is a fiduciary or contractual relationship, a duty created by law, or fraud or misrepresentation by the defendant bank. Courts have held banks strictly liable for their failure to return a check by an applicable deadline. Colonial's (D) allegation that First National (P) acted in bad faith in orchestrating the events that caused it to miss the midnight deadline are unfounded. At the very most, First National (P) took advantage of the laws in its favor in an attempt to shift the kite loss to Colonial (D), but such actions do not constitute bad faith. First National's (P) motion for summary judgment on the issue of Colonial's (D) breach of U.C.C. § 4-302 is granted.

EDITOR'S ANALYSIS: It would seem that the federal regulations would provide for a more equitable compromise than having the liability fall solely on one of two victims. Many would argue that Colonial (D) received the short end of the stick in this check-kiting scheme. Nonetheless, it must be remembered that it had the means to protect itself and failed.

NOTES:

OAK BROOK BANK v. NORTHERN TRUST COMPANY
Depository bank (P) v. Payor bank (D)
256 F.3d 638 (7th Cir. 2001).

NATURE OF CASE: Appeal from grant of summary judgment to payor bank in action for ineffective dishonor of a check.

FACT SUMMARY: Northern Trust Company (Northern) (D) decided to dishonor checks presented to it by Oak Brook Bank (Oak Brook) (P), and returned the checks to a federal reserve bank (a "returning" bank) at 4:46 p.m. on the second day after it received the checks. Oak Brook (P) claimed that Northern (D) failed to make the deadline required under the U.C.C. for getting a check to a returning bank, thus requiring Northern (D) to pay the checks.

CONCISE RULE OF LAW: A federal reserve bank's banking day is that part of the day that the bank's check-processing department is open for the receipt of checks.

FACTS: On February 10, a check kiter who had accounts in both Oak Brook Bank (Oak Brook) (P) and Northern Trust Company (Northern) (D) deposited in his Oak Brook (P) account checks (none for less than $2,500) totaling some $450,000 drawn on his Northern (D) account, which had only a minute balance. The checks were presented to Northern (D) for payment the next day, February 11. On February 13, Northern (D) decided to dishonor them and it informed Oak Brook (P) of that decision by phone shortly before 4 p.m. By that time, however, Oak Brook (P) had credited the kiter's account and he had withdrawn all but about $7,000 of the money in the account. At 4:30 p.m., Northern (D) sent the dishonored checks by courier to the Federal Reserve Bank of Chicago, a returning bank, which received them 16 minutes later, at 4:46 p.m. In addition to suing the kiter, Oak Brook (P) sued Northern (D), charging that the dishonor was ineffective because the return of the checks was untimely under the U.C.C., and that, therefore, Northern (D) had to make good Oak Brook's (P) loss. The district court granted summary judgment in favor of Northern (D), and the Court of Appeals granted review.

ISSUE: Is a federal reserve bank's banking day that part of the day that the bank's check-processing department is open for the receipt of checks?

HOLDING AND DECISION: (Posner, Cir. J.) Yes. A federal reserve bank's banking day is that part of the day that the bank's check-processing department is open for the receipt of checks. The U.C.C. requires the payor bank that wishes to dishonor a check to dispatch it (for example by putting it in the mail), either to the depositary bank or to a "returning" bank for forwarding to the depositary bank, by midnight on the next banking day after the banking day on which the payor bank had received the check. Failure to make the deadline requires the payor bank to pay the check. Northern (D) missed this deadline, because it received the

checks on February 11, but did not dispatch them to the Federal Reserve Bank until February 13. However, Federal Reserve Board's Regulation CC extends the U.C.C.'s deadline from midnight to when the payor bank dispatches the dishonored check on its return journey, provided the bank "uses a means of delivery that would ordinarily result in receipt by the bank to which it is sent...on or before the receiving bank's next banking day following the otherwise applicable deadline." The "otherwise applicable deadline" in this regulation refers to the U.C.C.'s deadline of midnight on the day after the payor bank receives the check—here, midnight of February 12. The next banking day was the 13th, so Northern (D) had to get the checks to the Federal Reserve Bank by the end of the Federal Reserves Bank's "banking day" on the 13th. The issue is whether it made this deadline. Regulation CC defines "banking day" as "that part of any business day on which an office of a bank is open to the public for carrying on substantially all of its banking functions." Oak Brook (P) argues that by 4:46 p.m. on February 13, the Federal Reserve Bank was no longer carrying on "substantially all of its banking functions." More precisely, it argues that whether it was or not is a contestable issue and so the grant of summary judgment for Northern (D) was premature. Regulation CC also states that a federal reserve bank is a bank within the meaning of the regulation only insofar as it is a "paying bank," which in the context of federal reserve banks, means that all its banking functions are check processing, including returns. So the issue narrows to whether the Federal Reserve Bank of Chicago was open to the public (Oak Brook (P) concedes that this means to other banks, which are a federal reserve bank's only "public") at 4:46 p.m. on February 13 for processing checks. February 13 was a Friday. Only one or two persons are on duty in the check-processing department. The processing of returned checks includes receipting the checks, sorting them by type and region, dispatching them to the depositary bank, and confirming the amount returned. When only one or two employees are on duty in the department, only receipting is completed; sorting is begun but not completed; dispatching, crediting, and, confirming are not even begun. If, therefore, as Oak Brook (P) argues, all these are separate functions, it cannot be said that the Federal Reserve Bank performs substantially all of its banking functions on Friday afternoons after 4 p.m., and therefore, Northern (D) missed the deadline and must pay the checks. This argument, however, is rejected on practical grounds, because it would be impractical for payor banks to monitor the internal operations of returning banks in order to make sure that sending a check by courier at a given

Continued on next page.

hour on a given day would be an occurrence that was within the returning bank's "banking day." Faced with such uncertainty, payor banks would tend to go back to the old U.C.C. deadline, which Regulation CC does not supersede, but merely supplements. Accordingly, a federal reserve bank is open to the public for substantially all of its banking functions whenever the check-processing department is open for the receipt of checks, which in the case of the Federal Reserve Bank of Chicago is 24 hours of every day that the bank is open. In this case, therefore, Northern (D) beat the deadline, because it had until midnight of the 13th to get the checks to the Federal Reserve Bank. Affirmed.

EDITOR'S ANALYSIS: As Judge Posner explains, in 1987, concerned about delay in depositors' access to funds that they deposited by check, Congress, in the Expedited Funds Availability Act, 12 U.S.C. § 4001-10, shortened the "hold period" of depositary banks, that is, the period after a check is deposited before the depositor can withdraw the money from his account. The shortening of the hold period increased the risk of nonpayment to these banks, and to deal with that problem the Act authorized the Federal Reserve Board to issue regulations governing the system of bank payments. Pursuant to this grant of authority the Board issued Regulation CC, which (seemingly ironically) added an additional day for returns to allow the payor bank to use a more expeditious means of return, such as a same-day, or next-day courier. This would effectively get the check back much faster than mail dispatched before the U.C.C.'s midnight deadline.

NOTES:

ESSEX CONSTRUCTION CORPORATION v. INDUSTRIAL BANK OF WASHINGTON, INC.

Depositor (P) v. Bank (D)

913 F. Supp. 416 (D. Md. 1995).

NATURE OF CASE: Action for damages alleging failure to provide timely notice of a dishonored check.

FACT SUMMARY: Industrial (D) failed to provide timely notice that a deposited check did not clear, and Essex (P) wrote two checks against the amount in reliance on the deposited funds.

CONCISE RULE OF LAW: A collecting bank retains the right to revoke or charge back funds that are provisionally credited to a customer until the collecting bank's settlement with the payor bank becomes final.

FACTS: On March 31, 1995, Essex (P) deposited into its account at Industrial (D) a check for $120,710 from East Side Manor Cooperative Association drawn against an account at Signet Bank. At the time of the deposit, Industrial (D) provisionally credited Essex's (P) account for the full amount but provided written notice that only $100 of the funds would be available for withdrawal prior to April 6. On April 6, Signet notified Industrial (D) that East Side had stopped payment on the check, so Industrial (D) placed a permanent hold on the full amount of the check. On April 7, Industrial (D) mailed written notice and the returned check to Essex (P). On that same day, however, Essex (P) wrote two checks in the amount of $21,224 and $18,084 against the funds it thought were available in its Industrial (D) account. On April 11, Essex (P) received Industrial's (D) written notice that the East Side check had been dishonored. Essex (P) brought an action for damages in the amount of the dishonored check against Industrial (D), alleging that Industrial (D) had violated District of Columbia banking laws by failing to provide timely notice of the dishonored check. Essex (P) and Industrial (D) filed cross-motions for summary judgment.

ISSUE: Does a collecting bank retain the right to revoke or charge back funds that are provisionally credited to a customer until the collecting bank's settlement with the payor bank becomes final?

HOLDING AND DECISION: (Motz, C.J.) Yes. A collecting bank retains the right to revoke or charge back funds that are provisionally credited to a customer until the collecting bank's settlement with the payor bank becomes final. Essex (P) appears to have misunderstood the different duties and requirements of payor and collecting banks. Essex's (P) right to the provisionally credited funds became irrevocable only upon final payment by Signet, which was a condition that never transpired. Although telephoning Essex (P) likely would have constituted better customer service, Industrial (D) complied with the appropriate requirements by mailing the check on April 7. Furthermore, even if Industrial (D) were guilty of Essex's (P) allegations, Essex (P) would only be entitled to the actual damages resulting from Industrial's (D) failure to provide timely notice of the dishonor, not the full amount of the dishonored check. Industrial's (D) motion for summary judgment is granted.

EDITOR'S ANALYSIS: It seems that many would agree that two weeks is a long time to wait to receive notice whether a check has cleared or been dishonored. Nonetheless, there are several steps that a party could take to expedite the process or avoid the issue altogether. Essex (P) could have called the bank before it wrote the checks against the deposit to be certain that it had cleared, or it could require a cashier's check for future payments.

NOTES:

FIRST UNION NATIONAL BANK v. BANK ONE, N.A.

Depository bank (P) v. Payor bank (D)

47 U.C.C. Rep.Serv.2d 645, 2002 WL 501145 (E.D. Pa. 2002).

NATURE OF CASE: Motion for partial summary judgment in action by depository bank to recover face value of under-encoded check paid by drawee bank to intermediate collecting bank.

FACT SUMMARY: First Union (P) claimed that Mellon (D), an intermediate collection bank, owed it the face amount of a $507,598 check that had been under-encoded to $0 because Mellon (D) had received payment from Bank One, N.A. (Bank One) (D), the payor bank, for the correct amount, but had never remitted this amount to First Union (P).

CONCISE RULE OF LAW: A collecting bank must account to its customer for final payment on an item that the customer coded incorrectly where the final payment amount is greater than the encoded amount but the payor bank has suffered no loss.

FACTS: First Union National Bank (First Union) (P) under-encoded in the amount of $0 a check with a face amount of $507,598, and presented the check to Mellon (D), an intermediate collecting bank, which in turn presented it to Bank One, N.A. (Bank One) (D). Initially, Bank One (D) settled with Mellon (D) for $0. At some point, Bank One (D) discovered the error and paid to Mellon (D) the correct amount, which Mellon (D) did not remit to First Union (P). After First Union (P) presented Bank One (D) with a photocopy of the check, Bank One (D) paid it the correct face amount of the check. On Bank One's (D) behalf, First Union (P) brought suit to recover from Mellon (D) the face amount of the check that Bank One (D) had already paid to Mellon (D). First Union (P) moved for summary judgment against Mellon (D) on its claim that Mellon (D) breached it duty as a collecting bank to account to its customer under Article 4 of the U.C.C. First Union also alleged unjust enrichment.

ISSUE: Must a collecting bank account to its customer for final payment on an item that the customer coded incorrectly where the final payment amount is greater than the encoded amount but the payor bank has suffered no loss?

HOLDING AND DECISION: (Buckwalter, J.) Yes. A collecting bank must account to its customer for final payment on an item that the customer coded incorrectly where the final payment amount is greater than the encoded amount, but the payor bank has suffered no loss. U.C.C. § 4-215(d) provides that, "if a collecting bank receives a settlement for an item which is or becomes final, the bank is accountable to its customer for the amount of the item and any provisional credit given for the item in an account with its customer becomes final." First Union (P) argues that under this statute, Bank One (D), the drawee bank,

made final payment on the check, an item in the amount of $507,598, and that final payment triggered accountability along the chain of collection. Therefore, according to First Union (P), Mellon (D), the collecting bank that received settlement for an item which became final, is accountable to First Union (P), its customer, for the amount of the item, $507,598, and the fact that First Union encoded the item in the wrong amount was irrelevant, because once final payment occurred, the drawee bank and each collecting bank along the chain of collection became strictly accountable to its respective customer for the amount of the item, here $507,598. Mellon (D) counters that for purposes of § 4-215(d) the "amount of the item" for which a collecting bank is accountable is the encoded amount of the check, as long as the encoded amount is less than the face amount of the check or, alternatively, whichever is less. Therefore, because Bank One (D) first made final payment on the under-encoded check in the amount of $0.00, that is the amount for which Mellon (D) is accountable. Under some case law, the encoding bank is estopped from claiming more than the encoded amount of the check. However, estoppel is an equitable remedy, and in an encoding error situation has been used only where the payor bank has suffered a loss that it cannot recover by charging its customers account. Here, the situation is different insofar as Bank One (D), the payor bank, was able to successfully charge its customer's account for the face amount of the check, and remitted that amount to Mellon (D). Thus, equitable estoppel does not entitle Mellon (D) to hold onto funds properly debited from the maker of a check midway along the chain of collection because of an encoding error made by the depository bank. Moreover, there is no support for the broad proposition that final payment of the amount of an item for § 4-215 purposes is the encoded amount, rather than the face amount of the check. The principle, therefore, is that ultimate liability for encoding errors should rest on the shoulders of the depository bank that makes the error when deciding who should bear the loss between the depository bank, the collecting bank and the drawee bank. However, in the usual case, as here, the parties can be put back into their original positions, with no party sustaining a loss. Here, the payee has been credited with the face amount of the check by the depository bank, which is awaiting to collect the funds through the collection chain. The drawer has been debited by the drawee bank in the face amount of the check. The drawee bank has remitted the face amount of the check to the intermediary collecting bank. All that is needed to complete the chain is for the intermediary collecting

Continued on next page.

bank to remit the funds to the depository bank. Therefore, Mellon (D) did not properly account to First Union (P) after receiving final settlement on the face amount of the check in violation of § 4-215(d), and Mellon (D) must remit $507,598 to First Union (P). Because Mellon (D) is liable under § 4-215(d), the court does not need to address First Union's (P) claim of unjust enrichment. Judgment for First Union (P).

EDITOR'S ANALYSIS: In a related issue, the court in this case held that First Union's (P) mistaken presentment of the check through the collection process a second time (when it presented the photocopy of the check after it learned of the error) did not amount to a breach of presentment warranty under the U.C.C. The court reasoned that the fact that Bank One's (D) obligations had already been discharged and there was nothing left to enforce on the check was knowledge better available to Bank One (D), the drawee bank, and the bank that had paid the check on the first trip through the collection process. Consequently, the court concluded that it would be inappropriate to shift the loss to the presenting bank for this error.

NOTES:

MINSKOFF v. AMERICAN EXPRESS TRAVEL RELATED SERVICES COMPANY, INC.

Account holder (P) v. Credit card company (D)

98 F.3d 703 (1996).

NATURE OF CASE: Suit to recover unauthorized payments.

FACT SUMMARY: Minskoff (P) brought suit to recover unauthorized payments made to American Express (D) by one of Equities' employees.

CONCISE RULE OF LAW: A cardholder's failure to examine credit card statements that would reveal fraudulent use of the card constitutes a negligent omission that creates apparent authority for charges that would otherwise be unauthorized.

FACTS: Equities, a real estate holding and management firm, opened an American Express corporate card account for which one card was issued in the CEO, Minskoff's (P), name. Equities hired Blumenfeld to assist Minskoff (P). American Express (D) received an application for an additional card to issue from the corporate account in Blumenfeld's name. American Express (D) issued the card and sent it to the Equities address. American Express sent twelve monthly billing statements for the corporate account to Equities, which paid the charges. American Express (D) then sent Minskoff (P) an invitation to apply for a platinum card. Blumenfeld accepted and also submitted a request for a supplemental card without Equities' knowledge. Minskoff (P) initiated suit seeking to recover $276,334.06 that had been paid to American Express (D) in satisfaction of unauthorized charges by Blumenfeld and a declaration they were not liable for the outstanding balance on the platinum account. The district court dismissed and Minskoff (P) appealed.

ISSUE: Does a cardholder's failure to examine credit card statements that would reveal fraudulent use of the card constitute a negligent omission that creates apparent authority for charges that would otherwise be unauthorized?

HOLDING AND DECISION: (Mahoney, Cir. J.) Yes. A cardholder's failure to examine credit card statements that would reveal fraudulent use of the card constitutes a negligent omission that creates apparent authority for charges that would otherwise be unauthorized. Minskoff (P) claims that because Blumenfeld obtained the cards through forgery and fraud, her use of the cards is per se unauthorized under section 1643 and Equities' liability is limited to $50. Section 1643 applies only in the case of an unauthorized use of a credit card. That term is defined as "use of a credit card by a person other than the cardholder who does not have actual, implied, or apparent authority for such use and from which the cardholder receives no benefit." In determining whether a use is unauthorized the general laws of agency apply. Apparent authority arises from the written or spoken words or any other conduct of the principal which, reasonably interpreted, causes a third person to believe that the principal consents to have an act done by the person purporting to act for him." Restatement (Second) of Agency § 27. The existence of apparent authority is a question of fact and inappropriate for summary judgment. The principal, however, may be estopped from denying apparent authority if (1) its intentional or negligent acts created an appearance of authority in the agent; (2) on which a third party reasonably and in good faith relied; and (3) such reliance resulted in a detriment to the third party. Here it is clear that Blumenfeld acted without actual or implied authority when she forged the platinum card acceptance form and supplemental card applications. Thus, Minskoff (P) cannot be held liable for her initial possession of the cards. However, this does not preclude a finding of apparent authority for Blumenfeld's subsequent use of the cards. Under New York law, consumers are obligated to exercise reasonable care and promptness to examine bank statements in order to discover any unauthorized use or alteration. This policy is equally applicable to credit card holders. Such a review of the card statements would have disclosed charges made by Blumenfeld with the unauthorized cards. Vacated and remanded.

EDITOR'S ANALYSIS: The Truth in Lending Act (TILA), 15 U.S.C. § 1643, is a federal statute banning the issuance of credit cards to persons who did not request them. The statute limits the cardholder's liability for unauthorized use of the card to $50.

NOTES:

IZRAELEWITZ v. MANUFACTURERS HANOVER TRUST CO.

Credit card holder/purchaser (P) v. Card issuing bank (D)
N.Y. Civ. Ct., 120 Misc. 2d 125, 465 N.Y.S.2d 486 (1983).

NATURE OF CASE: Action to compel posting of credit to an account.

FACT SUMMARY: Trust Co. (D), a credit card issuer, refused to credit the account of Izraelewitz (P), its cardholder, for merhandise returned in violation of a merchant's "no refund" policy.

CONCISE RULE OF LAW: A "no refund" policy is not a determinative factor per se in applying 15 U.S.C. § 1666i.

FACTS: Izraelewitz (P) used a credit card issued to him by Manufacturers Hanover Trust Co. (Trust Co.) (D) to purchase electronic diagrams from Don Britton Enterprises. Izraelewitz (P) subsequently returned the merchandise, and Trust Co. (D) credited the account and attempted to collect payment from Don Britton. Don Britton refused the charge back, informed Trust Co. (D) of its strict "no refund" policy, and represented that Izraelewitz (P) was aware of the policy. When Trust Co. (D) redebited Izraelewitz's (P) account, Izraelewitz (P) sued under 15 U.S.C. § 1666i, seeking to compel Trust Co. (D) to credit his account.

ISSUE: Is a "no refund" policy a determinative factor per se in applying 15 U.S.C. § 1666i?

HOLDING AND DECISION: (Harkavy, J.) No. A "no refund" policy is not a determinative factor per se in applying 15 U.S.C. § 1666i. 15 U.S.C. §1666i allows a cardholder to assert claims arising out of the credit card transaction against the card issuer where the cardholder has made a good faith attempt to resolve the dispute with the merchant. "No refund" policies do not per se violate public policy, but most bank-merchant agreements require that the merchant establish a fair policy for exchange of merchandise. Don Britton's business is selling original designs, so access to its designs must be carefully restricted. Furthermore, Don Britton's policy is conspicuously displayed in its catalog and enhanced by alternative backup and free engineering assistance plans. Judgment for Trust Co. (D).

EDITOR'S ANALYSIS: 15 U.S.C. § 1666i was enacted in 1974 along with a number of amendments to the Consumer Credit Protection Act. Section 1666 of the 1974 legislation defines "billing error." The definition includes an indication on the issuer's billing statement of goods or services rejected by the cardholder as not in accordance with the sales agreement.

NOTES:

108

14

CHAPTER 14
PAYMENT SYSTEMS: ELECTRONIC TRANSFERS

QUICK REFERENCE RULES OF LAW

1. **Payment Orders.** A receiving bank is not liable for a sender's damages that result from the failure of a wire transfer transaction effected through the Federal Reserve Wire Transfer Network (Fedwire) where the receiving bank has followed the sender's orders, which on their face are unambiguous. (Grossman v. Nationsbank, N.A.)

2. **Receiver Finality.** A communication to cancel or amend a payment order will be effective only if the notice is received at a time and in a manner that affords the receiving bank a reasonable opportunity to act on the communication before the bank accepts the payment order. (Aleo International, Ltd. V. Citibank)

3. **The "Money-Back Guarantee."** Section 402 of Article 4A of the New York Uniform Commercial Code imposes a privity requirement so that a sender seeking a refund for an uncompleted funds transfer may look only to the receiving bank to whom it issued a payment order and payment. (Grain Traders, Inc. v. Citibank, N.A.)

4. **Incorrectly Identified Beneficiary.** Under Florida law, acceptance of a wire transfer by the recipient bank is precluded where the name, bank account or other identifying information of the beneficiary is nonexistent or unidentifiable. (Corfan Banco Asuncion Paraguay v. Ocean Bank)

GROSSMAN v. NATIONSBANK, N.A.
Funds sender (P) v. Receiving bank (D)
225 F.3d 1228 (11th Cir. 2000).

NATURE OF CASE: Appeal from dismissal of complaint for failure to state a claim for bank's failure to complete a wire transfer transaction in accordance with the sender's instructions.

FACT SUMMARY: Grossman (P) alleged that Nationsbank, N.A. (Nationsbank) (D) failed to complete a wire transfer transaction through the Federal Reserve Wire Transfer Network (Fedwire) in accordance with his instructions, and was liable to him for resulting damages ($200,000).

CONCISE RULE OF LAW: A receiving bank is not liable for a sender's damages that result from the failure of a wire transfer transaction effected through the Federal Reserve Wire Transfer Network (Fedwire) where the receiving bank has followed the sender's orders, which on their face are unambiguous.

FACTS: To participate in an investment program with HMF Management (HMF), Grossman (P) opened an account at First Union National Bank (First Union). He received instructions from HMF for the wire transfer of his investment funds into the account at First Union. These instructions directed that the funds be wired to bank name "Am South Bank" (Am South), and then for further credit to the First Union account. Grossman (P) went to Nationsbank (D), provided a copy of the wire-transfer instructions, and requested a wire transfer for $250,000 pursuant to those instructions, to be effected through the Federal Reserve Wire Transfer Network (Fedwire). Grossman (P) received confirmation that the funds had been sent per the wire-transfer order. However, the funds had not reached the account at First Union. Because he was not a signatory on the Am South account to which Nationsbank (D) was directed to wire the funds, Grossman (P) could not find out why Am South had not forwarded the funds to the First Union account. Nationsbank (D) also confirmed that it had, along with the funds, forwarded Grossman's (P) instructions to Am South. A few months later, Grossman (P) learned that the Am South account had been closed by HMF, its only signatory. However, HMF wired $50,000 to Grossman's (P) Nationsbank (D) account in return for an agreement from Grossman (P) authorizing HMF to deduct $50,000 from the principle sum of the investment that it would soon transfer to the First Union account. Grossman (P) brought suit alleging damages in excess of $200,000 as a result of Nationsbank's (D) failure to complete the wire transfer transaction in accordance with the instructions he had provided, or to advise him that such transaction could not be completed as structured. The district court dismissed his complaint for failure to state a claim, and the court of appeals granted review.

ISSUE: Is a receiving bank liable for a sender's damages that result from the failure of a wire transfer transaction effected through the Federal Reserve Wire Transfer Network (Fedwire) where the receiving bank has followed the sender's orders, which on their face are unambiguous?

HOLDING AND DECISION: (Per curiam) No. A receiving bank is not liable for a sender's damages that result from the failure of a wire transfer transaction effected through the Federal Reserve Wire Transfer Network (Fedwire) where the receiving bank has followed the sender's orders, which on their face are unambiguous. Federal Reserve Board Regulation J (Regulation J), which governs wire transfers effected through Fedwire, applies U.C.C. Article 4A to wire transfers conducted using Fedwire. Regulation J directs that Nationsbank's (D) duty as a receiving bank was to issue a payment order that complied with the sender's (Grossman's (P)), instructions. The instructions Grossman (P) provided to Nationsbank (D) did not identify the banks by the terms "intermediary bank" and "beneficiary's bank." The instructions were therefore non-specific. Grossman (P) argued that he instructed Nationsbank to send the funds to the account at First Union, using Am South as an intermediary bank. However, the instructions he gave Nationsbank (D) cannot be read as indicating a normal transfer using an intermediary bank, because funds traveling through an intermediary bank are not deposited in an individual account at the intermediary bank. The instructions Grossman (P) gave to Nationsbank (D) specifically stated that the money was to reach an account at Am South. The next line of the instructions read "for further credit to" the account at First Union, which indicates that the funds were first intended to be credited to the account at Am South, with instructions to be sent instructing that the funds then be transferred to the First Union account. Nationsbank (D) did exactly that. Because Nationsbank (D) followed the instructions that Grossman (P) provided, Nationsbank (D) complied with its duty under Regulation J. Therefore, Grossman (P) cannot state a claim for a violation of Regulation J, and the district court did not err in granting Nationsbank's (D) motion to dismiss. Affirmed.

EDITOR'S ANALYSIS: Fedwire is an electronic funds transfer system that permits large dollar fund transfers by computer-to-computer communications between banks, and Fedwire transfers usually involve the federal reserve system. Often, the actual transfer involves steps in which originator's bank sends a payment order to a federal reserve bank (in this function, technically an intermediary bank) and the reserve bank debits the account of the originator's bank at the reserve bank, and credits the reserve bank account of the beneficiary's bank. At that point, the reserve bank sends a payment order to the beneficiary's bank, which now has the money in its account and can credit the individual account of the beneficiary. However, the steps involving the federal reserve bank were not crucial to this case, so the court omitted them to simplify the facts.

ALEO INTERNATIONAL, LTD. v. CITIBANK
Transferring company (P) v. Transferring bank (D)
N.Y. Sup. Ct., 612 N.Y.S.2d 540 (1994).

NATURE OF CASE: Action alleging negligence for failure to stop an electronic fund transfer.

FACT SUMMARY: A vice president of Aleo (P) authorized Citibank (D) to make an electronic transfer of funds to an account in Germany and then filed suit after her attempt to halt the transfer was received too late to prevent its occurrence.

CONCISE RULE OF LAW: A communication to cancel or amend a payment order will be effective only if the notice is received at a time and in a manner that affords the receiving bank a reasonable opportunity to act on the communication before the bank accepts the payment order.

FACTS: Eyzerovich, a vice president of Aleo (P), authorized her local Citibank (D) branch in New York to make an electronic transfer of $284,563 to the Dresdner Bank in Berlin, Germany. Citibank (D) sent the payment order by electronic message at 5:27 p.m. New York time. The Dresdner Bank sent a message at 9:59 a.m. Berlin time (3:59 a.m. New York time) confirming that the transfer had been completed. At approximately 9 a.m. the following morning, Eyzerovich instructed Citibank (D) to stop the transfer. After Citibank (D) informed her that it could not do so, Aleo (P) filed suit.

ISSUE: Is a communication to cancel or amend a payment order effective if the notice is received at a time and in a manner that does not afford the receiving bank a reasonable opportunity to act on the communication before the bank accepts the payment order?

HOLDING AND DECISION: (Cahn, J.) No. A communication to cancel or amend a payment order will be effective only if the notice is received at a time and in a manner that affords the receiving bank a reasonable opportunity to act on the communication before the bank accepts the payment order. The Dresdner Bank had accepted the payment order before Eyzerovich attempted to stop the transfer. Citibank (D) may not be held liable for failing to honor an ineffective cancel request. Citibank's (D) motion is granted and the action is dismissed.

EDITOR'S ANALYSIS: Article 4A of the Uniform Commercial Code governs all aspects of electronic fund transfers. The application of Article 4A ensures that all steps in an electronic fund transfer will be governed by a single set of rules. Although the parties involved in the transfer may by mutual agreement choose a different jurisdiction's law, if they do not designate any choice Article 4A is controlling.

NOTES:

GRAIN TRADERS, INC. v. CITIBANK, N.A.
Fund transferor (P) v. Bank (D)
160 F.3d 97 (2d Cir. 1998).

NATURE OF CASE: Diversity action.

FACT SUMMARY: Grain Traders (P) brought suit against Citibank (D) under Article 4A of New York's Uniform Commercial Code and the common law seeking a refund for an alleged uncompleted electronic funds transfer.

CONCISE RULE OF LAW: Section 402 of Article 4A of the New York Uniform Commercial Code imposes a privity requirement so that a sender seeking a refund for an uncompleted funds transfer may look only to the receiving bank to whom it issued a payment order and payment.

FACTS: Grain Traders (P) initiated a funds transfer of $310,000 to Kraemer by issuing a payment order to its bank, BCN. The transfer instructed BCN to debit Grain Traders' (P) account in the amount of $310,000 and then to issue a payment order to Citibank (D). The payment order was to debit the $310,000 from BCN's account at Citibank (D) and to credit that amount to BCIL. Citibank (D) was then to issue a payment order to BCIL instructing it to transfer $310,000 to Banco Extrader, S.A. Extrader was then to credit the $310,000 to the account maintained at Extrader by Kraemer. BCIL and Extrader suspended payments at some point after Citibank (D) executed the payment order. BCIL's banking license was revoked and Extrader became insolvent. BCN contacted Citibank (D) and requested cancellation of its payment order and return of the funds. Grain Traders (P) brought suit seeking a refund from Citibank (D) under Article 4A. Both parties moved for summary judgment which was granted in favor of Citibank (D). Grain Traders (P) appealed.

ISSUE: Does section 402 of Article 4A of the New York Uniform Commercial Code impose a privity requirement so that a sender seeking a refund for an uncompleted funds transfer may look only to the receiving bank to whom it issued a payment order and payment?

HOLDING AND DECISION: (Walker, Cir. J.) Yes. Section 402 of Article 4A of the New York Uniform Commercial Code imposes a privity requirement so that a sender seeking a refund for an uncompleted funds transfer may look only to the receiving bank to whom it issued a payment order and payment. Section 402 governs the obligation of a sender of a payment order to make payment to the receiving bank after the order has been accepted and the obligation of the receiving bank to refund payment in the event the transfer is not completed. Under section 402(c), the sender's obligation to pay the receiving bank is excused in the event the transfer is not completed. If payment has already been made, a sender can seek a refund from the bank it paid under section 402(d). Grain Traders (P) sought to invoke this

"money-back guarantee" provision to obtain a refund from Citibank (D). The district court held that the refund action against Citibank (D), an intermediary bank, was barred because a section 402 refund action could only be maintained against the receiving bank to whom the sender had issued a payment order and whom the sender had paid. Thus, Grain Traders (P) could only look to BCN, the receiving bank, for recovery. This conclusion has support both in the plain language of Article 4A and the Official Comment to section 402. Thus, section 402 only allows each sender of a payment order to seek a refund only from the receiving bank it paid. Affirmed.

EDITOR'S ANALYSIS: The court also held that Grain Traders' (P) common law claims for conversion and money had and received were precluded since they sought to impose liability on Citibank (D) that would be inconsistent with Article 4A. The issue of whether Article 4A precluded such common law claims was a matter of first impression for the court, which agreed with other jurisdictions who interpreted the articles' provisions as precluding common law claims when such claims would impose liability inconsistent with the rights and obligations expressly provided by the article.

NOTES:

CORFAN BANCO ASUNCION PARAGUAY v. OCEAN BANK

Transnational bank (P) v. Florida bank (D)

Fla. Dist. Ct. App., 715 So. 2d 967 (1998).

NATURE OF CASE: Appeal from summary judgment for defendant on causes of action for violation of the U.C.C. and common law negligence.

FACT SUMMARY: Corfan (P) erroneously sent two wire transfers to the same person and brought suit against Ocean Bank (D) for repayment of one.

CONCISE RULE OF LAW: Under Florida law, acceptance of a wire transfer by the recipient bank is precluded where the name, bank account or other identifying information of the beneficiary is nonexistent or unidentifiable.

FACTS: Corfan (P) originated a wire transfer of $72,972 via its intermediary Swiss Bank to the account of Silva in Ocean Bank (D). Ocean Bank (D) noticed a discrepancy in the account numbers and did not inform Corfan (P) or Swiss of the error. Once the correct account number was confirmed by Silva, Ocean (D) accepted the wire transfer and credited his account. Corfan (P) became aware of the discrepancy and issued a second wire transfer of $72,972 to Silva's correct account number at Ocean (D). The second transfer did not indicate that it was a correction or replacement of the first transfer. The transfer was automatically credited to Silva's account. Several days later Corfan (P) inquired regarding the transfers indicating that only one was intended. Silva had already withdrawn both transfers from the account. When Ocean (D) refused to repay $72,972 to Corfan (P), Corfan (P) brought suit under the U.C.C. and for common law negligence. The trial court granted Ocean's (D) motion for summary judgment as to the U.C.C. count and dismissed the negligence count.

ISSUE: Under Florida law, is acceptance of a wire transfer by the recipient bank precluded where the name, bank account or other identifying information of the beneficiary is nonexistent or unidentifiable?

HOLDING AND DECISION: (Sorondo, J.) Yes. Under Florida law, acceptance of a wire transfer by the recipient bank is precluded where the name, bank account or other identifying information of the beneficiary is nonexistent or unidentifiable. The plain language of Florida Statutes § 4A-207(a) states that "if, in a payment order received by the beneficiary's bank, the name, bank account number, or other identification of the beneficiary refers to a nonexistent or unidentifiable person or account, no person has rights as a beneficiary of the order and acceptance cannot occur." Here the payment order referred to a nonexistent bank account number. Thus, under the clear and unambiguous terms of the statute, acceptance of the order could not have occurred. The trial court dismissed the negligence count on the

basis that the statutory scheme preempted any common law negligence claim. Since the duty claimed to have been breached by Ocean (D) in the negligence claim (the duty of care to follow the accepted banking practice of the community and to return the funds from the first transfer upon receipt due to a nonexistent account number) is exactly the same duty now governed by statute, the statutory scheme preempts the negligence claim and the dismissal of the claim is affirmed. Reversed in part and affirmed in part.

EDITOR'S ANALYSIS: It is common practice with respect to wire transfers for the recipient bank to ignore the name of the beneficiary and look only to the account number specified. U.C.C. § 4A-207 deals with this issue and allows the recipient bank to ignore the name identified as the beneficiary and to only look to the account number.

NOTES:

CHAPTER 15
FRAUD, FORGERY, AND ALTERATION

QUICK REFERENCE RULES OF LAW

1. **Negligence of Customer Contributing to Forgery.** Any person who, by his negligence, substantially contributes to an unauthorized endorsement is precluded from asserting the lack of authority against a drawee or other payor. (Thompson Maple Products, Inc. v. Citizens National Bank)

2. **Failure of Customer to Report Forgery.** For purposes of U.C.C. § 4-406, a bank exercises ordinary care in the payment of a check where it follows procedures used by comparably sized banks in the area in which it is located, even though it does not follow procedures used by all banks in the area. (Espresso Roma Corporation v. Bank Of America, N.A.)

3. **Validity of Contractual "Cutdown" Clauses.** A bank and its customer may agree contractually to shorten the one-year period provided in U.C.C. § 4-406(f) for reporting of an unauthorized signature or alteration on an item, provided the shortened period is not manifestly unreasonable. (National Title Insurance Corporation Agency v. First Union National Bank)

4. **Forgery—Action by Drawer.** A drawer has no action for money had or received or conversion against a collecting bank for cashing the drawer's check on a forged endorsement. (Stone & Webster Engineering Corp. v. First National Bank & Trust Co.)

5. **Imposters.** To invoke protection of the imposter rule, it must be proven that by impersonation of the payee the imposter induced a bank to issue a check. (Title Insurance Company of Minnesota v. Comerica Bank—California)

6. **The Double Forgery.** Uniform Commercial Code §§ 3-404 and -405 permit a plaintiff to assert a cause of action with respect to fictitious payee double forgeries if the person taking the check fails to exercise ordinary care. (Gina Chin & Associates, Inc. v. First Union Bank)

7. **Allocation of Loss By Contract.** There is no cause of action for recovery of funds paid on forged checks where a resolution is adopted authorizing the drawee's payment of checks bearing signatures resembling a machine-endorsed facsimile signature. (Jefferson Parish School Board v. First Commerce Corporation)

8. **Complete Instruments.** Whether a drawer failed to exercise ordinary care in preparing a check so as to prevent unauthorized alteration is a question of fact, a court's determination of which will be reviewed only for clear error, in an action brought by a drawee bank against a bank presenting the check for payment for the second bank's alleged breach of its presentment warranties. (HSBC Bank USA v. F & M Bank Northern Virginia)

9. **Restrictive Indorsements.** The unqualified language "for deposit only" following an indorsement on the back of a check requires a depositary bank to place the check's proceeds into the payee's account, and the bank violates that restrictive indorsement when it credits the check to any other account. (State of Qatar v. First American Bank)

THOMPSON MAPLE PRODUCTS, INC. v. CITIZENS NATIONAL BANK
Drawee company (P) v. Bank (D)
Pa. Super. Ct., 211 Pa. Super. 42, 234 A.2d 32 (1967).

NATURE OF CASE: Review of dismissal of breach of contract action.

FACT SUMMARY: Thompson (P), a small business, systematically failed to retain originals or otherwise control misappropriation of slips used to justify issuance of payment checks.

CONCISE RULE OF LAW: Any person who, by his negligence, substantially contributes to an unauthorized endorsement is precluded from asserting the lack of authority against a drawee or other payor.

FACTS: Thompson Maple Products, Inc. (Thompson) (P) employees filled out "scaling slips" in duplicate, recording the source, receipt, quantity, and quality of logs delivered by "haulers." Thompson (P) employees routinely gave both slips to the hauler. Other Thompson (P) employees then prepared checks in payment for delivered logs based on the information contained in the slips. Blank slips were readily accessible to haulers. One hauler filled out fraudulent slips to fictitious payees and forged their endorsements on the checks. Thompson (P) sued drawee Citizen's National Bank (D), charging breach of its contract of deposit. The trial court held that Thompson's (P) negligence contributed substantially to the unauthorized endorsements and dismissed. Thompson (P) appealed, contending that negligence in the conduct of a drawer's business was not contemplated by U.C.C. § 3-406.

ISSUE: If a person, by his negligence, substantially contributes to an unauthorized endorsement, is he precluded from asserting the lack of authority against a drawee?

HOLDING AND DECISION: (Hoffman, J.) Yes. If a person, by his negligence, substantially contributes to an unauthorized endorsement, he is precluded from asserting the lack of authority against a drawee. As between the payor banker and the customer, the bank ordinarily must bear losses caused by the forgery of a payee's endorsement. U.C.C. § 3-406, however, provides that negligence "which substantially contributes to . . . the making of an unauthorized signature" precludes the drawer from asserting a forgery. Section 3-406 rejects decisional law requiring that the negligence "directly and proximately affect . . . the conduct of the bank in passing the forgery." Here, Thompson (P) failed to exercise reasonable diligence in insuring honesty from its log haulers. Affirmed.

EDITOR'S ANALYSIS: U.C.C. § 3-406 applies to both "forged checks" and to checks bearing a "forged endorsement." A "forged check" is one bearing a forged drawer's signature and is negotiable as a valid instrument against the forger. A check bearing a "forged endorsement," by contrast, is ineffective against the payee.

NOTES:

ESPRESSO ROMA CORPORATION v.
BANK OF AMERICA, N.A.

Bank customer (P) v. Payor bank (D)

Cal. Ct. App., 124 Cal.Rptr.2d 549 (2002).

NATURE OF CASE: Appeal from dismissal on summary judgment of action for unauthorized payment of forged checks.

FACT SUMMARY: Boyd (P) and his corporations (P) (collectively "appellants") (P) alleged that Bank of America, N.A. (Bank) (D) was liable to them for having paid checks totaling more than $330,000 that had been forged by appellants' (P) former employee, Montanez. The Bank (D) asserted that appellants (P) were precluded by U.C.C. § 4-406 from asserting any claims against the Bank (D) for unauthorized payment of checks drawn on their accounts.

CONCISE RULE OF LAW: For purposes of U.C.C. § 4-406, a bank exercises ordinary care in the payment of a check where it follows procedures used by comparably sized banks in the area in which it is located, even though it does not follow procedures used by all banks in the area.

FACTS: From 1996 through April 1999, Boyd (P) and his corporations (P) (collectively "appellants") (P) employed Montanez, who assumed bookkeeping responsibilities and had access to blank checks. Starting in October 1997, Montanez downloaded company computer programs, stole blank checks, and printed company checks on his home computer that he used to pay his personal bills, and for personal purchases. The forged checks totaled more than $330,000. He concealed his actions by removing the forged checks from the bank statements when he sorted the mail. Boyd (P) did not discover the forgeries, or report them to the Bank (D) until May 1999. Appellants (P) brought suit against the Bank (D), and the Bank (D) moved for summary judgment based on § 4406 (U.C.C. § 4-406), which limits a payor bank's liability to its customer for making payment upon checks with alterations or unauthorized signatures. Pursuant to subdivision (f) of § 4406, the Bank (D) asserted that appellants (P) were absolutely precluded from asserting forgeries processed more than one year before the forgery was reported, because, by its terms, subdivision (f) applies, "[w]ithout regard to care or lack of care of either the customer or the bank," and precludes, "a customer who does not within one year after the statement or items are made available to the customer . . . discover and report the customer's unauthorized signature" from asserting it against the payor bank. The Bank (D) also relied upon the conditional preclusion established by § 4406(d) and (e). Section 4406(c) imposes a duty upon the customer promptly to review monthly statements or checks made available to the customer by the bank, to exercise reasonable care in discovering any unauthorized signature or alteration, and promptly to notify the bank of the discovery of such items. Pursuant to subdivision (d),

if the customer fails to comply with these duties, when the same person has forged checks on the account, the customer is precluded from making a claim against the bank for the unauthorized payment unless the customer notified the bank no more than 30 days after the first forged item was included in the monthly statement or canceled checks, and should have been discovered. This preclusion is conditional because the customer may avoid its application by establishing, under § 4406(e), that the bank "failed to exercise ordinary care in paying the item and that the failure contributed to [the] loss." The trial court granted summary judgment to the Bank (D), and the state court of appeals granted review.

ISSUE: For purposes of U.C.C. § 4-406, does a bank exercise ordinary care in the payment of a check where it follows procedures used by comparably sized banks in the area in which it is located, even though it does not follow procedures used by all banks in the area?

HOLDING AND DECISION: (Stein, Act. P.J.) Yes. For purposes of U.C.C. § 4-406, a bank exercises ordinary care in the payment of a check where it follows procedures used by comparably sized banks in the area in which it is located, even though it does not follow procedures used by all banks in the area. Although the Bank (D) sent appellants (P) statements and canceled checks every month, more than a year and a half elapsed before appellants (P) discovered and reported any of them, despite having the means to discover the forgeries. This is far beyond the 30 days specified in § 4406(d), so the Bank (D) has established a prima facie case that appellants are precluded under that section from making a claim against the Bank (D) for unauthorized payment. The burden shifts to appellants (P) under § 4406(e) to show that § 4406(d) should not apply because the Bank (D) "failed to exercise ordinary care in paying the item and that the failure contributed to [the] loss." "Ordinary care" in the case of a person engaged in business means observance of reasonable commercial standards, prevailing in the area in which the person is located, with respect to the business in which the person is engaged. In the case of a bank that takes an instrument for processing for collection or payment by automated means, reasonable commercial standards do not require the bank to examine the instrument if the failure to examine does not violate the bank's prescribed procedures and the bank's procedures do not vary unreasonably from general banking usage. Expert

Continued on next page.

testimony presented by the Bank (D) indicated that although the Bank (D) uses fraud filters, they were not designed to "catch a crooked employee who forges his employer's checks, which only the employer would know are forged." The Bank's (D) witness also declared that the Bank's (D) practices and procedures were consistent with those of all other large bulk file bookkeeping banks in California, and that the Bank (D) followed its procedures with respect to the checks at issue when it processed the checks. He concluded that the Bank (D) exercised ordinary care such that § 4406(e) would be inapplicable. Appellants' (P) argument that this declaration is insufficient to define the reasonable commercial standard in the area is rejected. Appellants (P) argue that the Bank (D) failed to demonstrate that its automated check processing did not vary unreasonably from general banking usage, because the expert stated that the Bank's (D) practices conformed to commercial standards for "bulk file bookkeeping" in all of California, and considered only the practices of similarly sized banks. Appellants (P), however, take the reference to the entire State of California, in isolation and out of context, because the expert specifically stated that he was also familiar with the practices of similarly sized banks in the "San Francisco Bay area." Thus, read as a whole, the expert's declaration expressed the opinion that the Bank's practices conformed not only with those of similarly sized banks in the Bay Area, but also with similarly sized banks in the State of California. Nor did the Bank (D) have to show that its practices were consistent with those of *all* banks in the area, not just those of similarly sized banks. To the contrary, the standard of reasonableness is set by comparable businesses. Size is a relevant factor in identifying comparable businesses because, in the banking context, a reasonable commercial standard for processing checks at a small bank with a relatively small volume of checks, and personal familiarity with its customers, would be quite different than what is reasonable for a large bank, such as the Bank (D), that processes upwards of a million checks per day. The expert's declaration therefore established that the reasonable industry standard prevailing in the area for similarly sized banks was to bulk process checks through an automated system that employs fraud filters, but does not include sight review of individual checks for signature verification. The Bank's (D) procedures conformed to this standard, which also was consistent with general bank usage as reflected by the practices of other bulk file bookkeeping banks in California, and it followed those procedures in this case. Therefore, the expert's declaration was sufficient to establish a prima facie case that the Bank (D) exercised ordinary care, thereby shifting the burden to appellants (P) to create a triable issue of fact. Appellants (P) presented their own expert, who made a fundamental error by failing to define the applicable reasonable commercial standard of care by looking at comparably sized banks using bulk file bookkeeping. Instead appellants' expert based his opinion—that the standard of care requires sight review of checks and other special handling—on the practices of large and small banks. Without a showing that *comparable* banks in the area select individual checks for sight review, the fact that the Bank's (D) system did not select individual checks for sight review, or signature verification, is insufficient to create a material issue of fact because § 3103(a)(7) specifies that "reasonable commercial standards do not require the bank to examine the instrument if the failure to examine does not violate the bank's prescribed procedures and the bank's procedures do not vary unreasonably from general banking usage." Even assuming that reasonable commercial standards did require that the Bank (D) have established criteria for selecting some checks for sight review, appellants (P) still fail to create a triable issue of fact because they provide no basis to infer that the failure to have such a system contributed to the loss. Even if the Bank (D) had used such a system of selection for sight review, appellants (P) provide no basis for inferring that any of the unauthorized checks would have been selected for sight review, resulting in earlier discovery of the forgeries. Therefore, they do not create a triable issue that the failure to have such a system contributed to the loss. Affirmed.

EDITOR'S ANALYSIS: As this case demonstrates, the abandonment of sight review does not mean that a bank has failed to exercise "ordinary care." For many years before the revision of Articles 3 and 4, courts were sharply divided on this issue, with many holding that failure to conduct sight review constituted negligence as a matter of law. Desiring to have Revised Article 4 accommodate a system of electronic presentment, the drafters adopted a definition of "ordinary care" in § 3-103(a)(9) that had been adopted in cases rejecting the notion that a bank committed negligence by failing to conduct sight review. It is this definition of ordinary care that is used in *Espresso Roma*.

NOTES:

NATIONAL TITLE INSURANCE CORPORATION AGENCY v. FIRST UNION NATIONAL BANK

Bank customer (P) v. Bank (D)

Va. Sup. Ct., 559 S.E.2d 668 (2002).

NATURE OF CASE: Appeal from denial of summary judgment for plaintiff and grant of summary judgment to defendant in action by bank customer to recover losses resulting from its bank's payment of counterfeit checks drawn on customer's account.

FACT SUMMARY: National Title Insurance Corporation Agency (National Title) (P) brought suit to recover losses resulting from the payment by First Union National Bank (First Union) (D) of two counterfeit checks ostensibly drawn on National Title's (P) account. First Union (D) claimed that the deposit agreement between them barred National Title's (P) claim because National Title (P) had not reported the unauthorized checks within the 60-day period provided for in the deposit agreement. National Title (P) argued that the 60-day period was unenforceable because the one-year period provided in U.C.C. § 4-406 was not subject to contractual modification.

CONCISE RULE OF LAW: A bank and its customer may agree contractually to shorten the one-year period provided in U.C.C. § 4-406(f) for reporting of an unauthorized signature or alteration on an item, provided the shortened period is not manifestly unreasonable.

FACTS: National Title Insurance Corporation Agency (National Title) (P) opened an escrow checking account with First Union National Bank (First Union) (D). The account was subject to a deposit agreement (Deposit Agreement) that governed the relationship between them. The Deposit Agreement provided that National Title (P) would carefully examine account statements and give notice of any unauthorized transactions, and provided that First Union (D) would not be liable for paying an item with an unauthorized signature or alterations unless the error was reported within 60 days of the mailing date for the first statement describing the item. Subsequently First Union (D) paid two checks ostensibly drawn on National Title's (P) account, both of which were counterfeit and not executed by an authorized signatory to the account. The checks were described in account statements mailed the month after they were honored, and National Title (P) did not report either of the unauthorized signatures to First Union (D) within 60 days of the mailing of the statements. After First Union (D) refused to credit National Title's (P) account in the amounts paid on the two checks, National Title (P) filed a motion for judgment seeking to recover its losses from First Union (D). First Union's (D) defenses included the assertion that the claim was precluded for failure to provide notice within the 60-day time period specified in the Deposit Agreement. On cross-motions for summary judgment, the trial court concluded

that contractual reduction of the one-year period for reporting unauthorized signatures set forth in U.C.C. §4-406(f) was permitted by law and that the 60-day period agreed upon by the parties in this case was not "manifestly unreasonable" under the provisions of U.C.C. § 4-103. Summary judgment was granted for First Union (D), and the state's supreme court granted review.

ISSUE: May a bank and its customer agree contractually to shorten the one-year period provided in U.C.C. § 4-406(f) for reporting of an unauthorized signature or alteration on an item, provided the shortened period is not manifestly unreasonable?

HOLDING AND DECISION: (Kisner, J.) Yes. A bank and its customer may agree contractually to shorten the one-year period provided in U.C.C. § 4-406(f) for reporting of an unauthorized signature or alteration on an item, provided the shortened period is not manifestly unreasonable. U.C.C. § 4-406(f) provides that a bank's customer is precluded from asserting against the bank an unauthorized signature or alteration on an item if the customer fails to report such fact to the bank within one year after a statement of account showing payment of the item is made available to the customer. The dispositive issue in this appeal is whether a bank and its customer may, by contractual agreement, shorten the one-year period provided in that provision. The preclusion in § 4-406(f) applies irrespective of whether the bank paid the item containing the unauthorized signature or alteration in good faith. National Title (P) first argues that § 4-406(f) is a statute of repose, i.e., a rule of substantive law, and that the one-year period set forth in that section is, therefore, not subject to contractual modification by the parties. Next, National Title (P) posits that the Deposit Agreement imports the time bar established in § 4-406(f) into § 4-406(c), thereby rendering the preclusion in subsection (f) meaningless. National Title (P) further asserts that the agreement impermissibly changes the comparative negligence provisions established in § 4-406(e) and reinstates the concept of contributory negligence into § 4-406(c). Finally, National Title (P) contends that the 60-day time limit for reporting an unauthorized signature or alteration on an item is "manifestly unreasonable," but that, if the Deposit Agreement is enforceable, the 60-day limit should be construed as the parties' definition of "reasonable promptness" in determining comparative negligence, rather than as an absolute bar to National Title's (P) claim against First Union (D). National Title's (P) arguments are rejected. First, the period provided in § 4-406(f) is a statutorily

Continued on next page.

prescribed notice that operates as a condition precedent to the customer's right to file an action against the bank to recover losses caused by the unauthorized signature or alteration. This condition precedent does not limit a customer's claim against a bank but requires that the customer first perform the duty to discover and report any unauthorized signature or alteration on an item before bringing suit against the bank. The characterization of § 4-406(f) as a condition precedent is not determinative of the question whether a customer and a bank can, by agreement, shorten the one-year period. The provisions of § 4-103 (a) provide the analytical framework for resolving that question. Section 4-103 (a) states that provisions in that title may be varied by agreement but the parties to the agreement cannot disclaim a bank's responsibility for its lack of good faith or failure to exercise ordinary care or limit the measure of damages for the lack or failure. The parties may determine by agreement the standards by which the bank's responsibility is to be measured if those standards are not manifestly unreasonable. This section (4-103 (a)) confers blanket power to vary all provisions of Article 4 by agreements of the ordinary kind. Thus, this statute allows a bank and its customer to vary by agreement the effect of the provisions of Article 4 as long as the agreement does not: (1) disclaim a bank's responsibility for its lack of good faith, (2) disclaim a bank's responsibility for its failure to exercise ordinary care, or (3) limit the measure of damages for the lack or failure. Here, the provision in the Deposit Agreement reducing the one-year period to a period of 60 days does not run afoul of these limitations on the authority to vary the effect of the provisions of Article 4. The agreement does not absolve First Union (D) of its duty to exercise ordinary care or good faith, nor does it limit the measure of damages. Instead, this provision merely varies the effect of § 4-406(f) in regard to the time period involved. This reduction in the length of the statutory notice period is consistent with the concept that a bank can be held potentially liable for paying an item containing an unauthorized signature or alteration only for a limited period of time. Thus, a bank and its customer may contractually shorten the one-year period contained in Code § 4-406(f). Notwithstanding this reduced time period, if the customer complies with its duty to exercise reasonable promptness in examining its account statement and reporting any unauthorized signature or altered item, the bank remains liable for paying an item bearing an unauthorized signature or alteration. Likewise, the comparative negligence provisions contained in § 4-406(e) remain in effect during the 60-day period after the bank makes available to the customer a statement showing payment of items from the account. Thus, the provisions at issue do not alter the scheme of liability between banks and their customers as set forth in § 4-406. Finally, the 60-day time limitation set forth in the Deposit Agreement is not "manifestly unreasonable." Other jurisdictions have likewise upheld the validity of reductions in the one-year period to periods similar to or shorter than 60 days. A condition precedent such as the one set forth in § 4-406(f) recognizes that a customer is in a better position than a bank to know whether a signature is authorized or an item has been altered. A reduction in the one-year period allowed in subsection (f) to a period of 60 days encourages diligence by a customer and is in accord with public policy by limiting disputes in a society where millions of bank transactions occur every day. Affirmed.

EDITOR'S ANALYSIS: The type of clause included in the deposit agreement between the parties in this case is known as a "cutdown" clause, because, as its name implies, it cuts the period of time for reporting an unauthorized signature or alteration down from one year to a shortened time period. Such clauses, which, as this case demonstrates, have been upheld when reducing the time period to 60 days or less, significantly increase the burden on customers to diligently monitor their statements and accounts in a timely manner, while significantly insulating banks from ongoing exposure to liability for their errors.

NOTES:

STONE & WEBSTER ENGINEERING CORP. v. FIRST NATIONAL BANK & TRUST CO.

Drawee company (P) v. Bank (D)

Mass. Sup. Jud. Ct., 345 Mass. 1, 184 N.E.2d 358 (1962).

NATURE OF CASE: Action for money had and received, for conversion, and for negligence.

FACT SUMMARY: Owing money to Westinghouse, Stone & Webster (P) made checks out to that company, but an employee of Stone & Webster (P) forged a Westinghouse endorsement and cashed the checks.

CONCISE RULE OF LAW: A drawer has no action for money had or received or conversion against a collecting bank for cashing the drawer's check on a forged endorsement.

FACTS: Having made out checks totalling $64,755.44 to Westinghouse, to whom it owed money for goods and services furnished, Stone & Webster (P) was unaware that they had never been delivered and that one of its employees had cashed them at First National (D) by forging the endorsement of Westinghouse. First National (D) then forwarded the checks to the bank where Stone & Webster (P) had its checking account, First National Bank of Boston, which charged the checks to the account and refused to thereafter recredit the account for those sums. Stone & Webster (P) then sued for money had and received, for conversion of the checks, and for "negligence" in cashing checks with forged endorsements. When a demurrer to the declaration was sustained, Stone & Webster (P) appealed.

ISSUE: When a collecting bank cashes a check on a forged endorsement, does the drawer have a right of action for money had and received or for conversion of the checks against the collecting bank?

HOLDING AND DECISION: (Wilkins, C.J.) No. A drawer does not have a right of action for money had and received or for conversion of the checks against a collecting bank which has cashed his check on a forged endorsement. The money the collecting bank, First National (D) in this case, receives from the payor bank, First National Bank of Boston, here, is from the funds of the payor bank, so an action for funds had and received cannot be properly brought by the drawer, Stone & Webster (P). As to conversion actions by the drawer against the collecting bank, the U.C.C. has left this point untouched, but the preferable view is that no such right of action exists. That is the only position which facilitates each party in such a transaction being able to assert the defenses it is allowed under the U.C.C. Although the U.C.C. allows a drawer to insist that his account be recredited with the amount of any unauthorized payment, the drawee-payor bank has defenses based on the drawer's substantial negligence or upon his duty to discover and report unauthorized signatures and alterations. A drawee-payor bank can then proceed against the

presenting collecting bank on the relevant warranties unless it waived or failed to assert a valid defense it had against the drawer. In essence, each transferee has rights against his transferor, and allowing Stone & Webster (P) to skip over the drawee-payor bank, First National of Boston, and go against the collecting bank, First National (D), would upset this balance of defenses between immediate transferors. It would also compel resort to litigation in almost every case involving forgery of commercial paper. Affirmed.

EDITOR'S ANALYSIS: A split in authority exists as to the right of a drawer to recover directly from a depository bank. Some courts have allowed recovery on the premise that the depository bank's warranty to the payor bank against forged endorsements applies to the drawer, as third-party beneficiary.

NOTES:

TITLE INSURANCE COMPANY OF MINNESOTA v. COMERICA BANK-CALIFORNIA

Holder of loan interests (P) v. Paying bank (D)

Cal. Ct. App., 27 Cal. App. 4th 800 (1994).

NATURE OF CASE: Appeal in action for damages alleging negligence.

FACT SUMMARY: Title Insurance Company of Minnesota (P) filed suit against Comerica Bank (D) after Comerica (D) failed to discover that a check had been indorsed and presented for payment by an impersonator of the true payee.

CONCISE RULE OF LAW: To invoke protection of the imposter rule, it must be proven that by impersonation of the payee the imposter induced a bank to issue a check.

FACTS: Title Insurance Company of Minnesota (TICM) (P) was assigned the interests of two loans made to Helen Nastor secured by deeds of trust by First National Mortgage Company (FNMC). FNMC issued a check payable to Nastor for the amount of the first loan and gave the check to Helen's son, Rudy Nastor, for delivery to Helen. Later the same day, a woman impersonating Helen indorsed the check and presented it to Comerica Bank (D), where FNMC held an account. Comerica (D) paid the impersonator the full amount of the check. FNMC made a second loan to Helen, part of the proceeds of which were used to pay off the first loan. After FNMC did not receive any payment on the second loan, it initiated foreclosure proceedings against Helen's property. Helen's attorney informed FNMC that its deed of trust on the property was invalid because it was executed by Rudy using a forged power of attorney. FNMC made a claim for payment under the second title insurance policy and TICM (P) paid FNMC the full amount of the second loan. TICM (P) then sued Comerica (D) for negligence, seeking recovery of the amount of the second loan. TICM (P) alleged that Comerica (D) breached its duty of due care by failing to utilize reasonable practices and procedures to ensure that only properly endorsed checks were paid. If proper procedures had been followed, Comerica (D) would have caught the imposter cashing the first check and FNMC would never have made the second loan. The trial court applied the "imposter rule," which provides that an indorsed check is effective if the bank was induced to issue the check by an impersonator of the payee. TICM (P) appealed, arguing that the imposter rule was erroneously applied and was not applicable in this case.

ISSUE: To invoke protection of the imposter rule, must it be proven that the imposter induced a bank to issue a check by impersonation of the payee?

HOLDING AND DECISION: (Mihara, J.) Yes. To invoke protection of the imposter rule, it must be proven that by impersonation of the payee the imposter induced a bank to issue a check. The impersonation by Helen's imposter did not induce

FNMC to issue the check; the check had already been issued and was merely presented for payment by the impostor. Rudy obtained issuance of the check to Helen not by impersonating her, but by falsely representing that he was authorized to act on her behalf. Although his actions were fraudulent, they do not constitute impersonation and therefore the imposter rule is not applicable. The trial court improperly dismissed TICM's (P) suit. Reversed.

EDITOR'S ANALYSIS: The impostor rule is intended to protect a bank in circumstances in which it is wrongly induced to issue a check by an impersonator. Although there was clearly an illegal representation made in this case, it was not the specific type that the impostor rule was designed to prevent. Nonetheless, this ruling is not the end of the line. Comerica (D) will still have the opportunity to prove that its general business practices were reasonable and standard in light of the fraudulent actions by Rudy and Helen's impersonator.

NOTES:

GINA CHIN & ASSOCIATES, INC. v. FIRST UNION BANK

Employer (P) v. Bank (D)

Va. Sup. Ct., 500 S.E.2d 516 (1998).

NATURE OF CASE: Action to recover funds lost as a result of forgery.

FACT SUMMARY: Chin's (P) employee double-forged Chin's (P) checks and deposited them in her account at First Union (D).

CONCISE RULE OF LAW: Uniform Commercial Code §§ 3-404 and -405 permit a plaintiff to assert a cause of action with respect to fictitious payee double forgeries if the person taking the check fails to exercise ordinary care.

FACTS: Chin (P), a food wholesaler, maintained checking accounts at certain banks. An employee of Chin (P) forged the signature of one of Chin's (P) officers on a number of checks payable to Chin's (P) suppliers. The employee then forged the payees' indorsements and deposited them in an account at First Union (D). Chin (P) filed a motion for judgment against First Union (D) alleging First Union (D) was negligent when it accepted checks drawn on Chin's (P) accounts bearing both forged signatures of the drawer and forged indorsements of the payees. The trial court sustained First Union's (D) demurrer and entered summary judgment. Chin (P) appealed.

ISSUE: Do Uniform Commercial Code §§ 3-404 and -405 permit a plaintiff to assert a cause of action with respect to fictitious payee double forgeries if the person taking the check fails to exercise ordinary care?

HOLDING AND DECISION: (Lacy, J.) Yes. Uniform Commercial Code §§ 3-404 and -405 permit a plaintiff to assert a cause of action with respect to fictitious payee double forgeries if the person taking the check fails to exercise ordinary care. First Union (D) claims that under U.C.C. §§ 3-404 and -405, Chin (P) does not have a cause of action because those sections only apply to instances involving a forged indorsement of the payee and not to circumstances where both the payee's indorsement and the signature of the drawer were forged. This conclusion is erroneous. Section 3-404(b) provides that if the payee on a check is fictitious or not the person intended, a forged payee's indorsement is nevertheless effective for one who takes the check in good faith. Section 3-405 provides that where an employee vested with the responsibility for processing, signing or indorsing the employer's check makes a fraudulent indorsement, the indorsement is effective if taken or paid in good faith. Both sections provide, however, that if the person taking the check fails to exercise ordinary care, the person bearing the loss may recover from the person failing to exercise ordinary care to the extent the failure to exercise ordinary care contributed to the loss. In the absence of any specific exemptions, we hold that the sections are applicable in double forgery situations. Thus Chin (P)

was not precluded from asserting a cause of action under §§ 3-404 or -405. Chin (P) alleged that First Union's (D) acceptance of the forged checks was negligent, "in contravention of established banking customs and standards" and "due to the negligent failure of [the bank] to supervise its employee." Since these allegations are sufficient to state a cause of action, the trial court erred in sustaining the demurrer. Reversed and remanded.

EDITOR'S ANALYSIS: The revisions to U.C.C. §§ 3-404 and -405 introduced the concept of comparative negligence to the U.C.C.. This reflects the drafters' intention that all participants in the transaction have a duty to exercise ordinary care in the drawing and handling of instruments. Failure to exercise such care results in liability to the negligent party.

NOTES:

JEFFERSON PARISH SCHOOL BOARD v. FIRST COMMERCE CORPORATION

Account holder (P) v. Bank (D)

La. Ct. App., 669 So. 2d 1298 (1996).

NATURE OF CASE: Suit to recover payment on checks.

FACT SUMMARY: Jefferson (P) sued First NBC (D) to recover the amount of several checks which it determined to be counterfeit.

CONCISE RULE OF LAW: There is no cause of action for recovery of funds paid on forged checks where a resolution is adopted authorizing the drawee's payment of checks bearing signatures resembling a machine-endorsed facsimile signature.

FACTS: Jefferson (P) maintained a checking account with First NBC (D). Various instruments purporting to be checks made by Jefferson (P) and drawn on the subject account were presented for payment and paid by First NBC (D). Jefferson (P) examined the checks and determined they were counterfeit. The checks were returned to First NBC (D) who maintained that Jefferson (P) should bear the loss. Jefferson (P) filed suit seeking recovery of the amount of the checks. The district court granted First NBC's (D) motion for summary judgment and Jefferson (P) appealed.

ISSUE: Is there a cause of action for recovery of funds paid on forged checks where a resolution is adopted authorizing the drawee's payment of checks bearing signatures resembling a machine-endorsed facsimile signature?

HOLDING AND DECISION: (Jones, J.) No. There is no cause of action for recovery of funds paid on forged checks where a resolution is adopted authorizing the drawee's payment of checks bearing signatures resembling a machine-endorsed facsimile signature. Jefferson's (P) only assignment of error claims that the court erred in dismissing the suit based on the adoption of the facsimile signature resolution. The assignment of error has no merit. The language of the facsimile agreement is clear and unambiguous, authorizing the bank (D) to honor all checks "purporting to bear" the facsimile signatures, "regardless of what means" the signature is affixed so long as the signatures "resemble the facsimile specimens." This result is consistent with § 4-103(1) in effect at the time of the agreement and case law. In Perini, the court held there was no cause of action for recovery of funds paid on forged checks where a resolution was adopted authorizing the drawee's payment of checks bearing signatures resembling the machine-endorsed facsimile signature. Since there is no dispute that the signatures are nearly identical to the facsimile signatures there is no issue of material fact. Affirmed.

EDITOR'S ANALYSIS: The version of section 4-103(1) in effect at the time of the agreement allowed for the variation of its provisions by agreement "except that no agreement can disclaim a bank's responsibility for its own lack of good faith or failure to exercise ordinary care or can limit the measure of damages for such lack of failure; but the parties may agree to determine the standards by which such responsibility is to be measured if those standards are not manifestly unreasonable." Here the court found the agreement to be reasonable; however, other courts have reached the opposite result.

NOTES:

HSBC BANK USA v. F & M BANK NORTHERN VIRGINIA

Drawee bank (P) v. Presenting bank (D)

246 F.3d 335 (4th Cir. 2001).

NATURE OF CASE: Appeal by a presenting bank from a judgment for the drawee bank.

FACT SUMMARY: Donald Lynch purchased a check in the amount of $250.00. The drawee/payor on the check was HSBC Bank (P). Prior to the check's deposit at F & M Bank (D), the amount was altered from $250.00 to $250,000.00 by adding three zeros and changing the period to a comma in the numerical portion of the check and adding the letters "Thoud" in the written portion. The alteration was unauthorized. The check was presented for payment to HSBC (P). F & M (D) warranted that the check had not been altered. HSBC (P) honored the check and paid $250,000.00 to F & M (D). HSBC (P) sued F & M (D) for recovery.

CONCISE RULE OF LAW: Whether a drawer failed to exercise ordinary care in preparing a check so as to prevent unauthorized alteration is a question of fact, a court's determination of which will be reviewed only for clear error, in an action brought by a drawee bank against a bank presenting the check for payment for the second bank's alleged breach of its presentment warranties.

FACTS: Donald Lynch purchased a check from Allied Irish Bank (AIB) in Ireland. The check was made payable to Advance Marketing and Investment Inc. (AMI) in the amount of US $250.00, which was handwritten as "Two Hundred + Fifty" on the center line of the check (with "US Dollars" handwritten on the line below), (i.e., the written portion of the check), and "US$250.00" handwritten on the upper right-hand side of the check (i.e., the numerical portion of the check). The manner in which AIB made out the check left just less than one-half inch of open space in the numerical portion and one inch of open space in the written portion. The drawee/payor on the check was HSBC Bank USA (P). Prior to the check's deposit into AMI's account at F & M Bank Northern Virginia (D), the amount of the check was altered from $250.00 to $250,000.00 by adding three zeros and changing the period to a comma in the numerical portion of the check and adding the letters "Thoud" in the written portion. The alteration was unauthorized, and the check was endorsed "A.M.I., Inc." F & M (D) presented the check for payment to HSBC (P). In so doing, F & M (D) warranted that the check had not been altered. HSBC (P) honored the check as presented and paid $250,000.00 to F & M (D), and debited AIB's account for that amount. HSBC (P) was subsequently advised by AIB of the check's unauthorized alteration and recredited AIB's account for the amount of the unauthorized alteration. HSBC (P) sued F & M (D). F & M (D) alleged a claim for breach of the presentment warranty.

ISSUE: Is whether a drawer failed to exercise ordinary care in preparing a check so as to prevent unauthorized alteration a question of fact such that a court's determination will be reviewed only for clear error, in an action brought by a drawee bank against a bank presenting the check for payment for the second bank's alleged breach of its presentment warranties?

HOLDING AND DECISION: (Hamilton, Sr. Cir. J.) Yes. Whether a drawer failed to exercise ordinary care in preparing a check so as to prevent unauthorized alteration is a question of fact, a court's determination of which will be reviewed only for clear error, in an action brought by a drawee bank against a bank presenting the check for payment for the second bank's alleged breach of its presentment warranties. Here, the district court's finding that the drawer, in leaving roughly one-half inch of open space following the numerical portion of the check and roughly one inch of open space following its written indication of the amount of the check, had not failed to exercise ordinary care in preparing the check, so as to preclude the drawer from asserting an unauthorized alteration when the check was paid not in the amount of $250.00 originally specified, but in the altered amount of $250,000.00, was not clearly erroneous. The drawer had left so little space following its written designation of the check's amount that the party altering the check was unable to insert the word "thousand," but had to use the abbreviation "thoud." The only evidence submitted by F & M (D) in support of its burden of proving that HSBC (P) had failed to exercise ordinary care in making out the check was the check itself. The district court physically examined the check, including the just less than one-half inch of open space in the numerical portion of the check and the one inch of open space in the written portion of the check. Based upon this physical examination, the district court found that the open spaces in the numerical and written portions of the check were sufficiently filled in by AIB such that "any alteration that was made was obvious." Thus, ordinary care had been exercised by AIB in making out the check. Because the district court's finding that AIB exercised ordinary care in making out the check was not clearly erroneous, judgment is affirmed in favor of HSBC (P).

EDITOR'S ANALYSIS: It should be noted that U.C.C. § 3-406 does not give a general right to challenge negligence.

STATE OF QATAR v. FIRST AMERICAN BANK
Employer (P) v. Depositary banks (D)
885 F.Supp. 849 E.D. VA (1995).

NATURE OF CASE: Suit for conversion.

FACT SUMMARY: The State of Qatar (P) sued the depositary banks (D) for conversion of unauthorized checks deposited in one of its employee's personal account.

CONCISE RULE OF LAW: The unqualified language "for deposit only" following an indorsement on the back of a check requires a depositary bank to place the check's proceeds into the payee's account, and the bank violates that restrictive indorsement when it credits the check to any other account.

FACTS: One of Qatar's (P) employees defrauded Qatar (P) by having checks drawn on Qatar's (P) account in purported payment of false and duplicate invoices. The employee successfully deposited such checks, even though they were made payable to others, into his own personal account at First American (D). Qatar (P) sued the depositary banks for conversion.

ISSUE: Does the unqualified language "for deposit only" following an indorsement on the back of a check require a depositary bank to place the check's proceeds into the payee's account, and the bank violates that restrictive indorsement when it credits the check to any other account?

HOLDING AND DECISION: (Ellis, Dist J.) Yes. The unqualified language "for deposit only" following an indorsement on the back of a check requires a depositary bank to place the check's proceeds into the payee's account, and the bank violates that restrictive indorsement when it credits the check to any other account. The only category of checks in dispute are those bearing the forged indorsement of the payee named on the face of the check, followed by a stamped "for deposit only" restriction. First American (D) may be held liable to Qatar (P) for handling a check's proceeds in violation of a restrictive covenant. Section 3-205(c) of the pre-1993 U.C.C. defines restrictive covenants to include the words "for collection," "for deposit," "pay any bank," or similar terms signifying a purpose of deposit or collection. While the phrase "for deposit only" is clearly a restrictive covenant, the U.C.C. does not define that term or state what conduct would be inconsistent with that restriction. Most courts have held that the restriction instructs depositary banks to deposit the funds only into the payee's account. That construction is adopted here. First American (D) violated the restrictive indorsements in depositing into the employee's account checks made payable to others and restrictively indorsed "for deposit only," and is liable for conversion in the amount of the total face value of the checks.

EDITOR'S ANALYSIS: The rationale behind the restriction is to direct that the funds be deposited into a specific account and not into just any account and thus avoid the risk of indorsing a check in a bank and having it stolen before it reaches its intended destination.

NOTES:

16

CHAPTER 16
THE BANK-CUSTOMER RELATIONSHIP

QUICK REFERENCE RULES OF LAW

1. **Proving Loss under 4-403(c).** Under § 4-403 of the U.C.C., which provides that a bank customer has the right to order his bank to stop payment on a check, the customer is limited to the facts of the particular transaction for which the check was issued. (Dunnigan v. First Bank)

2. **Priority Rules of Section 4-303.** A bank must comply with garnishment process within a reasonable time period, rather than having until midnight of the day following the day garnishment was served on it to comply. (W & D Acquisition, LLC v. First Union National Bank)

3. **Wrongful Dishonor.** A payor bank which has wrongfully dishonored an item is liable to its customer for damages proximately caused thereby, including loss of reputation and damage to credit standing. (Loucks v. Albuquerque National Bank)

4. **Service Charges and Fees.** Where circumstances suggest a bank-customer contract may be unconscionable, the parties are entitled under state law to present evidence as to the commercial settling, purpose, and effect of the contract. (Perdue v. Crocker National Bank)

DUNNIGAN v. FIRST BANK

Trustee in bankruptcy (P) v. Paying bank (D)
Conn. Sup. Ct., 217 Conn. 205, 585 A.2d 659 (1991).

NATURE OF CASE: Appeal from plaintiff's verdict in action alleging wrongful payment of a check.

FACT SUMMARY: After an error by a bookkeeper was discovered, Cohn Precious Metals attempted to stop payment on a check to Lamphere Coin for silver dollars which Cohn had overpaid by $19,606.

CONCISE RULE OF LAW: Under § 4-403 of the U.C.C., which provides that a bank customer has the right to order his bank to stop payment on a check, the customer is limited to the facts of the particular transaction for which the check was issued.

FACTS: On November 8, 1978, Lamphere Coin, a trader in coins and precious metals, delivered to Cohn Precious Metals silver dollars pursuant to a purchase order with a total value of $27,492. Cohn's bookkeeper incorrectly valued the unit price of the coins, resulting in an overpayment of $19,606 made by wire transfer on November 9. On November 10, Lamphere delivered another order of silver dollars to Cohn with a value of $21,175. On the same day, Cohn issued two checks to Lamphere in the amounts of $12,175 and $9,000. On November 14, after discovering the bookkeeper's error, Cohn directed First Bank (D) to stop payment on the two checks totaling $21,175. First Bank (D) stopped payment on the $9,000 check, but inadvertently honored the $12,175 check. Cohn retained the silver coins but never recovered its overpayment from Lamphere. Cohn's trustee in bankruptcy, Dunnigan (P), brought this action against First Bank (D) to recover the value of the wrongfully honored checks over Cohn's valid stop-payment order. The trial court rendered judgment for Dunnigan (P) for the amount of the check, and First Bank (D) appealed.

ISSUE: Under § 4-403 of the U.C.C., which provides that a bank customer has the right to order his bank to stop payment on a check, is the customer limited to the facts of the particular transaction for which the check was issued?

HOLDING AND DECISION: (Borden, Assoc. J.) Yes. Under § 4-403 of the U.C.C., which provides that a bank customer has the right to order his bank to stop payment on a check, the customer is limited to the facts of the particular transaction for which the check was issued. Section 4-403 also provides that the burden of establishing the fact and amount of loss resulting from the payment of an item contrary to a binding stop order is on the customer. Section 4-403 does not, however, contemplate taking into account a loss by the customer of credits that arose from prior unrelated transactions, as the trial court did in this case. Furthermore, Cohn has suffered no loss within the meaning of

§ 4-403 because the check was supported by good consideration in payment for the silver coins. The trial court incorrectly expanded the scope of § 4-403 in concluding that credits from prior transactions were relevant to the claim at issue. Reversed and remanded with direction to enter judgment for First Bank (D).

DISSENT: (Shea, J.) Cohn complied fully with § 4-403 in stopping payment on both checks; however, First Bank's (D) negligence permitted the paying of the $12,175 check. Contrary to the majority's opinion, there is nothing in § 4-403 that provides an exception excusing a bank's negligence in violating a properly ordered stop payment. The trial court's findings should be affirmed.

EDITOR'S ANALYSIS: As the dissent points out, the majority does seem to confuse two completely distinct issues. The stop-payment privilege of a bank customer can serve as a tactical advantage to the customer in dealing with a third party. When a bank interferes with a stop-payment order contrary to a customer's wishes, whether negligently or not, it can have severe ramifications for the customer, as illustrated in this case.

NOTES:

W & D ACQUISITION, LLC v. FIRST UNION NATIONAL BANK

Garnisher (P) v. Garnishee bank (D)

Conn. Sup. Ct., 262 Conn.704, 817 A.2d 91 (2003).

NATURE OF CASE: Appeal from summary judgment for defendant in scire facias action to recover funds.

FACT SUMMARY: W & D Acquisition, LLC (plaintiff) (P) claimed that First Union National Bank (defendant) (D) failed to secure funds within a "reasonable time" period pursuant to a garnishment order in defendant's (D) customer's accounts. Defendant (D) claimed that it had until midnight of the day following the day it was served with the garnishment to do so.

CONCISE RULE OF LAW: A bank must comply with garnishment process within a reasonable time period, rather than having until midnight of the day following the day garnishment was served on it to comply.

FACTS: W & D Acquisition, LLC (plaintiff) (P) obtained a prejudgment garnishment order for up to $70,000 against R.K.E. Associates (R.K.E.), which had two accounts with First Union National Bank (defendant) (D)—one with a balance of about $34,000 (account 1), the other with a balance of $30 (account 2). Defendant (D) was served with garnishment papers at noon on October 27, 1997, but did not secure the money in either account at that time. Later that afternoon, at around 3:26 p.m., an R.K.E. agent withdrew over $32,000 from account 1. By the close of business the next day, on October 28, 1997, as the result of various credits and debits, the balance in account 1 was reduced to about $30. Plaintiff (P) brought a writ of scire facias to recover the funds it alleged defendant (D) should have secured in response to the garnishment. Defendant (D) argued that under U.C.C. 4-104(a)(10), it was not obligated to comply with the garnishment until midnight of October 28, 1997, the day after it received the garnishment (the "midnight deadline"). The trial court determined that as a matter of law a bank has until the midnight deadline to comply with garnishment process, and granted summary judgment for defendant (D). The state's highest court granted review.

ISSUE: Must a bank comply with garnishment process within a reasonable time period, rather than having until midnight of the day following the day garnishment was served on it to comply?

HOLDING AND DECISION: (Borden, J.) Yes. A bank must comply with garnishment process within a reasonable time period, rather than having until midnight of the day following the day garnishment was served on it to comply. The statutory provision primarily at issue here is U.C.C. § 4-303(a), which strongly suggests that the relevant time period is a reasonable time depending upon all of the relevant facts and circumstances,

rather than a fixed period terminating on the bank's midnight deadline. This section provides that "[a]ny . . . legal process served upon . . . a payor bank comes too late to terminate, suspend, or modify the bank's right or duty to pay an item or to charge its customer's account for the item if the . . . legal process is received or served and a reasonable time for the bank to act thereon expires . . . after the earliest of the following: (1) [t]he bank accepts . . . the item; (2) the bank pays the item in cash. . . ." In other words, under this section, a banking institution is obligated to secure funds within a "reasonable time" after receiving garnishment process, a form of "legal process," to prevent distribution of those funds in response to an "item." The items at issue in this case include the withdrawal slip tendered by R.K.E.'s agent in exchange for $32,318.26 in cash as well as several checks drawn against account 1 in the hours that followed. Also, the section does not expressly provide that a banking institution must act before its midnight deadline. Another U.C.C. provision, § 1-204 further defines "reasonable time" as applying, in general, to the entire U.C.C. That section specifically provides: "What is a reasonable time for taking any action depends on the nature, purpose and circumstances of such action." Thus, textually, § 4-303(a) strongly indicates, by its open-textured language and by virtue of § 1-204(2), that its meaning is what is normally meant by the statutory use of the phrase "reasonable time," namely, a fact-specific inquiry depending on all of the circumstances of the case. This conclusion is supported by the official commentary to § 4-303, which provides in relevant part: "In the case of . . . legal process the effective time for determining whether [it was] received too late to affect the payment of an item and a charge to the customer's account by reason of such payment, is receipt plus a reasonable time for the bank to act on [the service of process]. . . . Usually, a relatively short time is required to communicate to the accounting department advice of one of these events but certainly some time is necessary. . . ." Thus, the official commentary unequivocally states that the time period is variable and depends upon the factual circumstances. It makes no mention of the bright-line rule created by the midnight deadline. This conclusion is consistent with the purpose of § 4-303(a), namely, to balance the interests of the garnishor in securing its potential debtor's funds against the need for the bank to have the necessary time in which to take the steps necessary to effectuate that security. Although, as the defendant (D)

Continued on next page.

suggests, a midnight deadline would give a bank more certainty and, in all likelihood, more time to take those steps, there is nothing in either the language or the purpose of the statute to justify that bright-line rule. Reversed and remanded.

EDITOR'S ANALYSIS: U.C.C. § 4-303(a) governs the priority between claims that affect the size of a customer's bank account after a check has been presented for payment, as well as the right of the check's holder to be paid. The events that can affect such priority, and which are the subject of § 4-303(a), include: the customer's death, incompetency, or bankruptcy; a stop-payment order; the bank's right of setoff; and legal process served on the bank by the customer's creditor—including garnishment, which was the subject of this case. The problem presented is at what point the check has reached the stage in the bank's payment process to take the amount of the check out of the customer's account for purposes of these events. One of the rules in this section, provided by § 4-303(a)(4), is that if the check has been effectively paid by expiration of the midnight deadline, any subsequent claim pursuant to these events comes too late to be prior to the check. It is this rule the defendant (D) bank relied on in this case, and which was rejected by the court as setting the time period for responding to a garnishment order.

NOTES:

LOUCKS v. ALBUQUERQUE NATIONAL BANK
Partnership (P) v. Bank (D)
N.M. Sup. Ct., 76 N.M.735, 418 P.2d 191 (1966).

NATURE OF CASE: Action seeking compensatory and punitive damages for wrongful dishonor of checks.

FACT SUMMARY: Albuquerque National (D) took money from a partnership account to cover a loan repayment due from an individual partner, which resulted in certain partnership checks "bouncing."

CONCISE RULE OF LAW: A payor bank which has wrongfully dishonored an item is liable to its customer for damages proximately caused thereby, including loss of reputation and damage to credit standing.

FACTS: Before he entered into partnership with Loucks (P) and formed the L & M Paint and Body Shop, Martinez (P) obtained a personal loan from Albuquerque National (D), a number of extensions thereon being granted even after the partnership was formed. With Martinez (P) still owing $402 on the loan, Albuquerque National (D) proceeded to take that sum out of the checking account which the partnership maintained at that bank, causing some partnership checks to "bounce." As a result, a number of people would no longer accept checks from the partnership, credit was denied the partnership by some, and one man actually came in and tore a map off the wall at the partnership's place of business because the check to pay for it had bounced. Loucks (P) and Martinez (P) sued to recover for damage to credit, reputation, and business standing, for an ulcer allegedly suffered by Loucks (P), and for loss of income and punitive damages. The court dismissed all causes of action except the one to recover the $402 taken out of the partnership account, for which recovery was ordered, and Loucks (P) appealed.

ISSUE: If a payor bank wrongfully dishonors a check, is the customer entitled to recover for the loss of reputation and damage to credit which was proximately caused thereby?

HOLDING AND DECISION: (Oman, J.) Yes. A payor bank is liable to its customer for damages proximately caused by the wrongful dishonor of an item, and that covers damage for loss of reputation and damage to credit. In this case, the partnership, not Loucks (P) and Martinez (P) as individuals, was the customer, so only damages suffered by the partnership are recoverable. This would not include recovery for Loucks' (P) alleged ulcer or for damage to the reputation and credit of Loucks (P) and Martinez (P) as individuals. Turning to the partnership damages, wrongful dishonor results in recovery for all damages proximately caused thereby to the customer, including consequential damages, but where dishonor occurs through mistake the damages are limited to actual damages proved. Here, the jury should have been allowed to decide if the dishonor was the result of mistake, if the partnership's reputation and credit standing were damaged by the dishonor, and the amount of such damage. However, the evidence does not indicate the maliciously intentional acts necessary to warrant punitive damages. Reversed and remanded.

EDITOR'S ANALYSIS: The American Bankers Association convinced a number of states to enact legislation providing that dishonor of a check through mistake or error and without malice creates no liability unless the depositor alleges and proves actual damages resulting therefrom. Furthermore, the liability is limited to the amount of damage thus proved.

NOTES:

PERDUE v. CROCKER NATIONAL BANK
Class of bank clients (P) v. Bank (D)
Cal. Sup. Ct., 38 Cal.3d 913, 702 P.2d 503 (1985).

NATURE OF CASE: Review of trial court order sustaining general demurrer to class action for recovery of bank fee overcharges.

FACT SUMMARY: Terms of small print on "signature cards," which bank required depositors to sign, were challenged as unconscionable.

CONCISE RULE OF LAW: Where circumstances suggest a bank-customer contract may be unconscionable, the parties are entitled under state law to present evidence as to the commercial setting, purpose, and effect of the contract.

FACTS: Crocker National Bank (D) required depositors to sign a "signature card" to authenticate subsequent endorsements. The cards stated, in very small (six point) type, that the signator was subject to all applicable present and future bank regulations. Copies of the relevant regulations were not provided, and the amount the bank charged to process checks drawn on accounts with insufficient funds ("NSF checks") was not disclosed. In 1978 Crocker Bank (D) charged depositors six dollars for each NSF check. The actual cost to Crocker Bank (D) of processing each check was thirty cents. Perdue (P) filed a class action suit challenging the validity of the NSF charges. Crocker Bank (D) demurred, and the trial court sustained without leave to amend. Perdue (P) appealed, contending the signature card contract was unconscionable.

ISSUE: Where circumstances suggest a bank-customer contract may be unconscionable, are the parties entitled under state law to present evidence as to the commercial setting, purpose, and effect of the contract?

HOLDING AND DECISION: (Broussard, J.) Yes. Where circumstances suggest a bank-customer contract may be unconscionable, the parties are entitled under state law to present evidence as to the commercial setting, purpose, and effect of the contract. Cal. Civ. Code § 1670.5 authorizes the court to refuse to enforce contracts it finds unconscionable. The statute entitles the parties to present evidence as to the commercial setting, purpose, and effect of a contract where it appears to the court that the contract may be unconscionable. The profit percentage here of 2,000 percent, while not automatically unconscionable, indicates a need for further inquiry. In addition, the contractual nature of the document is obscured by its description and use as a "signature card," and nothing in the contract inhibits the charging of unconscionable fees. The result is a totally one-sided transaction. Reversed.

EDITOR'S ANALYSIS: A checking account is a contractual relationship governed by Part 4 of U.C.C. § 4-401, federal statutes, and Federal Reserve regulations. Some federal provisions—for example the Expedited Funds Availability Act and Regulation CC—by their terms preempt the U.C.C. U.C.C. § 4-103(a) provides that bank-customer agreements may vary the "effect of the provisions" of Article 4.

NOTES:

GLOSSARY
COMMON LATIN WORDS AND PHRASES ENCOUNTERED IN THE LAW

A FORTIORI: Because one fact exists or has been proven, therefore a second fact that is related to the first fact must also exist.

A PRIORI: From the cause to the effect. A term of logic used to denote that when one generally accepted truth is shown to be a cause, another particular effect must necessarily follow.

AB INITIO: From the beginning; a condition which has existed throughout, as in a marriage which was void ab initio.

ACTUS REUS: The wrongful act; in criminal law, such action sufficient to trigger criminal liability.

AD VALOREM: According to value; an ad valorem tax is imposed upon an item located within the taxing jurisdiction calculated by the value of such item.

AMICUS CURIAE: Friend of the court. Its most common usage takes the form of an amicus curiae brief, filed by a person who is not a party to an action but is nonetheless allowed to offer an argument supporting his legal interests.

ARGUENDO: In arguing. A statement, possibly hypothetical, made for the purpose of argument, is one made arguendo.

BILL QUIA TIMET: A bill to quiet title (establish ownership) to real property.

BONA FIDE: True, honest, or genuine. May refer to a person's legal position based on good faith or lacking notice of fraud (such as a bona fide purchaser for value) or to the authenticity of a particular document (such as a bona fide last will and testament).

CAUSA MORTIS: With approaching death in mind. A gift causa mortis is a gift given by a party who feels certain that death is imminent.

CAVEAT EMPTOR: Let the buyer beware. This maxim is reflected in the rule of law that a buyer purchases at his own risk because it is his responsibility to examine, judge, test, and otherwise inspect what he is buying.

CERTIORARI: A writ of review. Petitions for review of a case by the United States Supreme Court are most often done by means of a writ of certiorari.

CONTRA: On the other hand. Opposite. Contrary to.

CORAM NOBIS: Before us; writs of error directed to the court that originally rendered the judgment.

CORAM VOBIS: Before you; writs of error directed by an appellate court to a lower court to correct a factual error.

CORPUS DELICTI: The body of the crime; the requisite elements of a crime amounting to objective proof that a crime has been committed.

CUM TESTAMENTO ANNEXO, ADMINISTRATOR (ADMINISTRATOR C.T.A.): With will annexed; an administrator c.t.a. settles an estate pursuant to a will in which he is not appointed.

DE BONIS NON, ADMINISTRATOR (ADMINISTRATOR D.B.N.): Of goods not administered; an administrator d.b.n. settles a partially settled estate.

DE FACTO: In fact; in reality; actually. Existing in fact but not officially approved or engendered.

DE JURE: By right; lawful. Describes a condition that is legitimate "as a matter of law," in contrast to the term "de facto," which connotes something existing in fact but not legally sanctioned or authorized. For example, de facto segregation refers to segregation brought about by housing patterns, etc., whereas de jure segregation refers to segregation created by law.

DE MINIMUS: Of minimal importance; insignificant; a trifle; not worth bothering about.

DE NOVO: Anew; a second time; afresh. A trial de novo is a new trial held at the appellate level as if the case originated there and the trial at a lower level had not taken place.

DICTA: Generally used as an abbreviated form of obiter dicta, a term describing those portions of a judicial opinion incidental or not necessary to resolution of the specific question before the court. Such nonessential statements and remarks are not considered to be binding precedent.

DUCES TECUM: Refers to a particular type of writ or subpoena requesting a party or organization to produce certain documents in their possession.

EN BANC: Full bench. Where a court sits with all justices present rather than the usual quorum.

EX PARTE: For one side or one party only. An ex parte proceeding is one undertaken for the benefit of only one party, without notice to, or an appearance by, an adverse party.

EX POST FACTO: After the fact. An ex post facto law is a law that retroactively changes the consequences of a prior act.

EX REL.: Abbreviated form of the term ex relatione, meaning, upon relation or information. When the state brings an action in which it has no interest against an individual at the instigation of one who has a private interest in the matter.

FORUM NON CONVENIENS: Inconvenient forum. Although a court may have jurisdiction over the case, the action should be tried in a more conveniently located court, one to which parties and witnesses may more easily travel, for example.

GUARDIAN AD LITEM: A guardian of an infant as to litigation, appointed to represent the infant and pursue his/her rights.

HABEAS CORPUS: You have the body. The modern writ of habeas corpus is a writ directing that a person (body) being detained (such as a prisoner) be brought before the court so that the legality of his detention can be judicially ascertained.

IN CAMERA: In private, in chambers. When a hearing is held before a judge in his chambers or when all spectators are excluded from the courtroom.

IN FORMA PAUPERIS: In the manner of a pauper. A party who proceeds in forma pauperis because of his poverty is one who is allowed to bring suit without liability for costs.

INFRA: Below, under. A word referring the reader to a later part of a book. (The opposite of supra.)

IN LOCO PARENTIS: In the place of a parent.

IN PARI DELICTO: Equally wrong; a court of equity will not grant requested relief to an applicant who is in pari delicto, or as much at fault in the transactions giving rise to the controversy as is the opponent of the applicant.

IN PARI MATERIA: On like subject matter or upon the same matter. Statutes relating to the same person or things are said to be in pari materia. It is a general rule of statutory construction that such statutes should be construed together, i.e., looked at as if they together constituted one law.

IN PERSONAM: Against the person. Jurisdiction over the person of an individual.

IN RE: In the matter of. Used to designate a proceeding involving an estate or other property.

IN REM: A term that signifies an action against the res, or thing. An action in rem is basically one that is taken directly against property, as distinguished from an action in personam, i.e., against the person.

INTER ALIA: Among other things. Used to show that the whole of a statement, pleading, list, statute, etc., has not been set forth in its entirety.

INTER PARTES: Between the parties. May refer to contracts, conveyances or other transactions having legal significance.

INTER VIVOS: Between the living. An inter vivos gift is a gift made by a living grantor, as distinguished from bequests contained in a will, which pass upon the death of the testator.

IPSO FACTO: By the mere fact itself.

JUS: Law or the entire body of law.

LEX LOCI: The law of the place; the notion that the rights of parties to a legal proceeding are governed by the law of the place where those rights arose.

MALUM IN SE: Evil or wrong in and of itself; inherently wrong. This term describes an act that is wrong by its very nature, as opposed to one which would not be wrong but for the fact that there is a specific legal prohibition against it (malum prohibitum).

MALUM PROHIBITUM: Wrong because prohibited, but not inherently evil. Used to describe something that is wrong because it is expressly forbidden by law but that is not in and of itself evil, e.g., speeding.

MANDAMUS: We command. A writ directing an official to take a certain action.

MENS REA: A guilty mind; a criminal intent. A term used to signify the mental state that accompanies a crime or other prohibited act. Some crimes require only a general mens rea (general intent to do the prohibited act), but others, like assault with intent to murder, require the existence of a specific mens rea.

MODUS OPERANDI: Method of operating; generally refers to the manner or style of a criminal in committing crimes, admissible in appropriate cases as evidence of the identity of a defendant.

NEXUS: A connection to.

NISI PRIUS: A court of first impression. A nisi prius court is one where issues of fact are tried before a judge or jury.

N.O.V. (NON OBSTANTE VEREDICTO): Notwithstanding the verdict. A judgment n.o.v. is a judgment given in favor of one party despite the fact that a verdict was returned in favor of the other party, the justification being that the verdict either had no reasonable support in fact or was contrary to law.

NUNC PRO TUNC: Now for then. This phrase refers to actions that may be taken and will then have full retroactive effect.

PENDENTE LITE: Pending the suit; pending litigation underway.

PER CAPITA: By head; beneficiaries of an estate, if they take in equal shares, take per capita.

PER CURIAM: By the court; signifies an opinion ostensibly written "by the whole court" and with no identified author.

PER SE: By itself, in itself; inherently.

PER STIRPES: By representation. Used primarily in the law of wills to describe the method of distribution where a person, generally because of death, is unable to take that which is left to him by the will of another, and therefore his heirs divide such property between them rather than take under the will individually.

PRIMA FACIE: On its face, at first sight. A prima facie case is one that is sufficient on its face, meaning that the evidence supporting it is adequate to establish the case until contradicted or overcome by other evidence.

PRO TANTO: For so much; as far as it goes. Often used in eminent domain cases when a property owner receives partial payment for his land without prejudice to his right to bring suit for the full amount he claims his land to be worth.

QUANTUM MERUIT: As much as he deserves. Refers to recovery based on the doctrine of unjust enrichment in those cases in which a party has rendered valuable services or furnished materials that were accepted and enjoyed by another under circumstances that would reasonably notify the recipient that the rendering party expected to be paid. In essence, the law implies a contract to pay the reasonable value of the services or materials furnished.

QUASI: Almost like; as if; nearly. This term is essentially used to signify that one subject or thing is almost analogous to another but that material differences between them do exist. For example, a quasi-criminal proceeding is one that is not strictly criminal but shares enough of the same characteristics to require some of the same safeguards (e.g., procedural due process must be followed in a parol hearing).

QUID PRO QUO: Something for something. In contract law, the consideration, something of value, passed between the parties to render the contract binding.

RES GESTAE: Things done; in evidence law, this principle justifies the admission of a statement that would otherwise be hearsay when it is made so closely to the event in question as to be said to be a part of it, or with such spontaneity as not to have the possibility of falsehood.

RES IPSA LOQUITUR: The thing speaks for itself. This doctrine gives rise to a rebuttable presumption of negligence when the instrumentality causing the injury was within the exclusive control of the defendant, and the injury was one that does not normally occur unless a person has been negligent.

RES JUDICATA: A matter adjudged. Doctrine which provides that once a court of competent jurisdiction has rendered a final judgment or decree on the merits, that judgment or decree is conclusive upon the parties to the case and prevents them from engaging in any other litigation on the points and issues determined therein.

RESPONDEAT SUPERIOR: Let the master reply. This doctrine holds the master liable for the wrongful acts of his servant (or the principal for his agent) in those cases in which the servant (or agent) was acting within the scope of his authority at the time of the injury.

STARE DECISIS: To stand by or adhere to that which has been decided. The common law doctrine of stare decisis attempts to give security and certainty to the law by following the policy that once a principle of law as applicable to a certain set of facts has been set forth in a decision, it forms a precedent which will subsequently be followed, even though a different decision might be made were it the first time the question had arisen. Of course, stare decisis is not an inviolable principle and is departed from in instances where there is good cause (e.g., considerations of public policy led the Supreme Court to disregard prior decisions sanctioning segregation).

SUPRA: Above. A word referring a reader to an earlier part of a book.

ULTRA VIRES: Beyond the power. This phrase is most commonly used to refer to actions taken by a corporation that are beyond the power or legal authority of the corporation.

ADDENDUM OF FRENCH DERIVATIVES

IN PAIS: Not pursuant to legal proceedings.

CHATTEL: Tangible personal property.

CY PRES: Doctrine permitting courts to apply trust funds to purposes not expressed in the trust but necessary to carry out the settlor's intent.

PER AUTRE VIE: For another's life; in property law, an estate may be granted that will terminate upon the death of someone other than the grantee.

PROFIT A PRENDRE: A license to remove minerals or other produce from land.

VOIR DIRE: Process of questioning jurors as to their predispositions about the case or parties to a proceeding in order to identify those jurors displaying bias or prejudice.

CASENOTE LEGAL BRIEFS